CASINO CAMPING

Guide to RV-Friendly Casinos

by Jane Kenny

Published by
Roundabout Publications
PO Box 19235
Lenexa, KS 66285

Phone
800-455-2207

Internet
www.TravelBooksUSA.com

Published by Roundabout Publications, P.O. Box 19235, Lenexa, KS 66285; 800-455-2207; www.travelbooksusa.com

Library of Congress Control Number: 2009942694

ISBN-10: 1-885464-36-3
ISBN-13: 978-1-885464-36-1

CASINO CAMPING

For Jack: my pilot and my best friend

Contents

Introduction

Today, more than ever, the good news for RV gaming aficionados is: you don't have to trek all the way to Las Vegas or Atlantic City for your gaming fun. Casinos are all over the country and this book locates them for you. Gaming is growing rapidly in the U.S. and our casino guide reflects many changes taking place in the 32 states listed.

A Guide To RV-Friendly Casinos

Casino Camping is primarily a guide for the many Americans who travel the country in recreational vehicles. Consequently, while the book includes details on *most* casinos in the country, some casinos are not listed because they are not accessible for recreational vehicles.

Quite a few casino resorts have full service RV Parks or are planning to add them to their facility. Those that don't have RV Parks usually allow free overnight parking; some even have electric hookups for RVs in the parking lot. Shuttle service between the parking area and the casino is available at most large casinos.

Traveling players like to plan their trips to include a night or two of gaming while en route. Others will spend more time at a casino location if it has full service accommodations plus other attractions and recreation in the area. Most RV Parks at casino resorts are new and modern. Guests not only get to camp out next to the casino, but they can often enjoy other luxury amenities throughout the resort – pool/spa, sauna, fitness center, golf course, etc. Many casinos currently have an RV Park in their plans for future expansion because market studies have indicated that gaming destination resorts are becoming as popular as fishing destinations for retirees in RVs.

Casino RV Parks are also popular destinations for RV club rallies. A chart for each state lists casinos that have RV Parks as part of their facility.

How This Guide Is Organized

Following introductory articles, this book is organized alphabetically by state. A map at the beginning of each state section identifies casino locations by city. Individual listings are cross-referenced to the map by city name. Each casino listing includes the following information where applicable:

- Name, address, phone numbers and web address,
- On site hotel or motel
- Amenities (pool, fitness room, business center, etc).
- RV Park or campground and last year's rates,
- Restaurants on site,
- Entertainment,
- Golf course,
- Discounts generally offered at the casino resort,
- Casino description (slots, table games, etc.),
- Driving directions,
- Parking information for RVers.

A chart (see sample below) follows each state map and provides information about each casino including:

1) City in which the casino is located
2) Name of casino
3) Availability of RV park
4) Availability of RV spaces in parking lot with electric hookups
5) Whether a casino is within 2 miles of an interstate exit
6) The page number for detailed information about the casino

		3	**4**	**5**	**6**
City **1**	Casino **2**	🚐	∿	⬯	📄
Camp Verde	Cliff Castle Casino	✔		✔	15
Chandler	Gila River Casinos			✔	16
Fountain Hills	Fort McDowell Casino	✔			17
Maricopa	Harrah's Ak-Chin Casino				17

A Word About Nevada and New Jersey

Nevada remains the casino capital of America with literally thousands of gaming sites throughout the state. And Nevada always has the welcome mat out for RVs. The Nevada section of this guide has details that will be of interest and value to everyone planning a trip to that state.

New Jersey's casinos are all located in Atlantic City, but there are no RV Parks at any of the Atlantic City casinos. Furthermore, overnight RV parking is prohibited anywhere in the city (including casino parking lots) by local ordinance. The New Jersey section of this book features a description of the casino areas in Atlantic City for RVers who may want to go in for a "casino-hopping" day trip and for gaming enthusiasts planning an Atlantic City vacation.

Other Popular Gaming Destinations

Other popular "casino hopping" destinations appear in the following state sections:

- Colorado – Black Hawk/Central City; Cripple Creek
- Connecticut – Foxwoods and Mohegan Sun
- Mississippi – Tunica County; the Gulf Coast
- Nevada – Las Vegas, Laughlin and Reno
- South Dakota – Deadwood

We hope you will find the fifth edition of this guide helpful and informative as you travel this beautiful land. Wishing you safe and happy travels.

Jane

What's The Difference Between Gaming and Gambling?

Don't go to a casino expecting to win big. Don't expect to make a killing at the table or hit the big jackpot on the slots. Sure it happens, but not for the overwhelming majority of players.

Lots of how-to articles and books have been written about winning at casinos – on topics such as How To Win At Poker, Blackjack Strategies, Winning At Slots, How To Beat The Odds, etc, etc. Advice from professional gamblers may have some merit for other professionals, but this book is designed for casual or recreational casino players.

The average recreational player is by no means a professional gambler. For a casual player, going to the casino should not be about winning or losing…it should be about playing games as a form of entertainment. In this regard we see a difference between gaming and gambling.

As we all learned from the time we first played Monopoly or little league baseball, every game has a winner and a loser. Those who play only to win – and expect to win every time they play – are unrealistic. They put themselves under a lot of stress and take all the fun out of playing games.

Our winning strategy for playing games at the casino is to set limits on money and time and then relax and have fun.

1) **Set a dollar limit and stick to it**. The amount you set – your bankroll – becomes your personal "price of admission" to the casino for that gaming session. If you use up the budgeted bankroll before the end of the session (length of session explained below), stop playing! Come back for another session in a few hours, a few days, weeks, or months – whatever is your style. It is a big mistake to pump more money into an already losing session.

2) **Set a time limit for the gaming session and stick to it**. Always remember that, no matter what game you play, the odds are in the

casino's favor. Longer sessions increase the casino's odds even more. By playing shorter sessions you'll probably keep part or all of your original bankroll longer. If you are winning when your time limit is up, be disciplined enough to end the session as a winner. You still have the original bankroll and won't need to pay your personal pre-set price of admission the next time you come to the casino.

3) **Never ever set your bankroll at more than you can afford to lose!** This simple bit of advice will keep you in the arena of recreational gaming. Keep in mind the odds are always in the casino's favor. Be sensible.

4) **Relax and have fun**. Once you've established the mindset of gaming as entertainment, you can go ahead and have fun at it, knowing you are disciplined enough to spend no more than the specified amount at no longer than the specified time period. Nowadays casinos offer more fun than ever. Slot machines have moved far beyond the boring reels of endless cherries and bars to interactive and entertaining electronic slots. There are machines that replicate popular TV game shows, machines that talk back to you and games that beguile the player with lively, imaginative graphics. And there are machines to accommodate every budget – pennies, nickels, quarters, dollars and even $10, $50 and $100 slots at some locations. Table game fans, too, have more variety. Today there's a wider range of games and, in many places, low minimums for the novice player.

Table players can benefit most from the "specific bankroll and session time" strategy. Disciplined players can relax and enjoy the camaraderie and games at the tables. And, by applying the strategy outlined above, they're more apt to leave a winner.

What does it mean to leave as a winner? A player who leaves with all or part of his bankroll in his pocket is a winner! Players who have the good common sense to leave when they are even or slightly ahead are winners. Be a winner!

For Some, Gambling Is Not An Option

Problem gamblers tell us that winning is easy…leaving is hard. If you can identify with this, read on.

For the large majority of people gambling is fun – it's not a problem. But for some it can become a problem that interferes with their life and literally takes over. If casino gambling is a form of entertainment for you, then you also need to be aware that there is a progressive illness called compulsive gambling.

Gamblers generally fall into three categories:

1. The casual or occasional gambler for whom casino gaming is a form of entertainment.

2. Professional gamblers who have a studied approach to games with an element of skill so that they have an advantage. Their motivation is economic gain. The professional gambler gambles to live; a compulsive gambler lives to gamble.

3. Problem and compulsive gamblers. The problem gambler cannot resist impulses to gamble and is on the way to becoming a compulsive (pathological) gambler. A person is a compulsive gambler if the gambling behavior takes over to the point where it disrupts and damages his or her personal and professional life. That person should seek help.

Gamblers Anonymous is an organization of compulsive gamblers who seek recovery from the illness. GA lists the following 20 questions and notes that if you answer yes to at least seven of them, you may be a problem gambler:

1. Do you lose time from work due to gambling?
2. Does gambling make your home life unhappy?

3. Does gambling affect your reputation?
4. Do you ever feel remorse after gambling?
5. Do you ever gamble to get money to pay debts or otherwise solve financial difficulties?
6. Does gambling cause a decrease in your ambition or efficiency?
7. After losing do you feel you must return as soon as possible to win back your losses?
8. After a win do you have a strong urge to return and win more?
9. Do you often gamble until your last dollar is gone?
10. Do you ever borrow to finance your gambling?
11. Do you ever sell anything to finance your gambling?
12. Are you reluctant to use your gambling money for other expenses?
13. Does gambling make you careless about the welfare of your family?
14. Do you ever gamble longer than you planned?
15. Do you ever gamble to escape worry or trouble?
16. Do you ever commit or consider committing an illegal act to finance your gambling?
17. Does gambling cause you to have difficulty sleeping?
18. Do arguments, disappointments or frustrations create within you an urge to gamble?
19. Do you have an urge to celebrate good fortune by a few hours of gambling?
20. Do you ever consider self-destruction as a result of your gambling?

Compulsive gambling is a diagnosable and treatable illness. It can be as debilitating as drug or alcohol addiction. A 24-hour help line is available at 1-800-522-4700.

Arizona

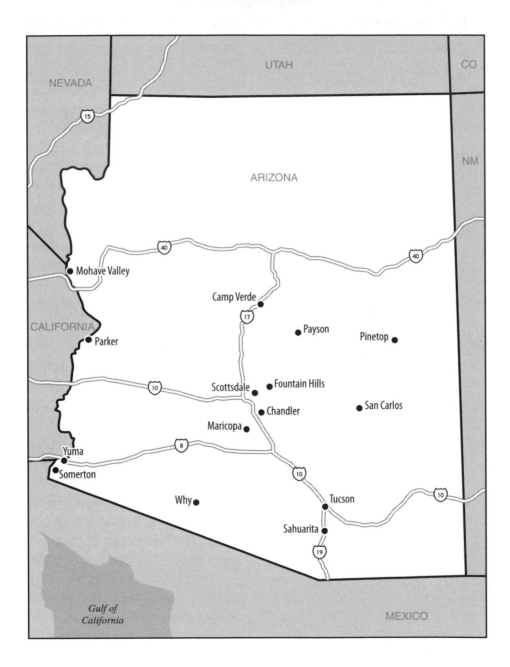

City	Casino	🚐	⚡	⛑	📄
Camp Verde	Cliff Castle Casino	✔		✔	15
Chandler	Gila River Casinos			✔	16
Fountain Hills	Fort McDowell Casino	✔			17
Maricopa	Harrah's Ak-Chin Casino				17
Mohave Valley	Spirit Mountain Casino	✔			18
Parker	Blue Water Casino				18
Payson	Mazatal Casino				19
Pinetop	Hon-Dah Casino	✔			19
Sahuarita	Desert Diamond			✔	20
San Carlos	Apache Gold Casino	✔			20
Scottsdale	Casino Arizona				21
Somerton	Cocopah Casino				21
Tucson	Casino Del Sol				22
Tucson	Casino of the Sun				22
Tucson	Desert Diamond			✔	22
Why	Golden Ha: San Casino				23
Yuma	Paradise Casino			✔	23

ARIZONA

Native American Tribes operate all the casinos in the state. Gaming compacts were first negotiated with Arizona's tribes in 1993 allowing them to offer slot machines in casinos on tribal lands. Later the compacts were amended to include table games.

CAMP VERDE

Cliff Castle Casino, Lodge & RV Park
555 Middle Verde Road
Camp Verde, Arizona 86322
928-567-7900 • 800-381-SLOT
928-554-8000 or 877-577-5507 (RV Park)
www.cliffcastlecasino.net

DESCRIPTION: Located 50 miles south of Flagstaff, Cliff Castle includes a casino, lodge and RV Park. The 24-hour casino features 570 slots, 10 gaming tables, poker room and four restaurants. The lodge has 84 rooms. Distant Drums RV Park, with 150 modern full-hookup sites, is located on the west side of the interstate. Amenities include a pavilion and swimming pool/spa. Last year's rates were $33-$39. Shuttle service is provided to the casino. Outdoor concerts are held in the Stargazer Pavilion. **DISCOUNTS**: Good Sam, FMCA, AARP and AAA discounts are honored. **DIRECTIONS & PARKING**: From I-17 exit 289, the casino is east of the interstate (follow signs). RV parking in the lower lot is free and overnight parking is permitted for self-contained units. On-call shuttle service is provided.

CHANDLER

Gila River Casinos
1200 South 56th Street (Lone Butte Chandler)
5512 West Wild Horse Pass (Wild Horse Chandler)
Chandler, Arizona 85226
520-796-7777 • 800-WIN-GILA
www.wingilariver.com

DESCRIPTION: Two separate casino buildings are both located adjacent to I-10 at exit 162. Wild Horse Casino Resort is west of the interstate and has 1,000 slots, 71 gaming tables, poker room, bingo, keno, non-smoking section, buffet restaurant, two delis and gift shop. Live entertainment is featured in the casino. The resort includes a hotel and spa. The Lone Butte casino is on the east side of the interstate and can be seen from the highway. **DIRECTIONS & PARKING**: From I-10, exit 162: *To Wild Horse* go west and follow signs. Follow signs to the parking lot designated for RVs. *To Lone Butte*: go east, then north on 54th St. Free overnight RV parking is available at both locations. The casino requests that Security be notified if you plan to stay overnight. Please observe a four-day stay limit.

FOUNTAIN HILLS

Fort McDowell Casino & RV Park
10424 North Fort McDowell Road
Fountain Hills, Arizona 85264
480-837-1424 • 800-THE-FORT
480-836-5310 (RV Park)
www.fortmcdowellcasino.com
www.eagleviewrvresort.com

DESCRIPTION: The resort includes a hotel and RV Park. Open 24/7, the casino has 775 slots, keno, bingo every day and five restaurants. There is 24-hour blackjack and poker in the card room with 24-hour tableside food service. The modern RV Park has 150 full-hookup sites. Last year's daily RV rates were $42-$47. DISCOUNTS: A Player's Club discount is given at restaurants. A free continental breakfast is offered daily at the RV Park. DIRECTIONS & PARKING: From State Road 87 north (the Beeline), exit at Fort McDowell Road (about 25 miles northeast of Phoenix). The casino is located at the northwest corner of Fort McDowell Road and SR-87. If staying overnight, RVs must check into the RV Park. There is NO free overnight parking at this casino.

MARICOPA

Harrah's Ak-Chin Resort Casino
15406 Maricopa Road
Maricopa, Arizona 85239
480-802-5000 • 800-HARRAHS
www.harrahs.com

DESCRIPTION: Open 24/7, the casino features 966 slots, keno parlor, 14 blackjack tables, 6-table poker room and bingo. The resort has a hotel and four restaurants, Native American crafts shop and smoke shop. Free entertainment is featured in the Oasis Lounge. DISCOUNTS: Various senior discounts are offered on Thursdays; Total Rewards cardholders receive buffet discounts every day. DIRECTIONS & PARKING: From I-10 exit 164, turn right on to Queen Creek Road for 17 miles to the casino.

After entering the Ak-Chin property, go to the parking area to the left, designated for large vehicles. Overnight parking is permitted.

MOHAVE VALLEY

Spirit Mountain Casino & RV Park
8555 South Highway 95
Mohave Valley, Arizona 86440
928-346-2000 • 928-346-1225 (RV Park)

DESCRIPTION: The 120-space RV Park has 3 cottages and 82 level, full hookup sites in an open desert setting. Big rigs are welcome. Last year's daily rate was $25, with weekly and monthly rates also available. The RV Park is open all year. It is located adjacent to a cozy casino that has 252 slots, video poker, keno (no table games) and a snack bar. Miniature golf and a driving range are on site. DIRECTIONS: From I-40 exit 1, take US-95 north for 12 miles into Mohave Valley. The casino is on the southbound side of US-95.

PARKER

Blue Water Casino
11300 Resort Drive
Parker, Arizona 85344
928-669-7777 • 888-243-3366
www.bluewaterfun.com

DESCRIPTION: The 24-hour casino features 475 slots, live keno, live action gaming tables, bingo and three restaurants. There is a hotel on site. The resort, located on the Colorado River, also includes a fourplex movie theater and miniature golf. DIRECTIONS & PARKING: Located about 160 miles west of Phoenix. From I-10 exit at US-95, go north for about 45 miles into Parker. Turn right at Riverside Drive and go 1.5 miles to the casino. Designated RV parking is in the upper lot. Overnight RV stays are limited to one night.

PAYSON

Mazatzal Casino
Highway 87 at Milepost 251
Payson, Arizona 85547
928-474-6044 • 800-777-7529
www.777play.com

DESCRIPTION: Open daily 24 hours, the casino features 400 slots, card room open daily 10am-1am and a restaurant. DISCOUNTS: Ask about Fun Books for discounts. Early bird specials are featured daily in the restaurant. Senior discount is extended on food. DIRECTIONS & PARKING: The casino is about 90 miles northeast of Phoenix. Go north on US Hwy-87 (the Beeline) to mile marker 251. Follow signs to overflow parking and park on the level lots across from the casino. The casino is within walking distance from all parking areas. Check with Security if you plan to stay overnight; there is a 3-night limit, no hookups.

PINETOP

Hon-Dah Casino Resort & RV Park
777 Highway 260/Jct Highway 73
Pinetop, Arizona 85935
928-369-0299 • 800-929-8744
928-369-7400 (RV Park)
www.hon-dah.com

DESCRIPTION: The resort, located in the White Mountains of eastern Arizona, includes a casino, hotel and RV Park with 258 level wooded sites (80 are pull-thrus) in a pine forest. Summer is busy and reservations are suggested since most sites are seasonally occupied. Last year's daily RV rate was $26; weekly and monthly rates available. The casino has over 900 slots, six gaming tables, poker room, two restaurants, a cigar bar and gift shop. DISCOUNTS: New Players Club members receive a Fun Book. DIRECTIONS & PARKING: Located at junction Hwy-260 & Hwy-73 (three miles south of Pinetop). From I-40 exit 286, take Hwy-77 south for 47 miles to Show Low, then US-60/77 south to Hwy-260 east for 15.5 miles. RVs are required to check into the RV Park. Dry camping is available for free overnight parking when the RV Park is full.

SAHUARITA

Desert Diamond: I-19
1100 West Pima Mine Road
Sahuarita, Arizona 85629
520-294-7777 • 866-332-9467
www.desertdiamondcasino.com

DESCRIPTION: The 24-hour casino has 600 slots, 18 blackjack tables, keno and three restaurants. There is a 2,500-seat event center. **DIRECTIONS & PARKING**: From I-19 exit 80, the casino is on the north side of Pima Mine Rd. Free overnight parking for large vehicles is at the north end of the lot; shuttle service is available to the casino.

SAN CARLOS

Apache Gold Casino Resort & RV Park
Highway 70
San Carlos, Arizona 85550
928-475-7800 • 800-APACHE 8
928-475-7800 Ext. 3659 (RV Park)
www.apachegoldcasinoresort.com

DESCRIPTION: The resort includes a casino, hotel, RV Park and golf course. The fully paved, mountain view RV Park has 60 extra wide, full hookup, pull-thru sites. All are walking distance to the casino. The park has a heated pool/spa, laundry and convenience store. Last year's rate was $20 per night. Live entertainment is featured in the Cabaret. Apache Gold has the #1 public golf course in Arizona, and there is excellent bass fishing nearby. The 24-hour casino has 500 slots, video poker, keno, blackjack tables, live action poker room and two restaurants. **DISCOUNTS**: Ask about seasonal promotions for RV Park guests. **DIRECTIONS**: From junction US-70 & US-60 in Globe, go east for six miles on US-70 (a major four-lane road). RV parking is also permitted in the casino lot; check with Security upon arrival.

SCOTTSDALE

Casino Arizona – Two locations in Scottsdale
Loop 101 at McKellips Road and
Loop 101 at Indian Bend Road
Scottsdale, Arizona 85256
480-850-7777 • 877-724-4687
www.casinoaz.com

DESCRIPTION: The two Casino Arizona locations in Scottsdale are both located adjacent to the northbound lanes of Loop 101. The casino at McKellips Road has 1,000 slots, 50 gaming tables, keno and five restaurants. The Talking Stick Resort at Indian Bend Road includes a larger casino, hotel and several dining venues. DIRECTIONS: The casinos are 15 miles northeast of Phoenix in Scottsdale, next to Loop 101 at McKellips Road (exit 50) or at Indian Bend Road (exit 44). For both casinos, turn east after exiting from Loop 101. RVs are welcome at the Talking Stick Resort. Please check in with Security if planning to stay overnight.

SOMERTON

Cocopah Casino
15136 South Avenue B (Rt-95)
Somerton, Arizona 85350
928-726-8066 • 800-237-5687
www.cocopahresort.com

DESCRIPTION: The 24-hour casino includes 500 slots, 10 blackjack tables, bingo every day and four restaurants. There is a hotel at the resort. DISCOUNTS: Ask at the Players Club about seasonal senior discounts. DIRECTIONS & PARKING: From I-8 near the California border, exit at 16th St. Take 16th Street to Avenue B (US-95). Go seven miles south on Avenue B toward Somerton. There are 30 spaces designated for RV dry camping at $5 per night. Pay at the gift shop. Shuttle service is provided to the casino.

TUCSON

Casino Del Sol
5655 West Valencia
Tucson, Arizona 85746
520-883-1700 • 800-344-9435
www.casinodelsol.com

DESCRIPTION: Open 24/7, the casino has 1,300 slots, 34 gaming tables including a poker room, bingo daily and seven restaurants. Live entertainment is featured in the AVA outdoor amphitheater. DISCOUNTS: Restaurant specials Tueday and Thursday; free coffee and donuts every morning in the lounge. DIRECTIONS & PARKING: From I-19 exit 95 (W Valencia Rd exit), go 8 miles west on Valencia. There is ample space for RVs near the AVA amphitheater. Free overnight parking is available for self-contained vehicles. The casino requests that RVs not use jacks in the parking lot.

Casino of the Sun
7406 South Camino De Oeste
Tucson, Arizona 85746
520-883-1700 • 800-344-9435
www.casinosun.com

DESCRIPTION: The smaller 24-hour sister casino to Casino Del Sol has 500 slots and two restaurants, a smoke shop and gift shop. DISCOUNTS: Ask about current Club Sol promotions and/or senior citizen discounts. DIRECTIONS & PARKING: From I-19 exit 95 (W Valencia Rd exit), go 7 miles west to Camino De Oeste. Turn left to the casino. There is ample space for RVs. Check in with Security if you plan to stay overnight.

Desert Diamond: Nogales Highway
7350 South Nogales Highway
Tucson, Arizona 85706

520-294-7777 • 866 332-9467
www.desertdiamondcasino.com

DESCRIPTION: The 24-hour casino has 1,000 slots, 49 gaming tables, bingo hall and live keno in a smoke-free gaming area, three restaurants and sports bar. There is a hotel on site. **DIRECTIONS & PARKING**: From I-19 exit 95 take Valencia Rd east to Nogales Hwy, then south on Nogales Hwy for 1 mile. Free overnight parking is available. The designated area for RVs is near the hotel; dry camping only. A security officer on bicycle will assist with parking and give you the required paperwork to be completed for your free stay.

WHY

Golden Ha: San Casino
Highway 86, Milepost 55
Why, Arizona 85321
520 547-4306 • 866-332-9467
520-547-4321 (Convenience Store)

DESCRIPTION: The casino is a popular stop on the way to Organ Pipe National Park and Rocky Point Mexico. It has 40 slots, a grill, full service gas station and convenience store. The casino is open 10am to midnight weekdays, until 2am weekends. **DIRECTIONS**: From I-8 exit 116 go south on State Rd 85 for 53 miles then State Rd 86 east to the casino at milepost 55 (1.5 miles east of Why, AZ).

YUMA

Paradise Casino
450 Quechan Dive
Yuma, Arizona 85364
760-572-7777 • 888-777-4946
www.paradise-casinos.com

DESCRIPTION: Paradise has two separate casino buildings – one on the Arizona side and one on the California side of the state line. They are in walking distance from one another. The Arizona casino has 475 slots, 12 gaming tables, bingo hall and a restaurant. The California casino has 200 slots, poker room and blackjack tables (no restaurant). **DISCOUNTS**: Club Paradise cardholders get discounts at the restaurant. **DIRECTIONS & PARKING**: From I-8 exit at 4th Ave. Follow casino signs. RVs may park on the dirt area designated for large vehicles. Overnight parking is permitted for persons in the casino.

California

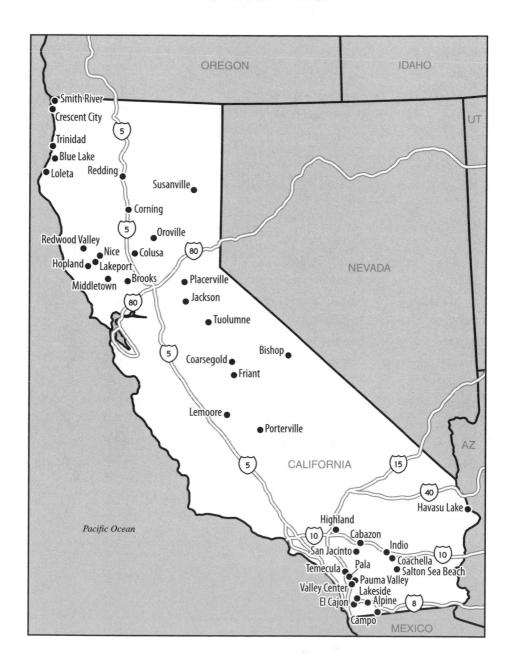

City	Casino	🚐	⚡	🛡	📄
Alpine	Viejas Casino			✔	27
Bishop	Paiute Palace Casino				28
Blue Lake	Blue Lake Casino				28
Brooks	Cache Creek Casino Resort				28
Cabazon	Morongo Casino Resort			✔	29
Campo	Golden Acorn Casino			✔	29
Coachella	Augustine Casino				30
Coachella	Spotlight 29			✔	30
Coarsegold	Chukchansi Gold Resort & Casino				31
Colusa	Colusa Casino				31
Corning	Rolling Hills Casino	✔		✔	32
Crescent City	Elk Valley Casino			✔	32
El Cajon	Sycuan Casino				33
Friant	Table Mountain Casino				33
Havasu Lake	Havasu Landing Resort	✔			34
Highland	San Manuel Indian Bingo & Casino				34
Hopland	Hopland Sho-Ka-Wah Casino				35
Indio	Fantasy Springs Casino			✔	35
Jackson	Jackson Rancheria Casino Resort	✔			35
Lakeport	Konocti Vista Casino	✔			36
Lakeside	Barona Valley Ranch Resort				37
Lemoore	Tachi Palace Casino				37
Loleta	Bear River Casino			✔	38
Middletown	Twin Pine Casino				38
Nice	Robinson Rancheria Casino	✔			39
Oroville	Feather Falls Casino	✔			39
Oroville	Gold Country Casino				39
Pala	Pala Casino				40
Pauma Valley	Casino Pauma				41
Placerville	Red Hawk Casino				41
Porterville	Eagle Mountain Casino				42
Redding	Win-River Casino				42
Redwood Valley	Coyote Valley Casino			✔	42

City	Casino	🚐	⚡	🛡	📄
Salton Sea Beach	Red Earth Casino				43
San Jacinto	Soboba Casino				43
Smith River	Lucky 7 Casino			✔	44
Susanville	Diamond Mountain Casino				44
Temecula	Pechanga Resort & Casino	✔		✔	44
Trinidad	Cher-Ae Heights Casino			✔	45
Tuolumne	Black Oak Casino				45
Valley Center	Harrah's Rincon Casino				46
Valley Center	Valley View Casino				47

CALIFORNIA

Gaming came to the state in March 2000, when Californians passed Proposition 1A which called for the state to arrange compacts with Indian tribal leaders aimed at permitting casinos on California's Indian lands. Currently, California has more than 40 Tribes hosting some form of gambling. Vegas-style casinos and casino resorts can be found throughout the state.

ALPINE

Viejas Casino
5000 Willows Road
Alpine, California 91901
619-445-5400 • 800-847-6537
www.viejas.com

DESCRIPTION: Located 25 miles east of San Diego, the casino features 2,500 slots, 108 gaming tables, poker room, racebook, bingo and six restaurants. Headline entertainment appears at concerts in the park. Retail factory outlet shops are nearby. **DIRECTIONS & PARKING**: From I-8 exit 33 (Alpine Blvd/Willows Rd) take Willows Rd north for 1.5 miles. The paved lot on the east side is designated for large vehicles. It is within walking distance to the casino.

BISHOP

Paiute Palace Casino
2742 North Sierra Highway (US-395)
Bishop, California 93514
760-873-4150 • 888-372-4883
www.paiutepalace.com

DESCRIPTION: Located in the heart of the Eastern Sierras, the 24-hour casino has 332 slots, 6 gaming tables and a café. There is a 24-hour gas station and convenience store on site. DISCOUNTS: A senior discount is extended at the restaurant. DIRECTIONS & PARKING: The casino is located directly on the southbound side of US-395, near the junction of US-6, on the north end of Bishop. Overnight parking is available in a well-lit RV/truck lot behind the casino building.

BLUE LAKE

Blue Lake Casino
777 Casino Way
Blue Lake, California 95525
707-668-9770 • 877-BLC-2-WIN
www.bluelakecasino.com

DESCRIPTION: Located ten miles north of Eureka, the 24/7 casino features 750 slots, 18 gaming tables, poker room, non-smoking areas, a restaurant, fast food and 24-hour café. Free live shows are featured in the Steelhead Lounge. DISCOUNTS: Weekly discounts for seniors. Ask about free gifts for joining the slot club. Red-Eye breakfast buffet in the café, midnight–10am. DIRECTIONS & PARKING: From US-101 exit 716A, take CA-299 east for 5.4 miles to the Blue Lake exit. Free overnight parking is available. There is a gas station on site.

BROOKS

Cache Creek Casino Resort
14455 Highway 16

Brooks, California 95606
530-796-3118 • 800-452-8181 (CA) • 800-992-8686
www.cachecreek.com

DESCRIPTION: The casino has 3,100 slots, 143 gaming tables, separate high limit area for blackjack and baccarat, non-smoking slots area and five restaurants. There is a hotel, mini mart and gas station on site. **DIRECTIONS & PARKING**: From I-505 exit 21 follow CA-16 west 12.5 miles. The casino is on the right in Brooks. Ample parking is available for RVs. Overnight is OK.

CABAZON

Morongo Casino Resort
49750 Seminole Drive
Cabazon, California 92230
951-849-3080 • 800-252-4499
www.morongocasinoresort.com

DESCRIPTION: The resort includes a 24-hour casino with over 2,500 gaming machines, 50 gaming tables, poker room, 12 restaurants and a hotel. **DISCOUNTS**: Winners Club members receive 10% off at the gift shop. **DIRECTIONS & PARKING**: From I-10 at exit 144, the casino can be seen from the interstate. Coming from the east on I-10, take the Cabazon/Main St. exit, go north, then west on Seminole Dr. Coming from the west, exit at Apache Trail, then north to Seminole Dr., then east to the casino. RVs should use the parking lot behind the old casino building. Overnight parking is permitted for self-contained RVs.

CAMPO

Golden Acorn Casino
1800 Golden Acorn Way
Campo, California 91906
619-938-6000 • 866-794-6244
www.goldenacorncasino.com

DESCRIPTION: Located 40 miles east of San Diego, the facility includes a truck stop, convenience store and a 24-hour restaurant with breakfast served anytime. The casino has 750 slots and 12 gaming tables. **DISCOUNTS**: Special discounts and promotions for seniors featured monthly. **DIRECTIONS & PARKING**: At I-8 exit 61, the casino is visible from the interstate. Lots of parking spaces are provided for large vehicles. RVs should park next to the large Golden Acorn sign. Overnight is OK for self-contained vehicles.

COACHELLA

Augustine Casino
84001 Avenue 54
Coachella, California 92236
760-391-9500
www.augustinecasino.com

DESCRIPTION: The 24/7 casino is located about five miles from I- 10; it has over 700 slots, a dozen gaming tables, non-smoking slots area and two restaurants (one open 24 hours). **DIRECTIONS & PARKING**: From 1-10, exit 146 (Dillon Rd), south on Dillon Rd for 1.5 miles, south on Van Buren St for 3 miles to the casino (corner of Van Buren & Avenue 54). RVs should park on the east side of the lot. Please check in with Security for parking authorization.

Spotlight 29
46-200 Harrison Place
Coachella, California 92236
760-775-5566 • 866-878-6829
www.spotlight29.com

DESCRIPTION: Owned by the 29 Palms Band of Indians, the 24/7 casino has 2,000 slots, 37 gaming tables, poker room, non-smoking slots area and three restaurants. Headline entertainment is featured in the showroom. **DIRECTIONS & PARKING**: The casino is 130 miles east of Los Angeles. From I-10, exit 146 (Dillon Rd/Coachilla), the casino can be seen from the eastbound lanes of the interstate. RV parking is next to the truck parking at the west end of the complex. Overnight is OK, but stays are limited to 24 hours.

COARSEGOLD

Chukchansi Gold Resort & Casino

711 Lucky Lane
Coarsegold, California 93614
559-692-5200 • 866-7-WIN-WIN
www.chukchansigold.com

DESCRIPTION: The 24-hour casino has 1,800 slots, 59 gaming tables, volcanic roulette, poker room and seven restaurants. The hotel has 200 rooms. Live entertainment and large screen TVs are in the Firehouse Blues lounge. DISCOUNTS: Ask about senior citizen specials at the buffet. DIRECTIONS & PARKING: From CA-99 exit 131 take CA-41 north for 36.3 miles then east on Lucky Lane .7 mile. There is a designated parking area for large vehicles. Check in with Security if you plan to stay overnight.

COLUSA

Colusa Casino

3770 Highway 45
Colusa, California 95932
530-458-8844 • 800-655-UWIN
www.colusacasino.com

DESCRIPTION: Located 75 miles north of Sacramento on the Wintun Reservation, the 24-hour casino has over 860 slots, 14 gaming tables, poker room and two restaurants. There is a hotel on site. DISCOUNTS: Senior Days are held every Tuesday and Friday. Seniors (50 and older) receive slot play credits. A senior slot tournament is held. DIRECTIONS & PARKING: From I-5 Williams exit 578, take CA-20 east for 8.4 miles, then north on CA-45 for 3.1 miles. RVs should park in the lot north of the casino. Overnight is OK.

CORNING

Rolling Hills Casino & RV Park
2655 Barham Avenue
Corning, California 96021
530-528-3500 • 888-331-6400
www.rollinghillscasino.com

DESCRIPTION: The resort includes a casino, hotel, lodge, RV Park and golf course. The self-serve RV Park has 48 full hookup, pull-thru sites on gravel pads. Daily rate is $25, self check-in with credit card or cash, first come/first serve. The casino, located in the Ramada Inn hotel, has over 700 slots, 12 tables, separate non-smoking areas and three restaurants. DISCOUNTS: Senior discounts Tuesday and Thursday for Shasta Club members (half-price dining.). DIRECTIONS & PARKING: The casino is located about 115 miles north of Sacramento. From I-5 exit 628 in Corning (at Liberal Ave), Rolling Hills is visible from the southbound lanes of the interstate. Free overnight parking is also available in the front lot.

CRESCENT CITY

Elk Valley Casino
2500 Howland Hill Road
Crescent City, California 95531
707-464-1020 • 888-574-2744
www.elkvalleycasino.com

DESCRIPTION: On the edge of the Redwood National Forest, the 24/7 casino has 313 slots, 7 gaming tables and a buffet restaurant. DISCOUNTS: Daily breakfast and lunch specials. DIRECTIONS & PARKING: From US-101 south end of Crescent City, go north on Humboldt Rd 1.5 miles then east at Howland Hill Rd. Free RV parking is available. Check with Security if you plan to stay overnight; the casino is accommodating for RV guests.

EL CAJON

Sycuan Casino
5469 Casino Way
El Cajon, California 92019
619-445-6002 • 800-279-2826
www.sycuancasino.com

DESCRIPTION: Ten miles east of San Diego, the two-story casino has 2,200 slots, 85 gaming tables, non-smoking area with separate entrance, bingo and four restaurants, including a 24-hour deli and snack bar in the bingo hall. There is a lodge at the resort and live entertainment is featured in the Showcase Theater. DISCOUNTS: Ask about Senior Day discounts and specials. DIRECTIONS & PARKING: From I-8 El Cajon/Second St exit, south on Second and left on Washington for one mile. The street name changes to Dehesa, proceed for six more miles to the casino. RVs should park in the overflow lot – walking distance to the casino.

FRIANT

Table Mountain Casino & Bingo
8184 Table Mountain Road
Friant, California 93626
559-822-7777 • 800-541-3637
www.tmcasino.com

DESCRIPTION: The 24-hour casino has 2,000 slots, 52 gaming tables, separate nine-table poker room and two restaurants. The Trading Post shop features authentic Native American collectibles art work and crafts. DISCOUNTS: The Senior lunch buffet is offered at discounted prices on weekdays. DIRECTIONS & PARKING: From CA-99 exit 131 take CA-41 north for 9.9 miles, then exit 135 to Friant Rd east 11.2 miles, continue on Millerton Rd 4.4 miles then north on Table Mountain Rd .2 mile. Check in with Security if you plan to stay overnight.

HAVASU LAKE

Havasu Landing Resort, Casino & RV Park
5 Main Street
Havasu Lake, California 92363
760-858-4593 • 800-307-3610
www.havasulanding.com

DESCRIPTION: On the western shores of Lake Havasu near the Arizona state line, the resort includes a full-service RV park, mobile homes on the lake and a marina with boat slips. A market, deli and general store are on site. Last year's RV rates were $25-$30. The casino has 220 slots plus live blackjack and poker. Casino hours are 8:30am–12:30am/2:30am(Fri–Sat). Activities include boating, water skiing, swimming, fishing, hunting, jet skiing, windsurfing and sightseeing. DIRECTIONS: From I-40 exit 144 at Needles, take US-95 south for 19 miles and turn left at Havasu Lake Rd.

HIGHLAND

San Manuel Indian Bingo & Casino
777 San Manuel Boulevard
Highland, California 92346
909-864-5050 • 800-359-2464
www.sanmanuel.com

DESCRIPTION: The 24-hour casino has over 3,000 slots, 100 gaming tables, smoke-free poker room and six restaurants. Bingo is held every day except Thursday. Free entertainment is featured nightly in the Tukut Lounge. There is live headline entertainment on weekends. DIRECTIONS & PARKING: From I-10, exit 72, go 4 miles north on I-215 to CA-30 east. Follow signs to Highland/Mt. Resorts and merge onto CA-30E. Stay on 30E for about 3 miles and exit at Highland Avenue East. Go one mile to Victoria Avenue and turn left. Stay on Victoria to the casino. The upper parking lot is designated for RVs (steep grades). Security is on site and will assist with parking. Shuttle service is available 24 hours.

HOPLAND

Hopland Sho-Ka-Wah Casino
13101 Nakomis Road
Hopland, California 95449
707-744-1395 • 888-746-5292
www.shokawah.com

DESCRIPTION: The 24-hour casino has 550 slots, 9 gaming tables, a steakhouse, deli and sports bar. **DIRECTIONS & PARKING**: Hopland is 107 miles north of the Golden Gate Bridge. From US-101 go east on CA-175 for 3.6 miles to the casino. (Exxon station at the corner of the 101 & CA-175.) Upon arrival on casino property, check with Security and they will direct you to the parking area for large vehicles. Overnight parking is permitted.

INDIO

Fantasy Springs Casino
84-245 Indio Springs Drive
Indio, California 92203
760-342-5000 • 800-827-2WIN
www.fantasyspringsresort.com

DESCRIPTION: The 24/7 casino located in the Palm Springs Valley, has 2,000 slots, 40 gaming tables, poker room, off track betting and bingo every day. The resort also includes a hotel, seven restaurants and two lounges. A 24-lane bowling alley is on site. **DIRECTIONS & PARKING**: Located 125 miles east of Los Angeles, exit I-10 at Golf Center Pkwy (exit 144.) The casino is visible from the interstate. RV parking is behind the hotel. Overnight parking is permitted for self-contained RVs.

JACKSON

Jackson Rancheria Casino Resort & RV Park
12222 New York Ranch Road
Jackson, California 95642

209-223-1677 • 800-822-9466
www.jacksoncasino.com

DESCRIPTION: Located 60 miles southeast of Sacramento on the Miwuk Reservation, the resort includes a hotel and a 100-site full-service RV Park. The modern RV Park has a pool, recreation building, wi-fi throughout and a laundry. Last year's rates were $30-$45. Rallies are welcome. Shuttle service is provided. The 24-hour casino has 1,500 slots, 65 gaming tables, poker room, bingo on weekends and three restaurants and a food court. Free live music in the cabaret; headline entertainment in concert on weekends. **DISCOUNTS**: Good Sam and AAA discounts are offered. **DIRECTIONS & PARKING**: From CA-99 exit 254A take CA-88 (steep grades) north 38 miles, then north on CA-104/Ridge Road 6 miles to New York Ranch Rd south 1.2 miles.

LAKEPORT

Konocti Vista Casino & RV Park
2755 Mission Rancheria Road
Lakeport, California 95453
707-262-1900 • 800-386-1950
www.kvcasino.com

DESCRIPTION: Located on Clear Lake, California's largest natural lake, the resort includes a hotel and modern RV Park. There are 74 paved full hookup sites, showers and laundry. Last year's daily RV rates were $30; weekly rates are available; register at the hotel. RV guests are invited to use the pool and other hotel amenities. There is a 94-slip marina/boat launch and fishing off the dock. Casino hours are 8am-2am weekdays; 24 hours on weekends. The casino has 425 slots, video poker and 6 tables. A full service diner is open 6am–10pm. **DISCOUNTS**: The RV Park honors Good Sam, Escapees and Passport America discounts. Senior citizen discount at the diner. Ask about seasonal discounts and promotions. **DIRECTIONS & PARKING**: From US-101 in Hopland take CA-175 east 17.5 miles, then Soda Bay Rd east 1.8 mile and Mission Rancheria Rd north .5 mile. Free overnight parking is allowed on the gravel area next to the casino parking lot, but it is limited to two nights. If staying longer, please check into the RV Park.

LAKESIDE

Barona Valley Ranch Resort and Casino
1932 Wildcat Canyon Road
Lakeside, California 92040
619-443-2300 • 888-722-7662
www.barona.com

DESCRIPTION: Owned and operated by the Barona Band of Mission Indians, the casino features 2,000 slots, video poker, video roulette, modified craps, 70 live table games, poker room, off track betting parlor and bingo hall. The resort has a hotel, four restaurants and golf course. DISCOUNTS: Buffet discounts are given for Club Barona members. Free buffet for two on your birthday. DIRECTIONS & PARKING: Located 15 miles northeast of San Diego. From I-8 exit 23 go north on Lake Jennings Rd for 2.3 miles, continue on Mapleview St for .5 mile, east on Ashwood St for 1 mile then continue on Wildcat Canyon Road for 5.5 miles to the casino. Security will assist with parking.

LEMOORE

Tachi Palace Casino
17225 Jersey Avenue
Lemoore, California 93245
559-924-7751 • 800-942-6886
www.tachipalace.com

DESCRIPTION: The 24-hour casino, owned and operated by the Santa Rosa Rancheria Tachi Tribe, has five floors including 2,000 slots, 56 pit/table games, poker room, bingo every day and four restaurants. Live entertainment on weekends includes concerts and championship boxing. There is a hotel on site. DIRECTIONS & PARKING: From I-5 exit 309, go north on CA-41 for 20.7 miles, then east on Jersey Ave for 2.8 miles to the casino. Overnight parking is permitted for self-contained RVs.

LOLETA

Bear River Casino
11 Bear Paw Way
Loleta, California 95551
707-733-9644 • 800-761-2327
www.bearrivercasino.com

DESCRIPTION: The casino has 349 slots, 13 live action gaming tables, two restaurants and a sports bar. Karaoke is every Thursday. Hours are 9am-5am daily/24 hours on weekends. The adjacent Pump & Play has a gas station, convenience store and a smoke-free slots area. DISCOUNTS: Weekday specials are featured at the restaurant and complimentary doughnuts are offered Monday mornings. DIRECTIONS & PARKING: From US-101 exit 692 (Fernbridge/Ferndale), turn left on to Singley Rd. Follow signs. Parking is available for RVs; please notify Security if you plan to stay overnight.

MIDDLETOWN

Twin Pine Casino
22223 Hwy-29 at Rancheria Road
Middletown, California 95461
707-987-0197 • 800-564-4872
www.twinpine.com

DESCRIPTION: The resort has a hotel and 24/7 casino with over 500 slots, 12 gaming tables, poker room, steakhouse, marketplace, sports bar and entertainment. DIRECTIONS & PARKING: From US-101 in Hopland, follow CA-175 east 26.8 miles and south 19.7 miles, then CA-29 south 1.5 mile. Free overnight parking is available for RVs. Park along the fence and check in with Security if staying overnight. *Note:* This casino is well off the main highways and roads leading in are narrow and winding.

NICE

Robinson Rancheria Casino
1545 Highway 20
Nice, California 95464
707-262-4000 • 800-809-3636
707-274-5531 (RV Park)
www.robinsonrancheria.biz

DESCRIPTION: The 24-hour casino has 600 slots, 13 gaming tables, and 1,000-seat bingo hall, grill, snack shack and sports bar. The hotel has 48 rooms. Live entertainment is featured in the showroom. Starbuck's coffee is available in the gift shop. The Aurora RV Park and Marina, also owned by the Poma Indians, is 2.4 miles east of the casino on CA-20. Robinson Rancheria is on the north shore of Clear Lake where there is good fishing. **DISCOUNTS**: Senior Day on Wednesdays features match play and food doscounts. **DIRECTIONS & PARKING**: From US-101 north of Ukiah, take CA-20 east 21.8 miles toward Upper Lake/Williams. Robinson Rancheria is on the left as you enter Nice. Free overnight parking for RVs is permitted in the casino lot for one night only.

OROVILLE

Feather Falls Casino & RV Park
3 Alverda Drive
Oroville, California 95966
530-533-3885 • 877-652-4646
530-533-9020 (RV Park)
www.featherfallscasino.com

DESCRIPTION: The resort includes a hotel and a modern KOA RV Park with 43 full hookup spaces, group meeting hall, store, gift shop and laundry. Daily RV rates start at $36. The 24-hour casino has 1,000 slots, 11 single deck blackjack tables, poker room and two restaurants. Live entertainment is featured on weekends in the Cascade Showroom. **DISCOUNTS**: Casino coupons are given to all RV guests and group discounts given for rallies. **DIRECTIONS & PARKING**: Located 100 miles north of Sacramento. From Marysville, take CA-70 north for 22.7 miles to Ophir Road, then three miles east on Ophir Road. If staying overnight, RVs are asked to register at the RV Park.

Gold Country Casino
4020 Olive Highway
Oroville, California 95966
530-534-9892 • 800-334-9400
www.goldcountrycasino.com

DESCRIPTION: The 24-hour casino has 900 slots, 25 gaming tables, poker room and three restaurants. The hotel has 87 rooms/suites. DISCOUNTS: Senior Days on Tuesday and Thursday feature free coffee and donuts and a voucher for slot play. Cash Club members get cash back based on their play. DIRECTIONS & PARKING: From CA-99 in Oroville Junction go east on CA-162 (Oroville Dam Rd & Olive Hwy) for 10.4 miles. RVs should check with Security if they wish to stay overnight.

PALA

Pala Casino
11154 Highway 76
Pala, California 92059
760-510-5100 • 877-946-7252
www.palacasino.com

DESCRIPTION: The Vegas-style resort has a hotel and 24-hour casino with 2,250 slots, 87 gaming tables, poker room, two lounges and eight restaurants. Headline entertainment appears at the Pala Events Center and the Palomar Starlight Theater. DIRECTIONS & PARKING: Located 35 miles northeast of San Diego, from I-15 exit 46 at SR-76 (Pala/Oceanside). Take SR-76 east for five miles to the casino. RVs should park in the west lot, within walking distance to the casino. RV parking is limited to 24 hours.

PAUMA VALLEY

Casino Pauma
777 Pauma Reservation Road
Pauma Valley, California 92061
760-742-2177 • 877-687-2862
www.casinopauma.com

DESCRIPTION: The 24-hour casino has Vegas style gaming – 1,100 slots, 24 gaming tables, and three restaurants. Outdoor dining is available under the covered patio overlooking the Palamar Mountains. **DISCOUNTS**: Breakfast specials and senior lunch buffets are offered. Discounted prices on prime rib dinners are extended to Palm Club members. **DIRECTIONS & PARKING**: Located 35 miles northeast of San Diego. Take I-15, exit 46 to Hwy-76 (Oceanside/Pala exit) east for 12 miles to Pauma Reservation Rd. (Street sign is partially obstructed. Look for Jilburto's Taco Shop on the right and get into the left lane.) Turn left on to Pauma Reservation Rd for a half mile to the casino. Free parking is available for RVs. Turn right at the casino, then take the first right into the parking lot – walking distance to the casino.

PLACERVILLE

Red Hawk Casino
5250 Honpie Road
Placerville, CA 95667
530-677-7000
www.redhawkcasino.com

DESCRIPTION: The casino is on the Rancheria of the Shingle Springs Band of Miwok Indians in the foothills of the Sierras, 9 miles west of Placerville. It includes 2,000 slots, 75 gaming tables, high stakes room, six restaurants and retail stores. The entire lower level of the casino is non-smoking. **DIRECTIONS**: From the Capitol City Fwy in Sacramento, go east on US-50 for about 36 miles, follow signs to the casino. Check with Security about free overnight parking.

PORTERVILLE

Eagle Mountain Casino
681 South Tule Road
Porterville, California 93258
559-788-6220 • 800-903-3353
www.eaglemtncasino.com

DESCRIPTION: The casino features 1,500 slots, 13 table games, bingo, three restaurants and a snack bar. DIRECTIONS: From Hwy-99 exit 76 take CA-190 east for 21.1 miles then south on Road 284 for .5 mile and east on Indian Reservation Rd Overnight RV parking is available.

REDDING

Win-River Casino
2100 Redding Rancheria Road
Redding, California 96001
530-243-3377 • 800-280-8946
www.win-river.com

DESCRIPTION: Located 163 miles north of Sacramento, the casino has 1,000 slots, 24 gaming tables, poker room, bingo, a full service restaurant, deli and fast food. There is a Hilton Garden Inn on site. DIRECTIONS & PARKING: From I-5 exit 667, merge north onto CA-273 for 7.1 miles, then west on Canyon Rd and south on Redding Rancheria Rd for .3 mile. Ample parking is within walking distance to the casino. Please notify Security if you plan to stay overnight.

REDWOOD VALLEY

Coyote Valley Casino
7751 North State Street
Redwood Valley, California 95470
707-485-0700 • 800-332-9683
www.coyotevalleycasino.com

DESCRIPTION: The 24-hour casino has 270 slots, video poker, video keno, four gaming tables and high stakes bingo. Food is available at Angelina's Café. **DIRECTIONS & PARKING**: From US-101 exit 557 take West Rd east for .3 mile then State St south 1.1 mile. Free overnight parking is available.

SALTON SEA BEACH

Red Earth Casino
Highway 86 South
Salton Sea Beach, California 92275
760-395-1200

DESCRIPTION: The 24-hour casino features Vegas-style slots and gaming table, the Beach Club Café and Subway sandwich shop. The Travel Center has à convenience store. **DIRECTIONS & PARKING**: From I-10 exit 146 (Dillon Rd) exit toward Coachella/CA-86 South. Take CA-86 south for about 27 miles. Free overnight parking for RVs is limited to 3 days. There is a dump station at the travel center.

SAN JACINTO

Soboba Casino
23333 Soboba Road
San Jacinto, California 92581
951-665-1000 • 866-476-2622
www.soboba.net

DESCRIPTION: The 24-hour casino has over 2,000 slots, 20 table games, poker room, three restaurants and headline entertainment on weekends. **DISCOUNTS**: The steakhouse extends discounts to Players Club members. Also, ask about weekly Player Appreciation Days. **DIRECTIONS & PARKING**: Located 90 miles east of Los Angeles, from I-215 exit 22 take the Ramona Expressway east for 30 miles to Lake Park Dr. Turn left to the stop sign, then right on Soboba Road for about a mile to the casino. RVs should park toward the back of the lot. Overnight parking is OK.

SMITH RIVER

Lucky 7 Casino
350 North Indian Road
Smith River, California 95567
707-487-7777 • 866-777-7170
www.lucky7casino.com

DESCRIPTION: The 24-hour casino, located in the northwestern corner of the state just three miles south of the Oregon border, has over 200 slots, two gaming tables and a full service restaurant. **DIRECTIONS & PARKING**: The casino is visible from the northbound lanes of the 101 Freeway. Designated RV parking is within walking distance to the casino, and overnight parking is permitted.

SUSANVILLE

Diamond Mountain Casino & Hotel
900 Skyline Drive
Susanville, California 96130
530-252-1100 • 877-319-8514
www.diamondmountaincasino.com

DESCRIPTION: The casino has 240 slots, gaming tables, bingo, 24-hour café, steakhouse and sports bar. There is a hotel on site. **DISCOUNTS**: Ask about senior discounts at the café. **DIRECTIONS & PARKING**: The casino is located 160 miles northeast of Sacramento on US-395 in Susanville (between Lake Tahoe and Lasson Volcanic Park.) Parking is available for RVs; please notify Security if you plan to stay overnight.

TEMECULA

Pechanga Resort and Casino & RV Park
45000 Pechanga Parkway
Temecula, California 92592
951-693-1819 • 877-711-2WIN
877-997-8386 (RV Park)
www.pechanga.com

DESCRIPTION: The resort includes a hotel and RV Park with 168 sites (25 are pull thrus). The modern, full service RV Park has a heated pool, two Jacuzzi spas, recreation room, laundry, gas station, car wash and convenience store. Pechanga can serve as a home base for visitors exploring southern California. Last year's RV rates: $42-$52 per night. Reservations are suggested and rallies are welcome. Shuttle service is provided to the 24-hour casino that has 3,600 slots, 212 gaming tables, high stakes room and a non-smoking poker room. The gaming area has extensive non-smoking sections. There are eight restaurants; live entertainment is featured at the casino. Pechanga Resort is located in the picturesque Temecula Valley where outdoor non-gaming activities abound. **DISCOUNTS**: Good Sam, AAA and AARP discounts are honored. **DIRECTIONS**: From I-15, exit 50 (Indio/Route 79 South), Pechanga Indian Reservation signs are at the exit. Go south on Route 79 for .7 mile, right on Pechanga Parkway for 1.5 miles to the resort complex.

TRINIDAD

Cher-Ae Heights Casino
27 Scenic Drive
Trinidad, California 95570
707-677-3611 • 800-684-2464
www.cheraeheightscasino.com

DESCRIPTION: The 24-hour casino has 450 slots, 12 pit/gaming tables, poker room and bingo five days a week, restaurant and deli. **DIRECTIONS & PARKING**: From US-101 Trinidad exit 728 (Trinidad Beach sign at exit) immediately turn south on to Scenic Drive for one mile. *Note*: there are steep grades going up to the casino. Free overnight parking is available for RVs and 24-hour shuttle service is provided.

TUOLUMNE

Black Oak Casino at Tuolumne Rancheria
19400 Tuolumne Road North
Tuolumne, California 95379
209-928-9300 • 877-747-8777
www.blackoakcasino.com

DESCRIPTION: The 24/7 casino has 1,000 slots, keno, 24 gaming tables, non-smoking slots section and three restaurants. Live music is featured on weekends at the Willow Creek Lounge. There is a 24-lane bowling center on property. DISCOUNTS: Special prices on senior breakfast. Senior activities include weekly slot tournaments. DIRECTIONS & PARKING: In the Sierra foothills, the casino is 100 miles southeast of Sacramento. From CA-99 exit 233 take CA-219 east 4.8 miles, McHenry Ave north 1.8 mile, Patterson Rd east 3 miles, continue on CA-108 east for 40.6 miles to the Mono Way exit, then Tuolumne Rd east 6.9 miles. Check in with Security if you plan to stay overnight.

VALLEY CENTER

Harrah's Rincon Casino & Resort
33750 Valley Center Road
Valley Center, California 92082
760-751-3100 • 877-777-2457
www.harrahs.com

DESCRIPTION: The Vegas-style casino has 1,600 slots and video poker, over 60 table games, eight restaurants and coffee bar and casual grill. Live entertainment is featured in the Oasis Bar. The hotel has 651 rooms/suites. Concerts are held in the Open Sky Theater. DISCOUNTS: Total Rewards cardholders receive discounts at the buffet and gift shop. DIRECTIONS & PARKING: Located ten miles north of Escondido, from I-15, take exit 31 (Valley Parkway) going east. Valley Parkway turns into Valley Center Rd. (You will travel several miles through Escondido before the street changes to Valley Center Rd.) Follow Valley Center Road for about eight miles to Harrah's on the left. RVs should park behind the casino building. Overnight is OK.

Valley View Casino

16300 Nyemii Pass Road
Valley Center, California 92082
760-291-5500 • 866-843-9946
www.valleyviewcasino.com

DESCRIPTION: The 24-hour casino has 1,300 slots, 10 gaming tables, a buffet, steakhouse and café (open 24 hrs). **DISCOUNTS**: VIP Players Club members get discounts at the buffet. **DIRECTIONS & PARKING**: From I-15 take exit 31/Escondido at Valley Pkwy, then east on Valley Pkwy for 5 miles (it becomes Valley Center Rd). Follow signs to the casino. RV parking is available in the employee lot corner of Valley Center Rd & North Lake Wohlford Rd. Shuttle service is provided to the casino.

Colorado

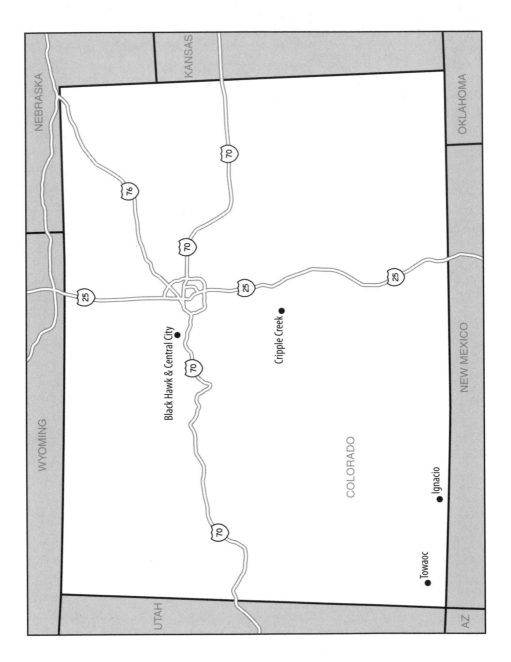

City	Casino	🚐	〽	⬭	📄
Black Hawk	Black Hawk Area Casinos				49
Cripple Creek	Cripple Creek Area Casinos				51
Ignacio	Sky Ute Casino Resort				52
Towaoc	Ute Mountain Casino	✔			53

COLORADO

Casinos in Colorado are located in two historic mining regions of the Rockies: Black Hawk/Central City (off I-70) and Cripple Creek (west of I-25). Two Indian casinos are in the southern region of the state off U.S. Highway 160.

BLACK HAWK / CENTRAL CITY

Black Hawk and *Central City* are among Colorado's oldest settlements. These towns grew as a result of the gold rush of 1859 and prospered during the latter half of the 19th Century. After the gold ran out, the area turned to coal (hard rock mining), which provided steady employment through the early part of the 20th Century. After that, the area declined somewhat. In 1990 the old mining towns had a major revival when a successful Colorado ballot initiative allowed limited stakes gambling in the commercial districts of the towns with the proceeds earmarked for historic preservation efforts statewide. Gaming began in Black Hawk/ Central City in 1991, ushering in a new "gold rush" for the historic mining towns.

With some two dozen casinos clustered in the charming little downtown areas, Black Hawk/Central City is a natural for "casino hopping." All casinos have slots, video poker, video blackjack and video keno. Most casinos have table games: blackjack, poker, let it ride and three-card poker. Casinos in Black Hawk and Central City are open every day 8am–2am. You can find more information about the city of Black Hawk at their web site: cityofblackhawk.org.

DIRECTIONS: From I-70 exit 244, east on Hwy-6 for 2.8 miles, north on Hwy-119 for 6.7 miles into Black Hawk. Note that Hwy-6 (between I-70 and Hwy-119) has two tunnels with 13 ft. clearances.

ACCOMMODATIONS: The larger casinos have hotels and there are also several charming B&B's in Black Hawk and Central City. For more information about accommodations, call 303-582-5221 for Black Hawk or 800-542-2999 for Central City, or refer to these sites: www. blackhawkcolorado.com *or* www.centralcitycolorado.com.

RV PARKING: There are parking lots and parking garages for cars throughout Black Hawk and Central City. RVs should use the Miners Mesa Parking Lot, located at the highest point in Black Hawk with a bird's eye view of the old mining town below. To get to Miners Mesa turn left at the first traffic light (Mill Street) and take Mill Street through the intersection of Main Street and continue up the hill for 1.8 miles. From the lot you can enjoy a spectacular 360° view of the mountains and even see the Continental Divide. Free overnight parking is provided for self-contained RVs. Free shuttle buses operate daily between 8am and 2am between the Miners Mesa lot and all the casinos in Black Hawk and Central City.

Black Hawk Casinos

Main Street
> Bull Durham Saloon & Casino, Canyon Casino, Colorado Central Station, Fitzgerald's Casino, Golden Gulch Casino, Gilpen Hotel Casino, Golden Gates Casino, Isle of Capri Hotel & Casino, The Lodge Casino Hotel, Jazz Alley Casino, Mardi Gras Casino, Riviera Casino, Wild Card Saloon and Winners Haven Casino.

Gregory Street
> Black Hawk Station Casino & Lodging, Bullwackers Casino, Don Cooper's Eureka Casino and Red Dolly Casino

Richman Street
> Mountain High Casino & Hotel and Richman Casino

Chase Street
   Silver Hawk Casino

Central City Casinos

Main Street
   Famous Bonanza, Easy Street Casino and Doc Holliday Casino

Gregory Street
   Fortune Valley Hotel & Casino

Dostal Alley
   Dostal Alley Saloon

CRIPPLE CREEK

Cripple Creek is the other area that was revitalized by the 1990 ballot initiative in Colorado. A unique Old West town, Cripple Creek is located in the mountains west of Colorado Springs. It is another interesting historic preservation/casino-hopping location. The Cripple Creek District Museum, in the heart of the old mining town, reflects the rich history of the area. The Pikes Peak Heritage Center is also at Cripple Creek. There are guided mine tours and gold panning adventures in season. The history of the Old West is also preserved at the theater in Cripple Creek. Some 18 casinos, located on the main thoroughfare in Cripple Creek, all offer electronic gaming and live action gaming tables. Information about Cripple Creek is available from their tourist office at 877-858-GOLD.

DIRECTIONS: From I-25 exit 141 go west on US-24 to Divide, CO, then south on Hwy-67 for 18 miles (two-lane road with sharp curves and steep grades) to Cripple Creek.

ACCOMMODATIONS: Many of the casinos have hotels, and there are B&B's in town as well. For information call Cripple Creek Tourism at 877-858-GOLD or refer to www.cripple-creekcolorado.com.

RV PARKING: Ample parking is provided for cars. However, there are no designated parking places for RVs at the Cripple Creek casinos and space for RV parking anywhere in town is very limited. There is free daytime parking available on the east side of Hwy-67 coming into town (spaces limited). For overnight, the mountainous terrain prevents camping on casino properties but there is one campground nearby, south of the casinos on Warren Avenue, between 2nd and 3rd.

Cripple Creek Casinos

General information about Cripple Creek casinos:

- Free shuttle service runs daily.
- Many casinos hand out Fun Books and coupons at the door.
- Some casinos offer free hot dogs, popcorn and drinks for players.
- Ask about daily specials and senior discounts at casino restaurants.

East Bennett Avenue
Black Diamond Casino, Brass Ass Casino, Bronco Billy's, Colorado Grande Gaming Parlor, Creeker's Casino, Double Eagle Hotel & Casino, Gold Digger's Casino, Gold Creek Casino, Gold Rush Hotel & Casino, Johnny Nolan's, J.P. McGill's Hotel & Casino, Midnight Rose Hotel & Casino, Uncle Sam's, and Womack's Legends Hotel & Casino

Third Street
Imperial Hotel & Casino

Myers Avenue
Wild Horse Casino

IGNACIO

Sky Ute Casino Resort
14324 Highway 172 North

Ignacio, Colorado 81137
970-563-3000 • 888-842-4180
www.skyutecasino.com

DESCRIPTION: The resort includes a modern hotel and 24-hour casino with slots, gaming tables, a smoke-free poker room and five restaurants. There is a bowling alley on site. The Southern Ute Cultural Center and museum (free admission) is nearby. **DIRECTIONS & PARKING**: From junction US-160 & US-550 (east edge of Durango), east two miles on US-160 to SR-172, then southeast on SR-172 for 18 miles. RV parking is available. If staying overnight, please notify Security.

TOWAOC

Ute Mountain Casino & RV Park

3 Weeminuche Drive
Towaoc, Colorado 81334
970-565-8800 • 800-258-8007
970-565-6544 (RV Park)
www.utemountaincasino.com

DESCRIPTION: The resort includes the casino, a hotel and RV Park with 76 level gravel sites (some have full hookup, some water & electric), central dump, laundry, and indoor swimming pool. Last year's daily rates were $23-$25. The RV Park is walking distance to the casino, but shuttle service is also provided. Ute Tribal Park tours are available. The casino is the largest in the four corners area with over 665 slots, five gaming tables, poker room, live keno, full service restaurant and a fast food counter. Hours are 8am–4am. **DISCOUNTS**: Food discount for seniors 55 and older. Good Sam, AARP and AAA discounts are honored. **DIRECTIONS & PARKING**: From junction US-160 and US-491 in Cortez, southwest for 11 miles on US-160/491. Free overnight parking for self-contained RVs is available at the travel center south of the casino or on the perimeter of the hotel's parking lot. The resort is near Mesa Verde and the Four Corners.

Connecticut

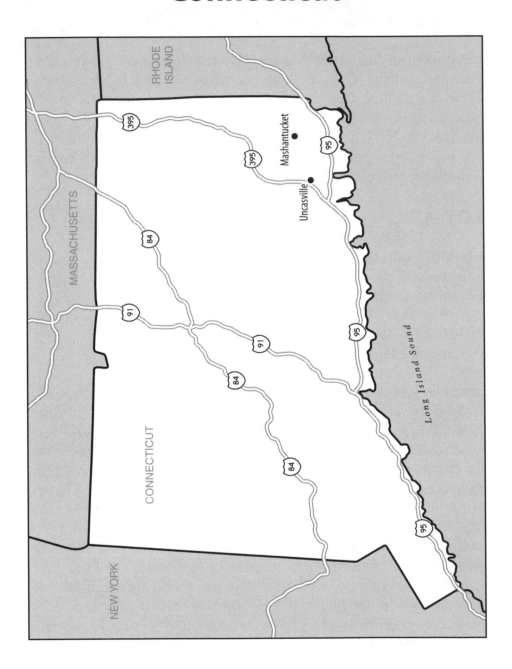

City	Casino	🚐	🏔	⬭	📋
Mashantucket	Foxwoods Resort Casino				55
Uncasville	Mohegan Sun Casino				56

CONNECTICUT

Connecticut is home to two spectacular casinos: Foxwoods and Mohegan Sun. They are located just across the Thames River from one another. Directions for "casino hopping" the ten miles from one to the other are also included below.

MASHANTUCKET

Foxwoods Resort Casino

39 Norwich Westerly Road
Mashantucket, Connecticut 06338
860-312-3000 • 1-800-FOXWOODS
www.foxwoods.com

DESCRIPTION: The famed Foxwoods, with over 340,000 square feet of gaming space, is the largest casino in the world. The Mashantucket Pequot Tribe opened the casino resort in 1992. There are three hotels on property. Foxwoods is so big you'll want to pick up a map at the information booth before exploring the property. Foxwoods has six casinos featuring 7,200 slots, including 500 slots in the non-smoking casino, 400 table games, a poker room, ultimate high-tech race book, keno and a high stakes bingo hall. The resort also has 24 restaurants, a Hard Rock Café, two 18-hole championship golf courses and many interesting specialty shops including the Wampum Trading Post Super Store and the Pequot Trader Outlet. DIRECTIONS: From I-95, exit 92, Route 2 west for eight miles to Foxwoods. From I-84, exit 55, Route 2 east to nine miles past Norwich. From I-395, exit 85 (in CT), go straight to the second traffic light, then south on Route 164. Follow Route 164 to the end (about seven miles) to Route 2 east for 1.5 miles. PARKING: One of the parking lots on property is designated for large vehicles. Check with Security when you come in. Free overnight parking is permitted for self-contained vehicles. Shuttle service to the casino operates 24 hours.

To get to Mohegan Sun from Foxwoods (approximately ten miles): Exit Foxwoods, turn left onto Route 2 West. Go about four miles to Route 2A. Rosie's Diner will be on your left. Turn left onto 2A. Go to the next stoplight and turn right. Follow Route 2A to next stoplight, which will be Route 12; then turn left. Go approximately 300 yards. Turn right on to Mohegan-Pequot bridge. Once across the bridge, follow signs to Mohegan Sun, which is the first exit on the right.

UNCASVILLE

Mohegan Sun Casino
1 Mohegan Sun Boulevard
Uncasville, Connecticut 06382
860-862-8000 • 1-888-226-7711
www.mohegansun.com

DESCRIPTION: Mohegan Sun Casino is also large and luxurious. It features a hotel tower with more than 1,200 rooms/suites, 30 restaurants and two casinos; 300,000 square feet of gaming includes slots, table games, poker room and a pari-mutuel simulcast facility. Mohegan Sun also has a large shopping mall and a food court with specialty food outlets. There is free entertainment nightly in the Wolf Den Showroom.
DIRECTIONS & PARKING: From I-95 exit 76, north on I-395 to exit 79A (Route 2A east). It is less than one mile to Mohegan Sun Blvd. The "winter" parking lot is designated for large vehicles. Free overnight parking is permitted for self-contained vehicles and 24-hour shuttle service is provided.

To get to Foxwoods from Mohegan Sun (approximately ten miles): Follow Mohegan Sun Blvd to Route 2A East. After crossing Mohegan-Pequot bridge, at the light, turn left onto Route 12. Make the next right onto Route 2A East. Follow it to the end. At the light turn right onto Route 2 East. Follow for four miles to Foxwoods on the right.

Delaware

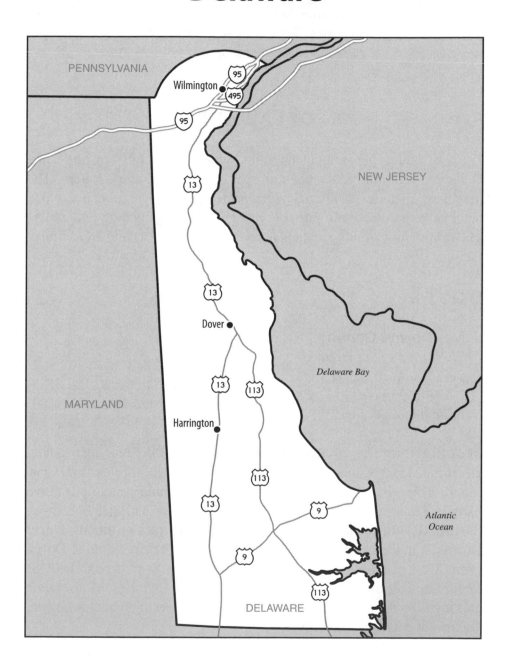

City	Casino	🚐	⚡	🛡	📄
Dover	Dover Downs Gaming				58
Harrington	Harrington Raceway & Midway Slots	✔			59
Wilmington	Delaware Park Racetrack & Slots			✔	59

DELAWARE

There are three pari-mutuel facilities with slot machines in the state. Delaware's gaming machines are operated by the state's lottery. The machines include traditional slots, video poker, video keno, video blackjack and electronic pit/table games including roulette and craps.. The minimum gambling age in Delaware is 21 for slots and 18 for horse racing.

DOVER

Dover Downs Gaming
1131 North DuPont Highway
Dover, Delaware 19901
302-674-4600 • 800-711-5882
www.doverdowns.com

DESCRIPTION: The 24-hour casino has over 3,100 slots/video poker, electronic table games, live racing in season and simulcasting year-round. There is a hotel, conference center and nine restaurants. Live harness racing takes place Nov-April. Dover International Speedway (NASCAR) is located at Dover Downs. DIRECTIONS & PARKING: Dover Downs is in the central part of Delaware within the city limits of Dover. From SR-1 exit 104 (north of Dover) merge onto Scarborough Rd/US-13 for one-half mile, then south on DuPont Hwy 1.4 miles. Motor home parking is on the gravel or grassy portion of the parking lot at the casino. Overnight parking is permitted.

HARRINGTON

Harrington Raceway & Midway Slots
Delaware State Fairgrounds
18500 South DuPont Highway/US-13
Harrington, Delaware 19952
302-398-7223 • 888-887-5687
www.midwayslots.com

DESCRIPTION: The state fairground has a casino, RV Park and raceway. The RV Park has several hundred sites with water and electric hookups. Last year's rate was $30 (special rates for rallies.). There is a dump station on site. The RV Park is within walking distance of the casino that has over 1,600 slots, electronic table games, daily simulcasting and three restaurants. Live harness racing is featured April-June, Aug-Oct and the Governor's Day Race during the Delaware State Fair in July. The casino is open 24 hours (closed on Easter and Christmas.) There is no hotel at this location. **DISCOUNTS**: Senior discounts are given to those 50 and older. **DIRECTIONS & PARKING**: Located 20 miles south of Dover at the State Fairgrounds on US-13. RV parking is also available at the far end of the lot along the fence where buses park. Overnight parking is permitted.

WILMINGTON

Delaware Park Racetrack & Slots
777 Delaware Park Boulevard
Wilmington, Delaware 19804
302-994-2521 • 800-417-5687
www.delawarepark.com

DESCRIPTION: Located in Wilmington, the facility features thoroughbred racing April-Nov, daily simulcasting, 3,000 slots in the casino and eight restaurants. Free weekly slot tournaments are held. There is no hotel at this location. The casino is open 24 hours. **DIRECTIONS & PARKING**: From I-95 exit 4B, take SR-7 north and follow signs to Delaware Park. RVs may park in the bus/truck parking lot. Please limit RV overnight stays to 24 hours.

Florida

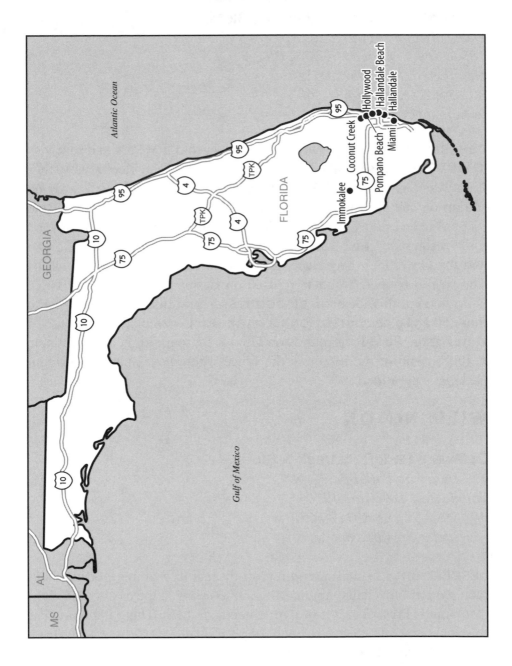

City	Casino	🚐	〰	⛉	🗎
Coconut Creek	Coconut Creek Casino				61
Hallandale	Gulfstream Park & Casino			✔	62
Hallendale Beach	Mardi Gras Gaming			✔	62
Hollywood	Hollywood Seminole Gaming				63
Immokalee	Seminole Gaming Palace and Casino				63
Miami	Miccosukee Indian Gaming				63
Pompano Beach	Pompano Park Harness Track & The Isle Casino			✔	64

FLORIDA

Florida has "racinos" (casinos located at race tracks) in Broward and Dade Counties. There are also poker rooms at many of the non-racino tracks throughout the state. Florida has an extensive casino cruise network of boats that sail every day – out to beyond the three-mile limit – for a few hours of gambling on the high seas. Florida's Indian tribes operate five gaming locations. *Note:* The **Seminole Hard Rock Casino** in Tampa DOES NOT permit RVs to park there due to space constraints.

COCONUT CREEK

Coconut Creek Casino
5550 NW 40th Street
Coconut Creek, Florida 33073
954-977-6700 • 866-2-CASINO
www.seminolecoconutcreekcasino.com

DESCRIPTION: The 24-hour casino is located on five acres of Seminole tribal land in the city of Coconut Creek. It has 1,500 gaming machines, poker room, two restaurants and a lounge. DIRECTIONS & PARKING: Coconut Creek is south of Boca Raton and north of Fort Lauderdale. From I-95 exit 39 go west on Sample Road for 4.5 miles to NW 54th Avenue, turn right and go one-half mile to the casino on the left. (The casino is one block east of US-441.) RVs should check with Security for assistance with parking. Although there is a limited parking area, RVs may park in the back of the west parking lot (not on Indian land) during daytime hours. Overnight parking is prohibited by the municipality and local law enforcement issues tickets to RVs that park overnight.

HALLANDALE

Gulfstream Park & Casino
901 South Federal Highway (US-1)
Hallandale, Florida 33009
954-454-7000 • 800-771-8873
www.gulfstreampark.com

DESCRIPTION: The casino has over 800 Vegas-style slots, 20 poker tables, daily simulcasting, three restaurants and fast food. Casino hours are 10am-3am weekdays/24hrs weekends. Live thoroughbred racing is held Jan-April, Wed-Mon. Post time is 1:10pm. DIRECTIONS & PARKING: From I-95 exit 18 (Hallendale Beach Blvd) go east to the corner of US-1. Follow signs. There is ample room for RV parking during the casino's hours of operation; check in with Security for parking authorization.

HALLENDALE BEACH

Mardi Gras Gaming
831 North Federal Highway
Hallendale Beach, Florida 33009
954-924-3200
www.playmardigras.com

DESCRIPTION: The casino features over 1,100 Vegas-style slots, 30 poker tables, simulcasting beginning at noon, restaurant, fast food and sports bar.. A 14-race greyhound program is featured every night; matinee on Monday. Hours of operation are 10:30am-3:30am. The poker room is open 24 hours. DIRECTIONS & PARKING: From I-95 exit 19 (Pembroke Road) go east to the track. Follow signs. Parking for RVs is available in the lot during the casino's hours of operation. Check in with Security for parking authorization.

HOLLYWOOD

Hollywood Seminole Gaming
4150 North State Road 7
Hollywood, Florida 33021
954-961-3220 • 866-222-7466
www.seminolehollywoodcasino.com

DESCRIPTION: On the Seminole Reservation the casino has 1,100 slots, 15 gaming tables, and bingo. The resort includes a hotel, eight nightclubs, 15 restaurants, entertainment venue, shopping mall and a Hard Rock Café. DIRECTIONS & PARKING: From I-95 exit 22, take Sterling Road west for three miles to SR-7/US-441. Go south on SR-7 to the casino. Parking for RVs is at the south end of the lot if there is room. Check with Security to determine if there will be space for large vehicles. RVs are often turned away due to lack of parking spaces.

IMMOKALEE

Seminole Gaming Palace and Casino
506 South 1st Street
Immokalee, Florida 33934
239-658-1313 • 800-218-0007
www.theseminolecasino.com

DESCRIPTION: The 24-hour casino features 1,100 slots, 15 live poker tables, two restaurants and a lounge. DIRECTIONS & PARKING: From I-75 exit 111, east on Hwy-846 (Immokalee Road) for 35 miles to the casino. There is ample space for RVs to park in the west corner of the lot near the fence. Overnight is OK.

MIAMI

Miccosukee Indian Gaming
500 SW 177th Avenue
Miami, Florida 33194
305-222-4600 • 800-741-4600
www.miccosukee.com

DESCRIPTION: The casino features 2,000 slot and video poker machines, table games, poker room and continuous live bingo. A hotel, conference center, three restaurants and snack bar are on site. **DIRECTIONS & PARKING**: From the Florida Turnpike Homestead Extension exit 25, go west on US-41 for 5.7 miles, turn right, then left into the parking lot. The casino is located on SR-997 just north of US-41 (a major east-west route across south Florida). It is 11 miles north of Homestead. RVs should park in the Racoon Lot – northwest section of the parking lot, walking distance to the casino. Overnight parking is OK.

POMPANO BEACH

Pompano Park Harness Track & The Isle Casino
1800 Southwest Third Street
Pompano Beach, Florida 33069
954-972-2000
www.pompanopark.com

DESCRIPTION: The Isle casino has 1,500 Vegas-style slots, 48 poker tables and daily simulcasting. Harness racing takes place year-round, 3-4 evenings a week. Post time is 7:25pm. Dining venues include a buffet, steakhouse, deli and Italian restaurant. Casino hours are 9am-3am weekdays/24hrs weekends. **DIRECTIONS & PARKING**: From I-95 exit 36, travel 1.5 miles west, then left on Powerline Road for .3 mile, then south to Third St. There is a designated parking area for RVs; follow signs.

Idaho

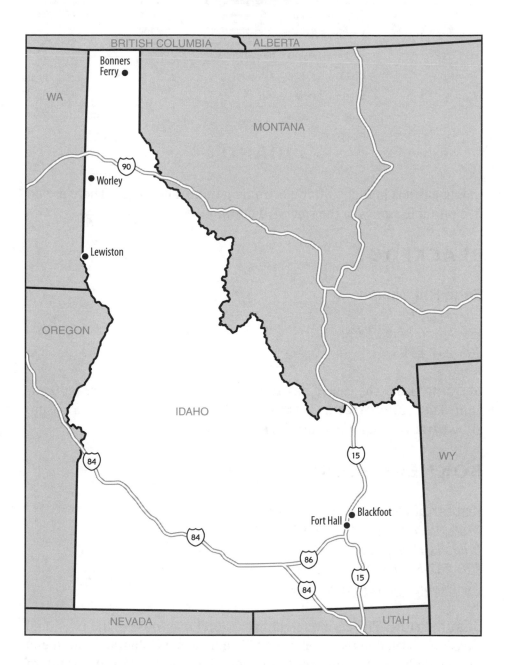

City	Casino	🚐	〰️	🛡️	📄
Blackfoot	Sage Hill Casino			✔	66
Bonners Ferry	Kootenai River Inn & Casino				66
Fort Hall	Fort Hall Casino & RV Park	✔		✔	67
Lewiston	Clearwater River Casino		✔		67
Worley	Coeur D'Alene Casino				68

IDAHO

Indian casinos in Idaho offer electronic gaming and bingo. There are no live pit/table games in the state. All casinos are open 24/7.

BLACKFOOT

Sage Hill Casino
Interstate 15, Exit 89
Blackfoot, Idaho 83221
208-237-4998

DESCRIPTION: The casino has 100 slots and a café. Hours are 6:30am-5am daily. **DIRECTIONS & PARKING**: Located at exit 89, the casino allows free overnight parking for RVs.

BONNERS FERRY

Kootenai River Inn & Casino
7169 Plaza Street (Kootenai River Plaza)
Bonners Ferry, Idaho 83805
208-267-8511 • 800-346-5668
www.kootenairiverinn.com

DESCRIPTION: The casino resort has a hotel overlooking the river, and a casino, located in the hotel, with 500 slots and a restaurant with menu service daily. **DIRECTIONS & PARKING**: The resort is 35 miles south of the Canada border. From I-90 exit 12, travel north on US-95 to Bonners

Ferry. The casino is on Hwy-95. Free overnight parking for RVs is available at the far end of the parking lot.

FORT HALL

Fort Hall Casino & RV Park
Simplot Road (I-15 at exit 80)
Fort Hall, Idaho 83203
208-237-8778 • 800-497-4231
www.forthallcasino.com

DESCRIPTION: The 24-hour casino features over 900 slot and video poker machines, bingo, a grill and snack bar. The RV Park is situated on the north side of the casino building and is within walking distance. There are 40 full-hookup spaces, free wi-fi, rest rooms and showers at the RV Park. RV guests should pull in, then register at the cage in the casino. Last year's daily rate was $20. DIRECTIONS & PARKING: From I-15 the casino is visible from the interstate at exit 80. Free overnight parking is also permitted for self-contained vehicles, but it is requested that you use the far perimeter of the parking lot.

LEWISTON

Clearwater River Casino Hotel & Campground
17500 Nez Perce Road
Lewiston, Idaho 83501
208-746-0723 • 877-678-7423
208-750-0231 (RV Park)
www.crcasino.com

DESCRIPTION: The resort, owned and operated by the Nez Perce Tribe, has a casino, hotel and RV Park with 33 full-hookup spaces. RV daily rate is $27 and weekly and monthly rates are available. The casino has over 600 slots, bingo 3 days a week, off track betting, full service restaurant and deli. DISCOUNTS: A birthday club celebration is held on the last day of the month. Complimentary drinks for players. DIRECTIONS: From I-90 exit 12, south on US-95 for 188 miles. The casino is located on US-

95/12 about four miles south of Lewiston. RV parking is also permitted near the casino building.

WORLEY

Coeur D'Alene Casino Resort Hotel
27068 South Highway 95
Worley, Idaho 83876
208-686-0248 • 800-523-2464
www.cdacasino.com

DESCRIPTION: The largest casino resort in Idaho has a hotel and conference center designed in dramatic western lodge style. The casino has 1,800 Vegas-style slots, video poker and five electronic blackjack tables with seven positions per table and a $5 minimum bet. There is a non-smoking slots area, bingo and OTB room. Food venues include the buffet, café and food court. The buffet restaurant features deluxe breakfast on Saturdays and Sunday brunch. The 18-hole Circling Raven golf course also has a 25-acre practice facility. DIRECTIONS & PARKING: From I-90 exit 12, south on US-95 for 25 miles. The casino is located directly on US-95 in Worley. RVs should use the parking lot entrance closest to the Chevron station.

Illinois

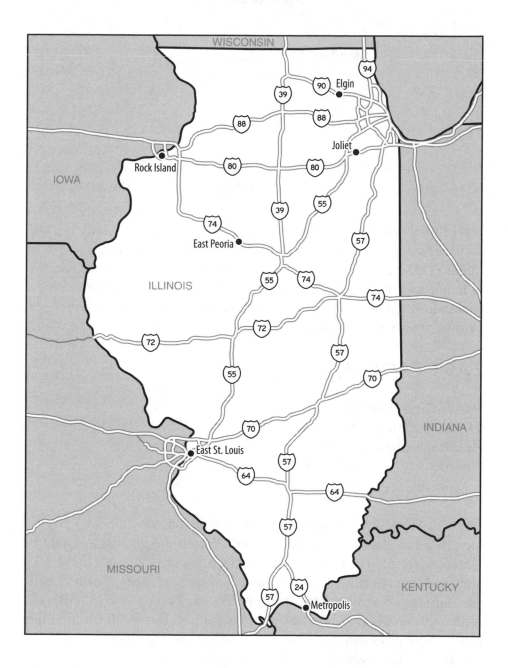

City	Casino	🚐	〽	⛉	🗎
East Peoria	Par-A-Dice Casino			✔	70
East St. Louis	Casino Queen	✔		✔	71
Elgin	Grand Victoria Casino				71
Joliet	Empress Casino Hotel	✔		✔	72
Metropolis	Harrah's Metropolis				72
Rock Island	Jumer's Casino Rock Island			✔	73

ILLINOIS

Most Illinois casinos are traditional riverboat style, permanently docked on waterways in the state. Chicago area casinos (4 in Illinois and 4 in Indiana) are permanently docked along Lake Michigan. Some casinos in major metropolitan areas do not have parking for RVs due to space constraints. They are not included in the book. *Note:* Four Chicago area casinos are listed in the Indiana section of this guide.

EAST PEORIA

Par-A-Dice Casino
21 Blackjack Boulevard
East Peoria, Illinois 61611
309-698-7711 • 800-727-2342
www.par-a-dice.com

DESCRIPTION: The riverboat casino docked on the Illinois River is located a mile from I-74 with easy on/off from the interstate. There is a hotel adjacent. The boat has four decks featuring 27 tables and 1,100 slots and four restaurants. The third deck is non-smoking. Casino hours are 9am–6am daily. DIRECTIONS & PARKING: From I-74 exit 95B, one mile north on Main St. The casino is on the left. Use the lot behind the hotel where designated RV spaces are along the back perimeter of the parking lot. The casino is within walking distance.

EAST ST. LOUIS

Casino Queen

200 South Front Street
East St. Louis, Illinois 62201
618-874-5000 • 800-777-0777
618-874-5000 – Ext. 8871 (RV Park)
www.casinoqueen.com

DESCRIPTION: The resort includes a hotel, a 132-space RV Park and a newly-expanded casino. The RV Park, open March thru Oct., features large pull-thru, full hookup sites. Last year's daily RV rates were $33. A modern casino has 1,100 slots, video poker machines, 34 pit/table games and three restaurants. Free shuttle service operates throughout the resort. The RV Park and the casino have spectacular views of the Gateway Arch and the St. Louis skyline. For sightseeing in St. Louis, resort guests can take the Metrolink from a nearby station. **DISCOUNTS**: Discounts honored at the RV Park include Good Sam, AAA and FMCA. **DIRECTIONS**: From I-70/I-55 westbound, use exit 2A (3rd Street) or eastbound use exit 1 (4th St) East St Louis, then follow brown riverboat casino signs. From I-255 exit 17B, take SR-15 west, following brown riverboat casino signs. Free RV parking is also permitted in the truck parking lot just outside of the RV Park entrance.

ELGIN

Grand Victoria Casino

250 South Grove Avenue
Elgin, Illinois 60120
847-468-7000
www.grandvictoria-elgin.com

DESCRIPTION: The dockside casino is on the Fox River some 20 miles west of Chicago. It has 1,100 slots, 29 pit/gaming tables and three restaurants. The casino, open daily 8:30am–6:30am, is within the hotel. **DISCOUNTS**: Seniors (65 and older) get discounts at the buffet. **DIRECTIONS & PARKING**: From I-90 tollway (milepost 24), take Rt-31 south for 2.3 miles to Chicago Ave. Left on Chicago Avenue for .3 mile to South Grove Avenue, then right for .25 mile. RV parking is available in the north lot. Please check in with Security.

JOLIET

Empress Casino Hotel & RV Park
2300 Empress Drive
Joliet, Illinois 60436
815-744-9400 • 888-436-7737
www.pngaming.com

DESCRIPTION: The resort includes an RV Park with 50 paved sites with electric, water and a central dump. There is also a hotel. A water park is within walking distance. Last year's daily RV rates were $24-$30 (winter rate for electric only, $12.). Shuttle service is provided from the RV Park to the modern casino. The Empress Barge, docked on the Des Plains River has over 1,200 slots/video poker, 20 gaming tables and three restaurants. Casino hours are 8:30am–6:30am daily. DIRECTIONS & PARKING: From I-80 exit 127, south on Empress Road for .6 mile to the end, turn left and go east on Rt-6 for .5 mile to the casino. Overnight parking is also permitted in the casino lot.

METROPOLIS

Harrah's Metropolis
203 South Ferry Street
Metropolis, Illinois 62960
618-524-2628 • 800-935-7700
www.harrahs.com

DESCRIPTION: This Harrah's is in southern Illinois on the Ohio River just across from Paducah, KY. The casino features 1,200 slots, 31 pit/table games, poker room and three restaurants: buffet, diner and steakhouse. A modern hotel has 258-rooms/suites. There is an interesting display of antique slot machines in the walkway between the hotel and the casino. Casino hours are 9am–7am daily. Live entertainment is featured in the

Riverfront Event Center. **DIRECTIONS & PARKING**: From I-24 exit 37, west on Rt-45 for 3.8 miles to Ferry Street in Metropolis. Turn left and follow Ferry Street to the casino. RV's should use the perimeter of the parking lot where there are designated spots; follow signage for oversize vehicle parking. Free overnight parking is permitted for self-contained vehicles.

ROCK ISLAND

Jumer's Casino Rock Island

777 Jumer Drive
Rock Island, Illinois 61204
309-756-4600 • 800-477-7747
www.jumerscasinohotel.com

DESCRIPTION: The resort has a hotel and casino with 1,100 slots, 30 gaming tables and four restaurants. The casino is open daily 7am-5am. **DIRECTIONS & PARKING**: The new casino is located at the intersection of I-280 (at exit 11) and SR-92. Check in with Security for parking directions. Overnight parking is permitted for self-contained RVs.

Indiana

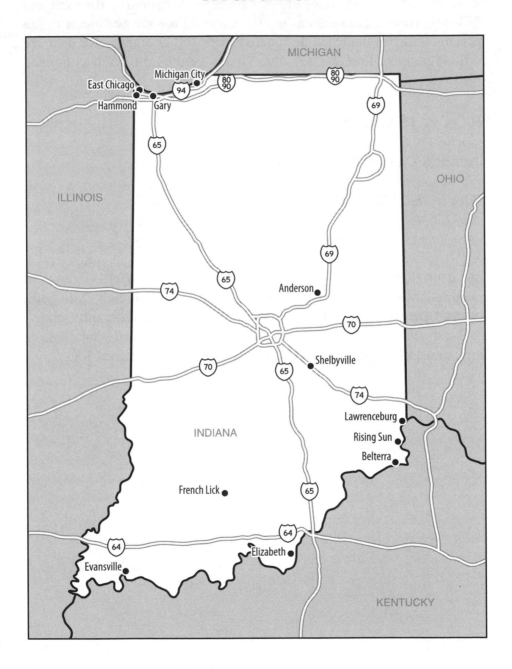

City	Casino	🚐	🏕	🛡	📄
Anderson	Hoosier Park Racing & Casino			✔	75
Belterra	Belterra Casino and Resort				76
East Chicago	Ameristar East Chicago				76
Elizabeth	Horseshoe Southern Indiana				77
Evansville	Casino Aztar				77
French Lick	French Lick Resort & Casino				78
Gary	Majestic Star Casinos				78
Hammond	Horseshoe Hammond Casino				79
Lawrenceburg	Hollywood Casino & Hotel				79
Michigan City	Blue Chip Hotel & Casino				80
Rising Sun	Grand Victoria Casino & Resort				80
Shelbyville	Indiana Downs Racing			✔	81

INDIANA

Indiana legalized casinos in 1993, and currently there are 12 casinos in the state. Four are located just east of Chicago on Lake Michigan, while six others are in the southern part of the state. Indiana's first "racinos" opened in 2008 at the state's two race tracks.

ANDERSON

Hoosier Park Racing & Casino
4500 Dan Patch Circle
Anderson, Indiana 46013
765-642-7223 • 800-526-7223
www.hoosierpark.com

DESCRIPTION: The 24-hour casino has 2,000 slots, video poker and electronic versions of blackjack, 3-card poker, roulette, non-smoking area and six restaurants. Live racing takes place April to November and racing simulcasting runs year round. **DIRECTIONS**: From I-69 exit 26 take IN-9 north for .7 mile then east on IN-236/E 53rd for .7 mile and north at Dan Patch Circle. Free parking is available for RVs and overnight is OK. Follow signs for truck & RV parking.

BELTERRA

Belterra Casino and Resort
777 Belterra Drive
Belterra, Indiana 47020
812-427-7777 • 888-235-8377
www.belterracasino.com

DESCRIPTION: The 24-hour casino includes 57 gaming tables, 1,600 slots and five restaurants. The resort has a hotel and a Tom Fazio-designed 7,000-yard golf course. **DIRECTIONS & PARKING**: From I-71 in Kentucky, exit 57 (Warsaw/Sparta), follow SR-35 to Warsaw, KY. At US-42 turn left toward the Markland Dam Bridge and turn left on to the bridge. After crossing the bridge, turn left at the stop sign and follow SR-156 to the casino. RVs should park in the large open area parking lot; overnight is OK.

EAST CHICAGO

Ameristar East Chicago
777 Resorts Boulevard
East Chicago, Indiana 46312
219-378-3000 • 866-711-4263
www.ameristar.com

DESCRIPTION: The casino features 2,000 slots, 76 pit/table games and a bingo hall. There is a hotel on site and a buffet, diner, steakhouse, café and fast food. **DIRECTIONS & PARKING**: From I-90 exit 10 (Cline Ave/IN-912) travel north to Pastrick Marina (exit 5C off IN-912 north), follow signs to Ameristar. RVs should contact Security after coming in. RV parking is available on the pier and also behind the hotel. Parking is limited and RVs must have a Star Club card and authorization to stay overnight.

ELIZABETH

Horseshoe Southern Indiana
11999 Avenue of the Emperors
Elizabeth, Indiana 47117
812-969-6000 • 888-766-2648
www.harrahs.com

DESCRIPTION: The 5,000-passenger riverboat is open 24/7. The casino has over 100 pit/gaming tables, 2,000 slots and four restaurants. There is a hotel at the resort. **DISCOUNTS**: Ask about current Senior Day (55+) discounts on Wednesdays. **DIRECTIONS & PARKING**: From I-64 exit 123 (New Albany), follow signs to Hwy-111. Take Hwy-111 south for 8.5 miles to Horseshoe on the right. RVs should drive past the parking garages and hotel complex, cross the bridge, then turn right on Stucky Road to the outdoor lot designated for large vehicles. Overnight RV parking is permitted.

EVANSVILLE

Casino Aztar
421 N.W. Riverside Drive
Evansville, Indiana 47708
812-433-4000 • 800-342-5386
www.casinoaztar.com

DESCRIPTION: Aztar is an old-fashioned paddle wheeler with over 1,000 slots, 52 gaming tables and seven restaurants. Casino hours are 8am–5am/24 hrs (Fri–Sun). There is a hotel at the resort and live entertainment is featured on weekends. **DISCOUNTS**: Senior Days feature exercise sessions, slot tournaments and half off the buffet. Call ahead for information. **DIRECTIONS & PARKING**: From I-64 exit 25, south on Rt-41 for approximately 15 miles to the Lloyd Expressway, then west to Fulton Avenue and south for three blocks. Free overnight parking is available in the lot for self-contained RVs.

FRENCH LICK

French Lick Resort & Casino
8670 West State Road 56
French Lick, Indiana 47432
812-936-9300 • 800-457-4042
www.frenchlick.com

DESCRIPTION: The resort's history dates back to the 1850's when people flocked to the area because of its mineral springs waters. The resort was recently renovated in turn-of-the-century style. It includes a hotel and spa and a casino with 1,300 slots, 50 pit/table games, 12-table poker room and a high limit gaming area. Two of the three golf courses are restorations of courses designed in 1907 and 1917. The resort also has six eateries, a six-lane bowling alley and retail shops. **DIRECTIONS & PARKING**: From Indianapolis, go south on SR-37 about 98 miles to Paoli, then take SR-56 west for 10 miles. From Louisville, take I-64 west to exit 122, then US-150 west to Paoli, then SR-56 west for 10 miles. RVs should park at the Pluto building (directly across the street from the hotel lobby) or in the area behind the casino boat.

GARY

Majestic Star Casinos
One Bluffington Harbor Drive
Gary, Indiana 46312
219-977-7777 • 888-225-8259
www.majesticstar.com

DESCRIPTION: With gaming on two riverboats, Majestic Star has 2,500 slots, 89 pit/table games, five food venues and is open 24 hours. A 300-room hotel overlooks Lake Michigan. **DIRECTIONS & PARKING**: From I-90 exit 10 (Cline Ave/IN-912) travel north following brown signs to Gary riverboats. After going under the Bluffington Harbor archway, large vehicles should pull into the turn off on the right and parallel park. (*Caution*: Do not go any further. There is a low clearance (both height and width) tunnel between the archway and the casinos.) There is limited space in the turnoff. So if it's full, call Security at 219-977-9999 and they will escort you to the overflow parking area behind the hotel.

HAMMOND

Horseshoe Hammond Casino
777 Casino Center Drive
Hammond, Indiana 46320
219-473-7000 • 866-711-7463
www.horseshoe.com/hammond

DESCRIPTION: The 24-hour riverboat casino has 3,200 slots, 129 pit/ table games and five restaurants. There is no hotel at this location. **DIRECTIONS & PARKING**: From I-80/94 exit 5 (or From I-90 exit 10), take SR-912 north to Calumet Ave/US-41, then north about 2 miles, then left onto US12/20 west for .5 mile. Turn left at the large sign, after the overpass, large vehicles should turn right at the "marina overflow parking" sign. (There is only a parking garage for cars at the riverboat.) RVs should park in the center section of the overflow lot – don't park along the fence. There is a post near the bus stop with a red sign at the phone for visitors to call for a ride to the casino.

LAWRENCEBURG

Hollywood Casino and Hotel
777 Hollywood Blvd
Lawrenceburg, Indiana 47025
812-539-8000 • 888-274-6797
www.pngaming.com

DESCRIPTION: Open 24 hours daily, the casino has 2,400 slots, 98 table games and six restaurants. A 300-room hotel is connected to the casino. **DIRECTIONS & PARKING**: From I-275 west exit 16, take US-50 west. From I-74 exit 164, south on Rt-1 for approximately 14 miles to US-50. Follow brown riverboat signs. The RV parking lot is on US-50 at

Lorey Lane (about a mile northwest of the casino). Overnight is OK; call Security at 812-539-6787 for shuttle service to the casino. (The shuttle no longer runs continuously.)

MICHIGAN CITY

Blue Chip Hotel & Casino
777 Blue Chip Drive
Michigan City, Indiana 46360
219-879-7711 • 888-879-7711
www.bluechipcasino.com

DESCRIPTION: The resort includes a hotel and casino with 1,900 slots, 56 pit/table games and four restaurants. **DISCOUNTS**: New Rewards Club members receive introductory coupons. **DIRECTIONS & PARKING**: From I-94 exit 40B, go 5 miles on US20/35, then stay on Rt-35 for 5.2 miles to US-12, then east and cross the bridge .3 mile to the casino lot. RVs should park in the northeast section of the parking lot. Free overnight parking is permitted. Shuttle service is provided to the casino.

RISING SUN

Grand Victoria Casino & Resort
600 Grand Victoria Drive
Rising Sun, Indiana 47040
812-438-1234 • 800-472-6311
www.grandvictoria.com

DESCRIPTION: This pretty paddle wheeler, open 24/7, has 34 pit/table games and 1,300 slots on four spacious levels all built around a large open stairwell; top level is non-smoking. There are four restaurants, coffee house and a sports bar at the casino. The resort has a hotel and Southern Indiana's only Scottish-links style golf course. **DISCOUNTS**: 10% for seniors, 55+ seasonally. Ask about the current senior discounts. **DIRECTIONS & PARKING**: From the Cincinnati area, take I-275 west to exit 16, then west on US-50 for 6.9 miles, then south on Rt-56 for 7.8 miles. This takes you through the historic town of Aurora and on a scenic byway along the picturesque Ohio River. Turn left at Grand Victoria Drive. RVs should park in the large lot on the right – sections 6 and 7. The parking lot is walking distance to the casino. Overnight parking is permitted for self-contained RVs.

SHELBYVILLE

Indiana Downs Racing & Indiana Live! Casino
4200 North Michigan Road
Shelbyville, Indiana 46176
317-421-0000 • 866-478-7223
www.indianadowns.com

DESCRIPTION: Open 24/7, the casino has 2,000 slots, electronic versions of popular table games and four restaurants. Live thoroughbred and quarter horse racing is held April to July. DIRECTIONS: From I-74 exit 109 go east on Fairland Rd .3 mile then north on Michigan Rd .2 mile. Free parking is available for RVs and overnight is OK.

Iowa

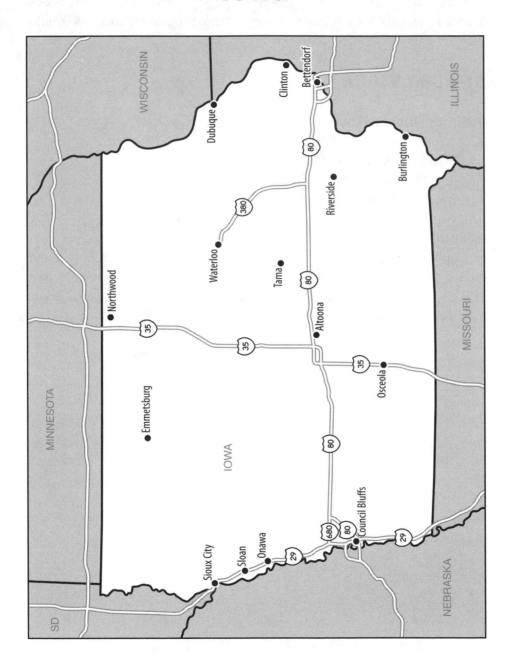

City	Casino	🚐	⚡	🛡	📄
Altoona	Prairie Meadows Racetrack & Casino			✔	83
Bettendorf	Isle of Capri – Bettendorf			✔	84
Burlington	Catfish Bend Casino				85
Clinton	Wild Rose Casino Resort				85
Council Bluffs	Ameristar Casino Council Bluffs			✔	85
Council Bluffs	Bluffs Run Raceway / Horseshoe Casino			✔	86
Council Bluffs	Harrah's Council Bluffs Casino			✔	86
Dubuque	Dubuque Diamond Jo Casino				87
Dubuque	Dubuque Greyhound Park & Casino				87
Emmetsburg	Wild Rose Casino & Resort	✔			87
Northwood	Diamond Jo Worth			✔	88
Onawa	Casino Omaha & RV Spaces		✔		88
Osceola	Terrible's Lakeside Casino Resort	✔		✔	89
Riverside	Riverside Casino				89
Sioux City	Argosy's Belle of Sioux City Casino			✔	90
Sloan	WinnaVegas Casino		✔		90
Tama	Meskwaki Bingo, Casino	✔			91
Waterloo	The Isle Casino – Waterloo				91

IOWA

Iowa's gaming includes permanently docked riverboats, land-based resorts, Indian casinos and pari-mutuel racinos. All casinos are Vegas-style.

ALTOONA

Prairie Meadows Racetrack & Casino
1 Prairie Meadows Drive
Altoona, Iowa 50009
515-967-1000 • 800-325-9015
www.prairiemeadows.com

DESCRIPTION: Prairie Meadows, the nation's first "racino," has 1,900 slots, 40 gaming tables, race book, smoke-free poker room, two restaurants and free entertainment. The casino is open 24/7. The track features live horse racing throughout the summer and simulcasting. DISCOUNTS: Club 55 for senior citizens offers discounts, special promotions and entertainment. DIRECTIONS & PARKING: Prairie Meadows is near I-80 exit 142 next to Adventureland. There is a specific parking area for large vehicles; "no overnight parking" signs are posted. RVs should not extend their jacks in the parking lot.

BETTENDORF

Isle of Capri – Bettendorf
1777 Isle Parkway
Bettendorf, Iowa 52722
563-359-7280 • 800-724-5825
www.isleofcapricasino.com

DESCRIPTION: The paddle wheeler on the Mississippi River is near I-74 with easy on/off access. The 24-hour casino has over 1,100 slots, 34 pit/gaming tables, poker room, two restaurants and fast food. Penguin's Comedy Club has live entertainment. An adjacent hotel has convention and meeting space. The marina has 70 docking spaces. *Note*: The casino shuttle bus also runs to the nearby Rhythm City Casino. DISCOUNTS: Ask about Senior Day (50+) discounts; these may include 50% off on gift shop items, two-for-one on meals or match play in the casino. DIRECTIONS & PARKING: From I-74 (in Iowa) exit 4 (State St/Riverfront), go east on State Street for .4 mile. Turn right at 17th St/George Theunen Drive to the casino complex –or– From I-80 (in Illinois) take exit 10 to I-74 west for 14 miles. After crossing the Mississippi River, take Iowa exit 4 (Grant St/State St), then north on State St to the George Theunen Bridge. The west lot is designated for overflow parking/RVs. Free overnight RV parking is permitted.

BURLINGTON

Catfish Bend Casino
3001 Winegard Drive
Burlington, Iowa 52601
319-372-1000 • 800-372-2946
www.catfishbendcasino.com

DESCRIPTION: Located next to Fun City, the casino has 700 slots, 18 table games and poker room. Casino hours are Mon-Thur 8am-3am/24 hrs (Fri-Sun). **DIRECTIONS & PARKING**: From I-80 exit 271 go south on IA-38 for 12.8 miles, then south on US-61 for 51 miles. Free RV parking is available; parking areas are crowded during the summer.

CLINTON

Wild Rose Casino Resort
777 Wild Rose Circle
Clinton, Iowa 52732
515-327-1776 • 800-457-9975
www.wildroseresorts.com

DESCRIPTION: The Wild Rose Resort, situated on 29 acres in Clinton, includes a casino in the hotel and an event center. The casino has 600 slots, 14 pit/gaming tables, a buffet and deli. **DISCOUNTS**: Weekly Senior Day features discounts at the restaurant and extra points at the casino. **DIRECTIONS & PARKING**: From I-80 exit 195B take US-61 north 14.9 miles to exit 137, then US-30 east for 16.2 miles and north at Mill Creek Pkwy/30th St. RV parking is available; overnight is OK.

COUNCIL BLUFFS

Ameristar Casino Council Bluffs
2200 River Road
Council Bluffs, Iowa 51501
712-328-8888 • 877-IMASTAR
www.ameristarcasinos.com

DESCRIPTION: Ameristar II, Iowa's largest riverboat, features 24-hour casino action on three levels with 1,500 slots, 30 pit/table games, three restaurants and a bakery. DISCOUNTS: Seniors (55+) receive a restaurant discount. DIRECTIONS & PARKING: From I-80 use exit 1A to I-29 north exit 52/Nebraska Ave and follow signs to riverboat casinos. RV parking is in the north lot. Overnight parking is OK for self-contained RVs.

Bluffs Run Raceway / Horseshoe Casino
2701 23rd Avenue
Council Bluffs, Iowa 51501
877-771-7463
www.horseshoecouncilbluffs.com

DESCRIPTION: Bluffs Run, a premier greyhound park, has live dog racing Tue–Sun in season and horse race simulcasting. The 24-hour casino has 1,900 slots, 62 table/poker games, keno, non-smoking section and three restaurants. DIRECTIONS & PARKING: From I-80/I-29 exit 1B, north .5 mile on 24th Street to 23rd Avenue, west on 23rd for .4 mile — or— From I-29 exit 52, follow casino signs. The track/casino complex is visible from the westbound lanes of I-80. Free overnight RV parking is permitted in the northeast lot of the casino for up to 12 hours.

Harrah's Council Bluffs Casino
One Harrah's Boulevard
Council Bluffs, Iowa 51501
712-329-6000 • 800-598-8451
www.harrahs.com

DESCRIPTION: On the Missouri River, Harrah's 24-hour riverboat casino features three decks of gaming with 1,000 slots, 21 pit/gaming tables, poker room, keno and three food venues, including a 24-hour diner. The hotel and 18-hole golf course are adjacent to the casino. DIRECTIONS & PARKING: Located at I-29 exit 53. RVs should park in the north lot and check with Security if you plan to stay overnight.

DUBUQUE

Dubuque Diamond Jo Casino
301 Bell Street
Dubuque, Iowa 52001
563-690-2100 • 800-582-5956
www.diamondjo.com

DESCRIPTION: Open daily 8am–3am/24hrs weekends, the casino has 1,000 slots, 17 pit/gaming tables, poker room and five restaurants. Headline entertainment on weekends. There is a picturesque walking path behind the hotel along the banks of the Mississippi River. DISCOUNTS: Players Club members get discounts on the buffet if 55+ and discounts in the gift shop every day. DIRECTIONS & PARKING: From US-20 Locust Street exit in downtown Dubuque, north on Locust .3 mile to Third St, east on Third for .4 mile, then south to the casino. RV parking is in the lot directly across the street from the casino.

Dubuque Greyhound Park & Casino
1855 Greyhound Park Drive
Dubuque, Iowa 52004
563-582-3647 • 800-373-3647
www.dgpc.com

DESCRIPTION: The gaming facility has 1,000 slots, 20 gaming tables, live greyhound racing May thru October, simulcast dog and horse racing and two restaurants. Hours are 8am–3am/24hrs weekends. Hilton Garden Inn is adjacent to the casino. DIRECTIONS & PARKING: The Greyhound Park & Casino is located off Hwy-151/61 at the Dubuque-Wisconsin Bridge. From US-20, exit at Downtown Dubuque to Hwy-151/61 north for 1.2 miles to the Greyhound Park exit. Parking for oversize vehicles is behind the casino building. Overnight RV parking is permitted.

EMMETSBURG

Wild Rose Casino & Resort
777 Main Street / US-18

Emmetsburg, Iowa 50536
712-852-3400
www.wildroseresorts.com

DESCRIPTION: The resort, on nine acres, includes a casino, hotel, convention hall and RV Park all next to a 12-acre lake. The RV Park has 68 sites with electric, water and central dump. Last year's rate was $15 and breakfast is included. The casino features 550 slots, 21 pit/gaming tables, buffet restaurant and authentic Irish Pub. **DIRECTIONS**: The casino is located on the east edge of Emmetsburg directly on US-18 in northern Iowa.

NORTHWOOD

Diamond Jo Worth
777 Diamond Jo Lane
Northwood, Iowa 50459
641-323-7777 • 877-323-5566
www.diamondjo.com

DESCRIPTION: The complex includes a motel and casino with 900 slots, 33 gaming tables, buffet, café and fast food. Casino hours are 8am-3am weekdays, 24hrs weekends. **DIRECTIONS**: The casino and motel are located on the Iowa/Minnesota border at I-35 exit 214 next to the southbound lanes near the Iowa Welcome Center. Free overnight parking is permitted for self-contained RVs. There is a dump station at the welcome center.

ONAWA

Casino Omaha & RV Spaces
1 Blackbird Bend
Onawa, Iowa 51040
712-423-3700 • 800-858-U-BET

DESCRIPTION: Casino Omaha features 550 slots, 10 gaming tables and a restaurant. Hours are 8am–3am/24hrs weekends. A convenience store and travel center are on property. **DIRECTIONS & PARKING**: From I-29 exit 112, west for .6 mile to the flashing yellow light, turn north onto Dogwood and go for .8 mile to the stop sign, then west on Hwy-K-42 for 2.3 miles. Turn left at the casino sign, then .9 mile to the casino. There are 14 free pull thru RV spaces with electric hookups on the east side of the parking lot.

OSCEOLA

Terrible's Lakeside Casino Resort and RV Park
777 Casino Drive
Osceola, Iowa 50213
641-342-9511 • 877-477-5253
www.terribleherbst.com

DESCRIPTION: The lakeside resort, next to I-35 in central Iowa, has a hotel and RV Park with 47 full hookup pull-thru sites, open all year. RV check-in is at the casino lobby; last year's daily rate was $20. The 24-hour casino has 1,000 slots, 24 gaming tables, poker room and two restaurants. The boat remains dockside. **DISCOUNTS**: Monday is senior day at Lakeside; ask about current discounts for seniors 50+. **DIRECTIONS**: From I-35 exit 34, west for .2 mile on Clay St to the resort. It is suggested that RVs use the RV Park. But if you wish to dry camp, park in the north area of the lot and do not put the jacks down.

RIVERSIDE

Riverside Casino
3184 Highway 22
Riverside, Iowa 52327
319-648-1234 • 877-677-3456
www.riversidecasinoandresort.com

DESCRIPTION: The resort includes a casino, hotel and golf course. The casino features 1,200 slots, 28 pit/table games, poker room, separate non-smoking section (slots and tables) and four restaurants. **DIRECTIONS & PARKING**: The resort is located just south of Iowa City. From I-80 exit

239A, take US-27/218 south for 15.8 miles to exit 80, then east on IA-22 for 1.3 miles. The designated parking area for RVs is the southeastern corner of the lot. Free overnight parking is permitted for self-contained RVs. Call the casino for a shuttle pickup if needed.

SIOUX CITY

Argosy's Belle of Sioux City Casino
100 Larsen Park Road
Sioux City, Iowa 51101
712-294-5600 • 800-424-0080
www.pngaming.com

DESCRIPTION: The triple-deck 1920's styled paddle wheel replica on the scenic Missouri River is open 24 hours and has 700 slots, 22 gaming tables, poker room and a restaurant. DIRECTIONS & PARKING: The casino, at I-29 exit 147, is visible from the southbound lanes of the interstate. The south end parking lot is designated for RVs. After you come into the riverfront from the interstate go three-quarters around the circle and park on the gravel lot (near the sign that says reserved for valet.) Overnight parking is OK; 24-hour casino shuttle service is available; call the casino.

SLOAN

WinnaVegas Casino & RV Spaces
1500 330th Street
Sloan, Iowa 51055
712-428-9466 • 800-468-9466
www.winnavegas-casino.biz

DESCRIPTION: Located in a quiet farm area 20 miles south of Sioux City, the 24-hour casino is owned and operated by the Winnebago Tribe of Nebraska and features 660 slots, 20 table games and bingo. The restaurant, open 7am–10pm, has buffet and menu service. DIRECTIONS & PARKING: From I-29 exit 127, west on 330th St. The casino is three miles from the interstate. There are 14 pull-thru electric hookup sites available for $7 per night. RV check-in is at the casino. Free RV parking is permitted in the north parking lot. There is a free dump station and a fresh water supply is available.

TAMA

Meskwaki Bingo, Casino & RV Park
1504 305th Street
Tama, Iowa 52339
641-484-2108 • 800-728-4263
www.meskwaki.com

DESCRIPTION: The resort includes a 52-space RV Park, hotel and 24-hour casino. The RV Park has electric at the sites, central dump and fresh water supply. The daily rate is $15 – register at the hotel front desk. The roomy casino features 1,600 slots, 45 pit/table games, live keno, racing simulcast, poker room, bingo every day, high limits gaming area, separate non-smoking slots area, three restaurants and a food court. Live entertainment is featured in the Garden Park Showroom. DIRECTIONS & PARKING: From I-80 exit 191/Tama, north on US-63 (two-lane) for 22.8 miles to US-30 (traffic light at junction of US-63/30), then west on US-30 - 4.4 miles. From I-35 exit 111, go 47 miles east on US-30, a major thoroughfare (opens to four lanes in some areas). The casino is located directly on US-30.

WATERLOO

The Isle Casino
777 Isle of Capri Boulevard
Waterloo, Iowa 50701
319-833-4753 • 800-843-4753

DESCRIPTION: The casino has 1,000 slots, 29 gaming tables, poker room, two restaurants and fast food. There is a hotel on site. DIRECTIONS & PARKING: From I-380 exit onto US-20 west. Take exit 71A to merge onto US-218 south for 1.4 miles, then west on Shaulis Rd for .7 mile. Follow signs to bus parking west of the casino building. Overnight parking is permitted.

Kansas

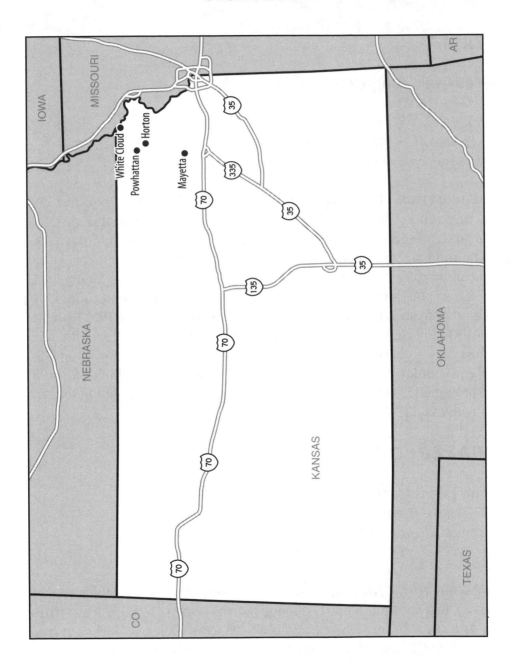

City	Casino	🚐	〽️	🛡️	📄
Horton	Golden Eagle Casino		✔		93
Mayetta	Harrah's Prairie Band Casino Resort	✔			94
Powhattan	Sac and Fox Casino		✔		94
White Cloud	Casino White Cloud		✔		95

KANSAS

Four Indian-owned casinos in northeastern Kansas are all located near US Highway 75, a major north/south route that intersects I-70 at milepost 358 near Topeka.

Plans are currently underway to add four state-owned casinos under a law passed by the state legislature in 2007 that would permit one casino in each of four Kansas counties.

HORTON

Golden Eagle Casino & RV Spaces
1121 Goldfinch Road
Horton, Kansas 66489
785-486-6601 • 888-464-5825
www.goldeneaglecasino.com

DESCRIPTION: Owned and operated by the Kickapoo Tribe, the casino, open 24/7, has 800 slots, 20 gaming tables, poker room, restaurant and 24-hour snack bar. RV spaces with full hookup are located on the west side of the parking lot. Last year's rate was $10; register in the gift shop. Bingo is held Wed–Sun. Live entertainment is featured on weekends. DISCOUNT: Celebrants get a free meal during their birthday and anniversary month. Senior Day is Thursday. DIRECTIONS & PARKING: From I-70 exit 358, go north on US-75 for 42.1 miles to SR-20, east for 4.9 miles; follow casino signs. Free overnight parking for self-contained RVs is also allowed, but Security should be notified.

MAYETTA

Harrah's Prairie Band Casino Resort & RV Park

12305 150th Road
Mayetta, Kansas 66509
785-966-7777 • 888-727-4946
877-2-RVPARK (RV Park reservations)
www.pbpgaming.com

DESCRIPTION: Located in the Kansas heartland, the 24-hour casino is owned by the Prairie Band Potowatomi Nation. The resort has a hotel and RV Park with 67 paved, full-hookup pull-thru sites, two bathhouses, laundry and wi-fi. Free 24-hour shuttle service is provided. Daily RV rate is $25. The casino has 1,100 slots, 33 pit/gaming tables, poker room and three restaurants. The on-site convention center is a venue for concerts and special events. DISCOUNTS: Ask about senior citizen discounts at the buffet. A discount of $5 is available at the RV Park for Players Club cardholders. DIRECTIONS & PARKING: From I-70 exit 358, north on US-75 for 17 miles, then west on 150th Avenue for 1.4 miles. Self-contained RVs are also permitted to boondock at the far end of the casino lot.

POWHATTAN

Sac and Fox Casino & RV Spaces

1322 US Highway 75
Powhattan, Kansas 66527
785-467-8000 • 800-990-2946
www.sacandfoxcasino.com

DESCRIPTION: Open 24 hours daily, the casino features 1,100 slots, 15 pit/gaming tables, buffet and deli, golf driving range and 24-hour truck stop. RV spaces with electric hookup are available in the parking lot; last year's rates were $10. Register at the casino. There is also a central dump station and fresh water available for RVs. DISCOUNTS: Seniors, 55 and older, get $1 off meals. Celebrants receive a free meal during their birthday and anniversary months. DIRECTIONS & PARKING: From

I-70 exit 358, the casino is on the northbound side of US-75, about 43 miles north of Topeka. Adequate parking is provided for large vehicles. If not registered for electric hookups, please notify Security if you plan to stay overnight.

WHITE CLOUD

Casino White Cloud & RV Spaces
777 Jackpot Drive
White Cloud, Kansas 66094
785-595-3430 • 877-652-6115

DESCRIPTION: This charming little Indian casino is surrounded by farmland in the northeastern corner of Kansas, near the Missouri and Nebraska borders. The casino has 350 slots, 9 gaming tables, a restaurant and deli. Casino hours are 9am–1am/3am weekends. There are six full-hookup RV sites adjacent to the parking lot; there is no charge for these spaces, but registration with Security is required before pulling in. There is no hotel at this location. DIRECTIONS: From I-70 exit 358 in KS, go north on US-75 for 54.4 miles, then east on US-36 for 20.2 miles, north on Timber Rd 1 mile, east on 240th St .5 mile, north on Thrasher Rd 5 miles, west on 290th St .5 mile, continue on Timber Rd 2 miles, then east on 310th St .6 mile. A shorter route out of St. Joseph, MO is to take US-36 west for 16.6 miles then SR-7 north 34 miles.

Note: Two Oklahoma casinos are located just south of the Kansas state line: First Council Casino on US-77 in Newkirk, Oklahoma (south of Arkansas City, Kansas), and Downstream Casino Resort in Quapaw, Oklahoma (west of Joplin, Missouri).

Louisiana

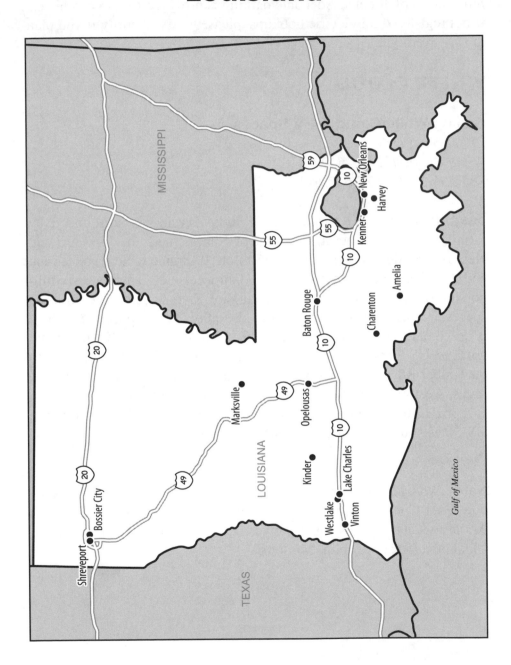

City	Casino	🚐	🗲	🛡	📄
Amelia	Amelia Belle Casino				97
Baton Rouge	Hollywood Casino Baton Rouge			✔	98
Bossier City	Boomtown Casino & Hotel			✔	99
Bossier City	Diamond Jack's Resort	✔		✔	99
Bossier City	Harrah's Louisiana Downs Racetrack & Casino			✔	99
Bossier City	Horseshoe Casino Hotel			✔	100
Charenton	Cypress Bayou Casino & RV Park	✔			100
Harvey	Boomtown Casino - Westbank				101
Kenner	Treasure Chest Casino			✔	101
Kinder	Coushatta Casino Resort & RV Park	✔			102
Lake Charles	L'Auberge du Lac Casino Resort	✔		✔	103
Marksville	Paragon Casino Resort & RV Park	✔			103
New Orleans	Harrah's New Orleans				104
Opelousas	Evangeline Downs Racetrack & Casino			✔	104
Shreveport	Eldorado Casino Shreveport			✔	105
Shreveport	Sam's Town Shreveport			✔	105
Vinton	Delta Downs Raceway & Casino			✔	105
Westlake	Isle of Capri Casino		✔	✔	106

LOUISIANA

When it comes to gaming, Louisiana has a wide variety of casino styles – ten riverboats, four land-based casinos and three racinos (casinos at race tracks). Most casinos in Louisiana are open 24/7.

When traveling in Louisiana, you'll also notice a number of smaller "casinos," mostly in travel centers, gas stations or bars. They have limited gaming machines, some OTBs, but generally no pit/table play.

AMELIA

Amelia Belle Casino
500 Lake Palourde Rd

Amelia, Louisiana 70340
985-631-1777 • 888-777-1143
www.ameliabellecasino.com

DESCRIPTION: The 1,200-passenger red, white & blue paddlewheeler is docked on Bayou Boeuf in Saint Mary's Parish about 50 miles west of New Orleans. It has over 800 slots, 25 gaming tables and a buffet restaurant featuring Cajun specialties. DISCOUNTS: Monday is Senior Day for club members 50+ featuring buffet discounts, extra points and free gifts. DIRECTIONS & PARKING: From US-90 exit 181, take the Amelia exit and follow signs. Parking for self-contained RVs is available toward the back of the lot.

BATON ROUGE

Hollywood Casino Baton Rouge
1717 River Road North
Baton Rouge, Louisiana 70802
225-709-7777 • 800-447-6843
www.pngaming.com

DESCRIPTION: The casino has 1,100 slots, video poker, 27 pit/gaming tables and a separate high limit area. Food venues include a steakhouse, buffet (overlooking the Mississippi River) and grille. Rhythms Lounge features live entertainment and has 17 TVs. There is no hotel at this location. DIRECTIONS & PARKING: From I-10 exit 155 to I-110, exit at North St. This is an exit ramp from the left lane! Take North St for .6 mile, then right on River Rd to the casino on the left. Free overnight parking for self-contained RVs is available in the lot along River Rd (next to railroad tracks). Security will assist with parking. A courtesy shuttle operates between the parking lot and the casino.

Note: The Belle of Baton Rouge casino is docked one mile down river from Hollywood Casino, and there is a hotel and parking garage at that location. It is in the downtown area where streets are narrow and outdoor parking space is limited. It is not recommended for RVs.

BOSSIER CITY

Boomtown Casino & Hotel
300 Riverside Drive
Bossier City, Louisiana 71111
318-746-0711 • 866-462-8696
www.boomtownbossier.com

DESCRIPTION: The western-themed riverboat casino has 1,200 slots on three levels, 33 gaming tables, high limit areas and three restaurants. The hotel has 188 rooms/suites. **DISCOUNTS**: Senior Day events may include slot tournaments and valuable coupons. There are also discounts available for slot club members at the buffet. **DIRECTIONS & PARKING**: From I-20 take exit 19B. On entering the Boomtown complex, RVs should go straight and turn left into the lot alongside the hotel. Please notify security if you plan to stay overnight as parking space is limited.

Diamond Jack's Resort & RV Park
711 Diamond Jacks Boulevard
Bossier City, Louisiana 71111
318-678-7777 • 866-552-9629
318-678-7661 (RV Park)
www.diamondjacks.com

DESCRIPTION: The resort has a hotel and RV Park with 32 level paved sites with full hookups. Last year's RV rates were $35-$40. The casino has 1,100 slots, 32 gaming tables and four restaurants (one open 24 hours). **DISCOUNTS**: The RV Park extends discounts to Diamond Jack's player's club cardholders. **DIRECTIONS & PARKING**: From I-20 take exit 20A to Isle of Capri Blvd. Free parking is available in the front lot when the RV Park is full.

Harrah's Louisiana Downs Racetrack & Casino
8000 East Texas Street
Bossier City, Louisiana 71111
318-742-5555 • 800-551-2361
www.ladowns.com

DESCRIPTION: The racetrack hosts live thoroughbred and quarterhorse racing May-Dec and daily simulcasting. The casino has 1,400 slots, video poker, and three restaurants. Harrah's Club, featuring southern cuisine, is located on the third level and has a track view. **DISCOUNTS**: Coupon books offered for first-time guests. **DIRECTIONS & PARKING**: Louisiana Downs is just off I-20 at exit 20A; it can be seen from the westbound lanes of the interstate. Overnight parking is permitted for self-contained RVs.

Horseshoe Casino Hotel
711 Horseshoe Boulevard
Bossier City, Louisiana 71111
318-742-0711 • 800-895-0711
www.horseshoe.com

DESCRIPTION: The Vegas-style casino has 1,500 slots, 65 pit/gaming tables and five restaurants. The hotel has 606 suites and a retail shopping concourse with upscale gift shops. A unique display in the lobby features $1 million in $100 bills. **DIRECTIONS & PARKING**: From I-20 exit 19B go north to the casino. Enter the casino complex and turn left at the first or second driveway into the RV parking lot. Overnight parking is permitted for self-contained RVs.

CHARENTON

Cypress Bayou Casino & RV Park
832 Martin Luther King Road
Charenton, Louisiana 70523
337-923-7284 • 800-284-4386
www.cypressbayou.com

DESCRIPTION: The casino has a self-park RV area with 11 modern full-hookup paved sites. When you come in, select a site and hook up. Last year's fee was $10 per night. A courtesy shuttle is available. The casino features 1,300 slots including video poker machines, 57 pit/table games, separate non-smoking slots area and five food venues. The casino is open 24 hours. There is no hotel at this location. Cypress Bayou is owned and operated by the Chitimacha Tribe of Louisiana. DIRECTIONS: From I-10 exit 103A, take US-90 east (along the future I-49 corridor) for 42.5 miles to SR-83, then east on SR-83 and left on SR-182 for .5 mile. Turn right on to Ralph Darden Memorial Parkway for two miles to the casino. The self-park RV area is east of the casino.

HARVEY

Boomtown Casino - Westbank
4132 Peters Road
Harvey, Louisiana 70058
504-366-7711 • 800-366-7711
www.boomtownneworleans.com

DESCRIPTION: The casino on three levels has 1,600 slots, video poker, 22 pit/gaming tables, poker room, separate non-smoking area for slot players, two restaurants and fast food. An interesting display on the history of gaming and a few vintage slot machines can be viewed in the casino lobby. There is no hotel at this location. DISCOUNTS: A senior discount is extended at the buffet. DIRECTIONS & PARKING: The casino is about 12 miles from the interstate. From I-10 eastbound, take exit 234B; From I-10 westbound, take exit 234C. Cross the bridge and continue on elevated Westbank Expressway (US-90 West Business Route) for six miles. Exit at Manhattan Blvd – exit 6. Continue on ground-level Westbank Expressway middle lane (do not enter tunnel). Follow the blue casino signs. The expressway ends at Peters Road. Turn left and follow Peters Road for 4.5 miles to the casino. The designated area for large vehicles is in the southeast corner of the parking lot. A courtesy shuttle is available.

KENNER

Treasure Chest Casino
5050 Williams Boulevard
Kenner, Louisiana 70065
504-443-8000 • 800-298-0711
www.treasurechestcasino.com

DESCRIPTION: The paddlewheeler located in Kenner (a suburb of New Orleans) has 1,000 slots on three decks, 16 pit/gaming tables, non-smoking area, a buffet and casual dining. Free nightly entertainment is featured. There is no hotel at this location. **DISCOUNTS**: Senior members of Prime Rewards, 50 and older, are eligible for monthly specials. **DIRECTIONS & PARKING**: From I-10 exit 223, north on Williams Blvd (SR-49) for 1.5 miles to the casino on the shores of Lake Pontchartrain. RVs should park in the Pontchartrain Center lot. A courtesy shuttle runs between parking lots and the casino.

KINDER

Coushatta Casino Resort & RV Park

777 Coushatta Drive
Kinder, Louisiana 70648
337-738-1370 • 800-584-7263
888-774-7263 (RV Park)
www.gccoushatta.com

DESCRIPTION: The resort includes a hotel and RV Park with 100 paved, full hookup sites and 100 chalets. The RV Park has a two-acre lake, swimming pool, horseshoes, tennis, basketball and volleyball courts, a lodge with fireplace, game room and large screen TV, laundry and a covered deck. Last year's RV rates were $19-$24. The 24-hour casino includes 2,800 slots, 92 gaming tables, poker room, high stakes gaming salons and a non-smoking area. The resort also has six restaurants and an 18-hole golf course, Koasati Pines, the longest championship course in the state. Free shuttle service is provided to and from the casino and the golf course. **DISCOUNTS**: AARP, Good Sam, FMCA or Escapees discounts are honored. **DIRECTIONS & PARKING**: From I-10 exit 44, go north 23 miles on US-165 to the resort located five miles north of Kinder. Free parking is available for RVs on the service road just outside the RV Park entrance or on the perimeter of the parking lot (space permitted).

LAKE CHARLES

L'Auberge du Lac Casino Resort
777 Avenue L'Auberge
Lake Charles, Louisiana 70601
337-395-7777 • 866-580-7444
www.ldlcasino.com

DESCRIPTION: The Texas Hill Country-themed resort has the largest single-level riverboat casino in the world, a hotel, 15 modern RV sites, six restaurants and a golf course. The casino features 1,600 slots and 62 table games. The RV sites (located southwest of the hotel building), have water and electric hookups with a central dump. Last year's daily rate was $25 and advance reservations are suggested. **Note**: RV spaces may be temporarily closed for part of 2010 due to construction of the new Sugarcane Bay addition to the resort complex. Call ahead for information. **DIRECTIONS & PARKING**: From I-10 exit 25, take the I-210 Loop to exit 4 then north on Nelson Road for .5 mile, left into the casino complex; follow signs to RV/truck parking. Several dry camping spaces are also available (curbside) in the RV area for free overnight parking.

MARKSVILLE

Paragon Casino Resort & RV Park
711 Paragon Place – Highway 1
Marksville, Louisiana 71351
318-253-1946 • 800-946-1946
www.paragoncasinoresort.com

DESCRIPTION: The resort includes a 335-room hotel and RV Park. There are 185 paved pull-thru RV sites with full hookups including cable TV. The RV Park has a pool, laundry, horseshoes, volleyball and a guest lodge with a big screen TV. Last year's RV rates were $17-$22. Five food venues include casual and fine dining, Cajun bistro, diner and the buffet. The resort includes an 18-hole championship golf course. Free shuttle service is provided to the casino and golf course. The 24-hour casino has over 2,200 slot machines with Las Vegas odds, 55 gaming tables, poker room, keno, race book and high denomination slot and table play. There is a designated non-smoking slots area. **DISCOUNTS**: The RV Park honors Good Sam and Passport America discounts. Seasonal promotions may include valuable gifts or match play for new Players Club members. Ask at the Players Club about current promotions. **DIRECTIONS**: From I-49 exit 80 in Alexandria, take US-71 south for 4.5 miles, LA-3170 east for 5.5 miles then LA-1 south for about 18 miles to the casino complex on the right.

NEW ORLEANS

Harrah's New Orleans
Canal at The River
New Orleans, Louisiana 70130
504-533-6000 • 800- 427-7247
www.harrahs.com

DESCRIPTION: The Vegas-style casino has 2,200 slots and 127 gaming tables. The hotel has 450 rooms. Harrah's is a land-based casino located in downtown New Orleans near the French Quarter. **NOTE**: There is NO parking for RVs at Harrah's in downtown New Orleans.

OPELOUSAS

Evangeline Downs Racetrack & Casino
2435 Creswell Lane Extension
Opelousas, Louisiana 70570
337-594-3000 • 866-472-2466
www.evangelinedowns.com

DESCRIPTION: The racino has 1,600 slots, a buffet, fine dining, 24-hour café and a raised centerpiece casino lounge with seating for 110. Live quarterhorse racing takes place in spring and fall; thoroughbred racing in summer. Simulcasting is offered all year. There is no hotel at this location. **DIRECTIONS**: From I-10 exit 103, take I-49 to exit 18. Turn right on Creswell. The entrance to the racino is on the left just past the Wal-Mart on the Creswell extension. RVs should park in the north lot.

SHREVEPORT

Eldorado Casino Shreveport
451 Clyde Fant Parkway
Shreveport, Louisiana 71101
318-220-0711 • 877-602-0711
www.eldoradoshreveport.com

DESCRIPTION: The casino offers over 1,500 slot machines, 61 gaming tables and a spacious pavilion with four restaurants including a buffet, steakhouse and 50's style diner. The hotel has 403 suites. **DIRECTIONS & PARKING**: From I-20 exit 19A, Spring St, proceed north to Milam St, right on Milam to Clyde Fant Pkwy. Limited RV parking spaces are available. Pull up to the valet area and they will assist with parking when space is available.

Sam's Town Shreveport
315 Clyde Fant Parkway
Shreveport, Louisiana 71101
318-424-7777 • 866-861-0711
www.samstownshreveport.com

DESCRIPTION: Located on the Red River in downtown Shreveport, the casino has 1,100 slots, 28 pit/gaming tables and a hotel. Restaurants include a buffet, café, and steakhouse. **DIRECTIONS & PARKING**: From I-20 exit 19A, Spring St, go north four blocks and turn right on Fannin, east to casino. RV parking is tight and limited. Spaces are available in the Expo Hall lot across from the casino.

VINTON

Delta Downs Raceway & Casino
2717 Delta Downs Drive
Vinton, Louisiana 70668
337-589-7441 • 800-589-7441
www.deltadowns.com

DESCRIPTION: The casino has 1,600 slots and video poker machines on a roomy gaming floor. There is a 230-room hotel on site. The Outlook Steakhouse offers fine dining with a view of the track. A buffet restaurant is open for lunch and dinner. Live racing includes thoroughbreds Oct-April and quarter horse racing April-July. There is daily simulcasting. **DIRECTIONS & PARKING**: From I-10 exit 4 or exit 7, follow signs to the racetrack located on CR-3063, three miles from the interstate. RV parking is in the large lot east of the hotel. Follow signs to the designated bus/RV parking area. Overnight parking is permitted for self-contained RVs.

WESTLAKE

Isle of Capri Casino & RV Spaces
100 Westlake Avenue
Westlake, Louisiana 70669
337-430-0711 • 888-475-3847
www.isleofcapricasino.com

DESCRIPTION: There are eight RV spaces with electric hookups in the parking lot adjacent to the 493-room hotel. The spaces are tight and there is no room to extend slideouts. Daily rate last year was $10 for the electric hookup and advance reservations are required. The casino has 1,900 slots, 75 pit/gaming tables and four restaurants. **DISCOUNTS**: Senior Days are held mid-week with special discounts and promotions. **DIRECTIONS & PARKING**: From I-10 exit 27, the Isle of Capri can be seen from the eastbound lanes of the interstate. Follow the green casino signs after exiting I-10. Free overnight RV parking is also available in the lot on the north side of the casino complex along the fence by the I-10 bridge.

Maine

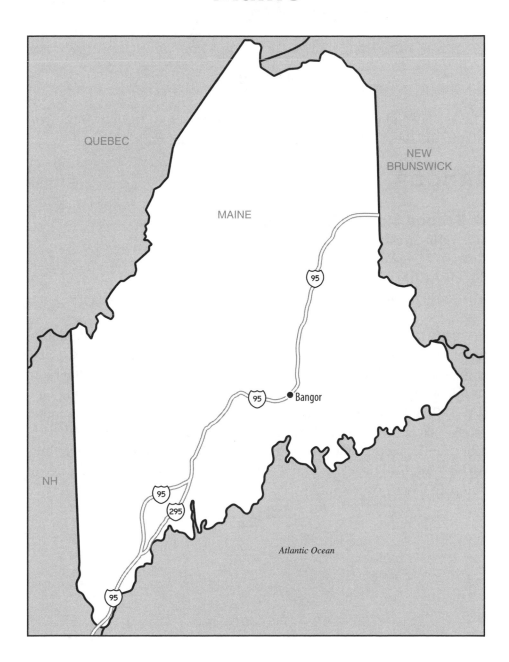

City	Casino	🚐	〽	🛡	📄
Bangor	Hollywood Slots at Bangor Raceway			✔	108

MAINE

The Hollywood Casino is located on Main Street in downtown Bangor next to the Bangor Raceway/OTB in historic Bass Park.

BANGOR

Hollywood Slots at Bangor Raceway

500 Main Street
Bangor, Maine 04401
207-561 6100 • 877-779-7771
www.hollywoodslotsatbangor.com

DESCRIPTION: The casino, adjacent to a hotel, has 1,000 slots, buffet restaurant, snack bar and retail shops. Live harness racing takes place at the raceway May-July. The raceway also has a full service restaurant, simulcasting and OTB. Casino hours are: Mon-Thur, 9am-1am/2am (Fri-Sat), and Sun noon-1am. **DIRECTIONS & PARKING**: From I-95 exit 182A, take I-395 E/ME-15 South for 1.3 miles to exit 3, then US-1A east .5 mile, merge onto Main St .2 mile. RVs should use the overflow parking lot. Call the casino for shuttle service. Please notify Security if you plan to stay overnight.

Michigan

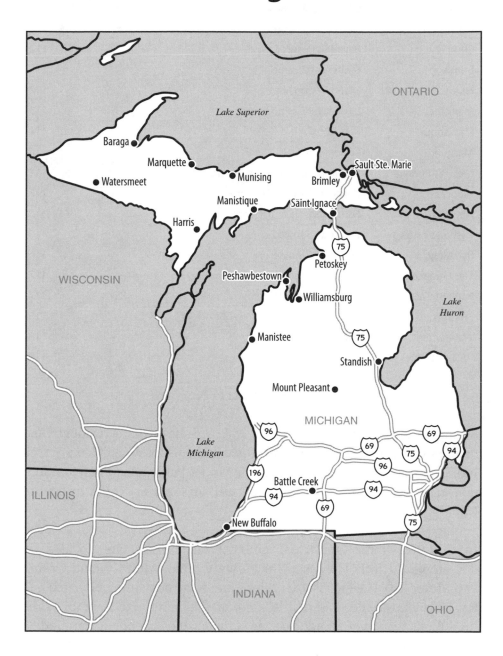

City	Casino	🚐	〰	🛡	📄
Baraga	Ojibwa Casino Resort	✔			111
Battle Creek	Firekeepers Casino			✔	111
Brimley	Bay Mills Resort Casino	✔			112
Brimley	Kings Club Casino				112
Harris	Island Casino Resort	✔			112
Manistee	Little River Casino Resort	✔			113
Manistique	Kewadin Casino				114
Marquette	Ojibwa Casino II		✔		114
Mount Pleasant	Soaring Eagle Casino & Resort				114
Munising	Kewadin Casino - Christmas				115
New Buffalo	Four Winds Casino Resort			✔	115
Peshawbestown	Leelanau Sands Casino		✔		116
Petoskey	Odawa Casino Resort				116
Saint Ignace	Kewadin Shores Hotel & Casino			✔	117
Sault Ste. Marie	Kewadin Casino Hotel	✔			117
Standish	Saganing Eagles Landing Casino				118
Watersmeet	Lac Vieux Desert Casino	✔			118
Williamsburg	Turtle Creek Casino				119

MICHIGAN

Michigan is known as "The Great Lakes State" where residents and visitors can enjoy 3,200 miles of Great Lakes shoreline. There are 18 Indian casinos in the state – nine in the Upper Peninsula (where outdoor non-gaming activities abound during all seasons) and nine in central Michigan.

In addition, three non-tribal commercial casinos are located in downtown Detroit. They are Greektown Casino, MGM Grand Casino and Motor City Casino. These casinos are in the busy inner city area and RV travelers should note that it is not advisable to take a motor home into the motor city. Parking garages at the casinos cannot accommodate oversize vehicles.

BARAGA

Ojibwa Casino Resort & RV Spaces
16449 Michigan Avenue
Baraga, Michigan 49908
906-353-6333 • 800-323-8045
www.ojibwacasino.com

DESCRIPTION: Located near Sandpoint Lighthouse on Keneenaw Bay, the casino features 300 slots, 10 gaming tables, bingo, a restaurant and bowling alley. The facility is open 24/7 all year. There is a hotel and 12 full hookup RV spaces; last year's charge was $20, first come, first served. Register at the hotel. DISCOUNTS: Senior Day on Mondays features specials and tournaments. DIRECTIONS & PARKING: From US-41 in Baraga, one mile west on M-38.

BATTLE CREEK

Firekeepers Casino
11177 Michigan Avenue East
Battle Creek, Michigan 49014
269-660-5722
www.firekeeperscasino.com

DESCRIPTION: The casino has 2,600 slots, 90 pit/table games, bingo, three restaurants and a food court. DIRECTIONS & PARKING: From I-94 take exit 104 toward 11 Mile Rd. Turn left at 11 Mile Rd for .3 mile then left onto E. Michigan Ave. for .7 mile. Parking is available for RVs. Check in with Security if staying overnight.

BRIMLEY

Two affiliated casinos in Brimley – Bay Mills and Kings Club – are owned by the Bay Mills Native American Community. The Bay Mills Reservation on the UP north shore is noted for its captivating views and rich Native American history. The two casinos are located just four miles from one another and a free shuttle operates between them. Bay Mills has a modern RV park.

Bay Mills Resort Casino & RV Park

11386 West Lakeshore Drive
Brimley, Michigan 49715
906-248-3715 • 888-422-9645
www.4baymills.com

DESCRIPTION: The resort includes an RV Park, open May-Oct, and a hotel. There are 76 shaded RV sites within walking distance to the casino. Last year's RV rates were $17-$25. The casino has three restaurants, 900 slots, 14 gaming tables, poker room and bingo. The 18-hole Wild Bluff championship golf course is located at Bay Mills. **DISCOUNTS**: Wednesday is Senior Day with double points given and buffet discounts for seniors 60 and older. **DIRECTIONS**: From I-75 exit 386, west on M-28 for 7.7 miles, then north into Brimley on M-24 for 2.5 miles and west on Lakeshore Dr. for 2 miles.

Kings Club Casino

12140 West Lakeshore Drive
Brimley, Michigan 49715
906-248-3700 • 888-422-9645
www.4baymills.com

DESCRIPTION: Affiliated with Bay Mills, the smaller casino has 200 gaming machines (no tables) and a deli. Casino hours are 10am-midnight. Shuttle service operates between the two casinos. **DISCOUNTS**: Seniors, 50+ receive discounts every Tuesday; ask for details. **DIRECTIONS**: From I-75 exit 386, west on M-28 for 7.7 miles, then north into Brimley on M-22 for 2.5 miles and west on Lakeshore Dr. for 4.3 miles.

HARRIS

Island Casino Resort & RV Park

W399 Highways 2 & 41
Harris, Michigan 49845

906-466-2941 • 800-682-6040
www.islandresortandcasino.com

DESCRIPTION: The resort includes a hotel and RV Park, open May-Nov, with 53 full hookup sites. Last year's daily rate was $15. Shuttle service is provided to the casino that has 1,700 gaming machines, 28 tables, poker room and three restaurants. RV guests may use the resort amenities including an indoor pool with a unique heated sand beach. Live entertainment is featured weekly. **DISCOUNTS**: Island Club members get discounts at restaurants and gift shop. **DIRECTIONS**: From Escanaba (on the northern shore of Lake Michigan), travel 13 miles west on Hwy-2 & 41 into Harris.

MANISTEE

Little River Casino Resort & RV Park
2700 Orchard Highway
Manistee, Michigan 49660
231-723-1535 • 888-568-2244
www.littlerivercasinos.com

DESCRIPTION: The resort includes a hotel and modern 96-space RV Park. Open April-Nov, the RV Park has an outdoor pavilion, guest lounge with TV and laundry. The park is walking distance to the casino; shuttle service is also provided. RV Park guests may use the hotel facilities: indoor pool/spa, sauna and fitness room. Full hookup rates were $29-$38 last year. The friendly casino features 1,350 slots, 35 table games, six-table poker room, restaurant and deli. **DISCOUNTS**: Good Sam and AAA honored. **DIRECTIONS & PARKING**: Manistee is near the east shore of Lake Michigan. From US-131 (major north/south route) Cadillac exit, take M-55 west to junction with US-31, then north for 3.1 miles on US-31. Casino is on the left. Overnight parking is also permitted in the parking lot (no hookups); there is a $5 charge for use of the central dump.

MANISTIQUE

Kewadin Casino – Manistique
1533D US-2 East
Manistique, Michigan 49854
906-341-5510 • 800-539-2346
www.kewadin.com

DESCRIPTION: The casino offers Vegas-style gaming in a hometown atmosphere. It has over 200 slots, 8 gaming tables, bingo, restaurant and bar. **DISCOUNTS**: Specials are offered for seniors, 50+ on Thursdays. **DIRECTIONS & PARKING**: From I-75 exit 344B west on US-2 for 89 miles. The casino is located west of the Mackinaw Bridge. Free RV parking is available in the casino lot.

MARQUETTE

Ojibwa Casino II & RV Spaces – Marquette
105 Acre Trail
Marquette, Michigan 49855
906-249-4200 • 888-560-9905
www.ojibwacasino.com

DESCRIPTION: The 24-hour casino features 300 slots, 10 gaming tables and a snack bar. **DISCOUNTS**: Monday specials for seniors 55+ may include free lunch, drawings and slot tournaments. **DIRECTIONS & PARKING**: From I-75 exit 344B follow US-2 north 65.5 miles, M-77 north 17.3 miles, M-28 west 32.7 miles and Kawbawgam Rd north. RV parking with free electric hookups is available in the casino lot.

MOUNT PLEASANT

Soaring Eagle Casino & Resort
6800 East Soaring Eagle Boulevard
Mount Pleasant, Michigan 48858
989-775-7777 • 888-732-4537
www.soaringeaglecasino.com

DESCRIPTION: The resort has 24-hour gaming in two buildings with 4,300 slots, 73 pit/gaming tables, poker room and four restaurants. A hotel is on site. **DIRECTIONS & PARKING**: From US-127, take M-20 east (Pickard) for 1.2 miles. Turn right on to Leaton Road and follow signs to the RV parking lot. A large parking area is designated specifically for RVs. Shuttle service is provided to the casinos 24 hours.

MUNISING

Kewadin Casino – Christmas
N 7761 Candy Cane Lane
Munising, Michigan 49862
906-387-5475 • 800-539-2346
www.kewadin.com

DESCRIPTION: In the northern UP along the shores of Lake Superior, this casino is located just west of Munising. Open seven days a week 8am–3am, it features over 200 slots and 6 gaming tables, Frosty's Bar & Grille and the Northern Lights gift shop. **DISCOUNTS**: Senior specials offered every Thursday if 50+. **DIRECTIONS & PARKING**: From I-75 exit 386, follow M-28 west for 117 miles. Free overnight parking is available for self-contained RVs.

NEW BUFFALO

Four Winds Casino Resort
11111 Wilson Road
New Buffalo, Michigan 49117
866-494-6371
www.fourwindscasino.com

DESCRIPTION: The casino has 3,000 slots, 96 gaming tables including a poker room, three restaurants and fast food. There is a hotel on site. **DIRECTIONS**: From I-94 exit 1 take MI-239 south for .2 mile and Wilson Rd east for .3 mile. Overnight parking is permitted for self-contained RVs at the far east end of the parking lot.

PESHAWBESTOWN

Leelanau Sands Casino & RV Spaces
2521 Northwest Bay Shore Drive
Peshawbestown, Michigan 49682
231-534-8100 • 800-922-2946
www.casino2win.com

DESCRIPTION: Open year round 7 days a week 8am-2am, the casino has over 400 slots, 7 gaming tables, poker room, restaurant and bar. DISCOUNTS: Ask about specials for seniors, 55 and older, on Tuesdays. DIRECTIONS & PARKING: From I-75 exit 254 follow M-72 west about 51 miles, then north on M-22 for 18.7 miles. The RV lot is across the street from the casino (next to the gas station). Electric hookups are $7 per night; go to the casino gift shop to pay for electric.

PETOSKEY

Odawa Casino Resort
1760 Lears Road
Petoskey, Michigan 49770
231-439-6100 • 877-442-6464
www.victories-casino.com

DESCRIPTION: The resort, nestled along the banks of the bay on eastern Lake Michigan, has a hotel has and a 24-hour casino with 1,500 slots, 17 gaming tables, four restaurants and a lounge with live entertainment. DISCOUNTS: Ask about senior specials on Wednesdays and Sundays if 55 and older. DIRECTIONS & PARKING: From I-75 take exit 290 toward Vanderbilt, go north on Old 27/CR-C48 for 2.7 miles, then west on East Thumb Lake Rd/CR-C48 for 12.2 miles. Turn north on US-131 and follow 12.8 miles to Petosky, then west on Lears Rd for .7 mile. Follow signs to Odawa Resort. RV parking is available for self-contained vehicles; follow signs.

SAINT IGNACE

Kewadin Shores Hotel & Casino – St. Ignace
3015 Mackinac Trail
Saint Ignace, Michigan 49781
906-643-7071 • 800-539-2346
www.kewadin.com

DESCRIPTION: The casino, open 24/7, has 800 slots, 18 gaming tables, poker room, keno and three restaurants. There is a hotel on site. **DISCOUNTS**: Northern Rewards players who are 50+ may receive specials on Thursdays. Ask at the club desk. **DIRECTIONS & PARKING**: St. Ignace is the gateway to the Upper Peninsula, near Mackinac Island and the Mackinac Bridge. From I-75 exit 348, take Mackinac Trail north for 1.4 miles. Ample parking is provided for RVs; overnight is OK.

SAULT STE. MARIE

Kewadin Casino Hotel & RV Park – Sault Ste. Marie
2186 Shunk Road
Sault Ste. Marie, Michigan 49783
906-632-0530 • 800-KEWADIN
www.kewadin.com

DESCRIPTION: The resort includes a hotel and 75-space RV Park with electric hookups (open May-Oct). Last year's RV rate was $10. RV guests are invited to enjoy the hotel's indoor pool. The casino features over 700 slots, 21 gaming tables, poker room, restaurant, deli and sports bar. The Bawating Gallery has the largest collection of Woodland Indian art in the Midwest. Sault Ste. Marie is Michigan's oldest city and local attractions include the Agawa Canyon and the world-famous Soo Locks. **DISCOUNTS**: Ask about senior discounts on Thursdays. **DIRECTIONS**: From I-75 exit 392 (before the bridge to Ontario) go east on Three Mile Rd for 2.4 miles then north on Shunk Rd for .9 mile.

STANDISH

Saganing Eagle's Landing Casino
2690 Worth Road
Standish, Michigan 48658
888-732-4537
www.saganing-eagleslanding.com

DESCRIPTION: The 24-hour casino has over 800 slots and fast food.
DIRECTIONS: From I-75 exit 188 take US-23 north 2.2 miles then M-13 south 1.6 miles and east on Worth Rd 2.6 miles.

WATERSMEET

Lac Vieux Desert Resort Casino & RV Park
N 5384 US-45 North
Watersmeet, Michigan 49969
906-358-4226 • 800-583-3599
800-895-2505 (RV Park)
www.lvdcasino.com

DESCRIPTION: The resort includes a hotel and RV Park with 14 sites with electric and water hookups. RV registration is at the hotel. Last year's rate was $15 per night; the RV Park is closed during winter months. The casino has 700 slots, 16 gaming tables, keno, poker room, a restaurant, snack bar and 9-hole golf course. Live entertainment is featured on weekends. **DISCOUNTS**: Various senior discounts on Tuesdays if 55 and older. Ask about them at the casino. **DIRECTIONS**: Located in the western UP, two miles north of the junction of US-2 and US-45 (about eight miles north of the Wisconsin border).

WILLIAMSBURG

Turtle Creek Casino

7741 M-72 East
Williamsburg, Michigan 49690
231-267-9546 • 888-777-8946
www.casino2win.com

DESCRIPTION: The 24/7 casino features 1,250 gaming machines, 28 gaming tables, a restaurant and café. **DIRECTIONS & PARKING**: From I-75 follow M-72 west 30 miles. Enter the casino property and go to the lot on the far left side. Shuttle service is available to the casino.

Minnesota

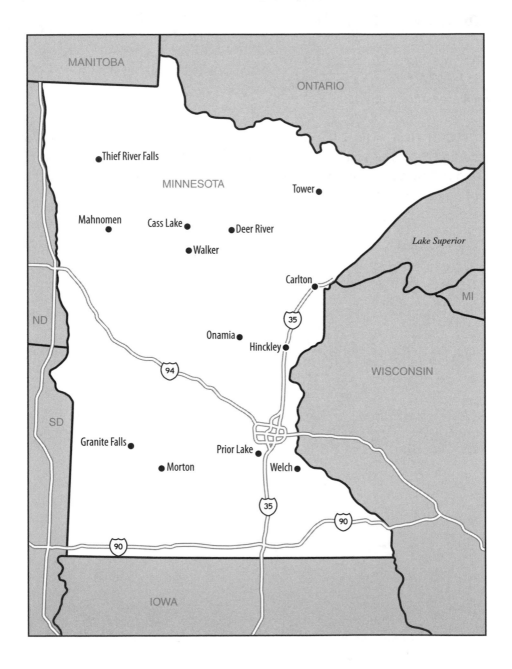

City	Casino	🚐	〽	⬭	📄
Carlton	Black Bear Casino & Hotel			✔	121
Cass Lake	Palace Casino Hotel		✔		122
Deer River	White Oak Casino				122
Granite Falls	Prairie's Edge Resort Casino	✔			123
Hinckley	Grand Casino Hinckley	✔		✔	123
Mahnomen	Shooting Star Casino Hotel	✔			124
Morton	Jackpot Junction Casino Hotel	✔			124
Onamia	Grand Casino Mille Lacs				125
Prior Lake	Mystic Lake Casino Hotel	✔			125
Thief River Falls	Seven Clans Casino				126
Tower	Fortune Bay Resort & Casino	✔			127
Walker	Northern Lights Casino		✔		127
Welch	Treasure Island Resort Casino	✔			128

MINNESOTA

Casinos in Minnesota are located throughout the state, many of them in the very heart of the "Land of the Lakes," where outdoor recreational activities abound. Minnesota casinos are RV-friendly with comfortable campgrounds or parking facilities. Casino resorts in the southern part of the state are lavish entertainment destinations featuring large Vegas-style casinos and upscale amenities.

Minnesota has had gambling since 1988 when the state's 11 Indian Tribes requested compacts to operate casinos with video games of chance. Later table games, blackjack and poker, were added.

CARLTON

Black Bear Casino & Hotel
1785 Highway 210
Carlton, Minnesota 55718
218-878-2327 • 888-771-0777
www.blackbearcasinohotel.com

DESCRIPTION: The 24-hour casino features 1,900 slots, video craps, 12 blackjack tables, poker room, bingo and three restaurants. The hotel has a skywalk to the casino. **DISCOUNTS**: Double points and specials at the poker room, grille and café on "2fer" Wednesdays. **DIRECTIONS & PARKING**: From I-35 exit 235, the casino is on the west corner of Hwy-210, visible from the southbound lanes of the interstate. Designated RV spaces are in the back parking lot (behind the hotel) and free overnight parking is permitted.

CASS LAKE

Palace Casino Hotel & RV Spaces
6280 Upper Cass Frontage Road
Cass Lake, Minnesota 56633
218-335-7000 • 800-228-6676
www.palacecasinohotel.com

DESCRIPTION: The 24-hour casino features 550 slots, video poker, keno, 10 blackjack tables, poker room, bingo, restaurant and snack bar. Bingo is called every day. There is a hotel on site. There are 25 RV spaces with free electric hookups for overnight parking plus a dump station and fresh water behind the casino. **DIRECTIONS & PARKING**: From I-35 exit 250, go west on US-2 into Cass Lake (about 130 miles.) There is a large casino sign on US-2, westbound lane. Go north on Hwy-75 for 1.3 miles. The free electric RV hookups are first-come, first-serve.

DEER RIVER

White Oak Casino
45830 US Highway 2
Deer River, Minnesota 56636
218-246-9600 • 800-653-2412
www.whiteoakcasino.com

DESCRIPTION: The casino, known as the "Best Little Casino in Minnesota," has 315 slots, seven gaming tables, a full service bar, gift shop and snack bar. There is no hotel at this location. **DISCOUNTS**: A free Fun Book is given on Senior Day (50+) Tuesdays. Fun Books are available for people under 50 on Thursdays. DIRECTIONS & PARKING: The casino is located directly on US-2, five miles northwest of Grand Rapids and 2.2 miles west of Deer River. There is limited RV space in the parking lot. Overnight RV parking is permitted. The RV area is within walking distance to the casino.

GRANITE FALLS

Prairie's Edge Resort Casino
5616 Prairie's Edge Lane
Granite Falls, Minnesota 56241
320-564-2121 • 866-293-2121
www.prairiesedgecasino.com • rvpark@prairieviewrvpark.com

DESCRIPTION: Owned and operated by the Upper Sioux Community, the resort includes a convention center, hotel and modern RV Park with 55 full-hookup spaces, some pull thrus. Last year's RV rates were $26; dry camping $17. The RV Park is closed in winter. The casino has 750 slots and friendly dealers at 15 blackjack and poker tables, three restaurants and a lounge. A smoke-free slots area is at the Prairie's Edge C Store. DISCOUNTS: Players Club discounts at the gas station. DIRECTIONS & PARKING: From Jct. US-212 & MN-23 in Granite Falls, go south on MN-23 for 3.7 miles, north on CR-39 for .2 mile and west on CR-17 for 2.4 miles. Free overnight RV parking is also available in the lot.

HINCKLEY

Grand Casino Hinckley & RV Park
777 Lady Luck Drive / Highway 48
Hinckley, Minnesota 55037
320-384-7777 • 800-472-6321
www.grandcasinosmn.com

DESCRIPTION: Resort accommodations include a hotel and two inns and RV Park with 220 sites and 50 cottages. Seasonally adjusted rates are from $15-$28. The RV Park is open all winter. Kids Quest child care center and a video arcade are located in the hotel. Food venues at the resort include three restaurants, fast food and snack bar. The casino has 2,300 slots, 46 live blackjack tables, poker room and bingo. Entertainment is featured daily and live outdoor concerts are held during summer months. The 18-hole Grand National Golf Course is located at the resort. 24-hour shuttle service runs throughout the resort. **DIRECTIONS**: From I-35 exit 183, east on SR-48 for one mile to the resort.

MAHNOMEN

Shooting Star Casino Hotel & RV Park
777 Casino Boulevard
Mahnomen, Minnesota 56557
218-935-2701 • 800-453-7827
www.starcasino.com

DESCRIPTION: Located on White Earth Indian Reservation, the resort has a hotel and a 47-site RV Park. RV sites are open May–Oct and last year's daily rate was $20. RV guests may use the amenities at the hotel including a spacious indoor pool and hot tub in an atrium, fitness room and arcade. The casino features 1,000 slots, 16 blackjack tables, poker room, bingo and non-smoking gaming area. There are four restaurants and two lounges with live entertainment. Headline concerts are held on weekends in the event center. **DISCOUNTS**: Monthly specials are featured at the restaurants. **DIRECTIONS & PARKING**: From I-94 exit 50, take US-59 about 75 miles north to Mahnomen. Free overnight parking for RVs is permitted in the overfill lot designated for buses.

MORTON

Jackpot Junction Casino Hotel & RV Park
39375 County Highway 24
Morton, Minnesota 56270
507-697-8000 • 800-946-2274
800-946-0077 (RV Park)
www.jackpotjunction.com

DESCRIPTION: The Lower Sioux Indian Community owns and operates the resort that includes a hotel and RV Park with 70 full hookup sites. There are showers and a convenience store within walking distance. The RV Park, open April-Oct, is walking distance to the casino. Rates are $11-$28 (with Jackpot Express Card.). RV rates are doubled for special events; advance reservations are suggested. The casino has 1,350 slots, 43 tables, a poker room and four food venues. The resort includes an 18-hole golf course, conference center, headline entertainment in the amphitheater on weekends and live entertainment in the lounge. DIRECTIONS: From I-90 exit 73, follow US-71 north about 69 miles to CR-2 for 1.25 miles and CR-24 south .4 mile.

ONAMIA

Grand Casino Mille Lacs
777 Grand Avenue /US-169 North
Onamia, Minnesota 56359
320-532-7777 • 800-626-LUCK
www.grandcasinosmn.com

DESCRIPTION: On the shore of Lake Mille Lacs, the resort includes two hotels and a spacious Vegas-style casino with 1,900 slots, 36 gaming tables, poker room, bingo and five restaurants. Headline entertainment is featured on weekends. The Mille Lacs Indian Museum, located nearby, features displays and exhibits dedicated to telling the story of the local band of Ojibwe and a restored trading post. DIRECTIONS & PARKING: Located about 90 miles north of the Twin Cities, take I-694 exit 29 to US-169 north. Just past Onamia, US-169 becomes a two-lane road. Stay on US-169 for eight more miles to the casino on the west side of the highway. RVs should follow signs to the designated area for oversized vehicles. Security will assist with parking. Overnight parking is permitted.

PRIOR LAKE

Mystic Lake Casino Hotel & RV Park
2400 Mystic Lake Boulevard

Prior Lake, Minnesota 55372
952-445-9000 • 800-262-7799
www.mysticlake.com

DESCRIPTION: The casino resort includes a hotel, RV Park and an 18-hole golf course. The modern 122-space Dakotah Meadows Campground features full hookup sites, Tipi rentals, a group pavilion, fuel center and a self-serve RV wash with catwalk. Last year's daily fees were $27-$30. The 24-hour casino has 4,000 slots, 96 blackjack tables, high stakes blackjack room, separate non-smoking slots section and four restaurants. A second casino, Little Six, is located a half-mile from the Mystic Lake complex with 615 slots and eight blackjack tables. Shuttle buses operate 24 hours throughout the resort complex. The famous Mall of America is nearby. DISCOUNTS: AAA and FMCA discounts honored. DIRECTIONS: Mystic Lakes is located 25 miles southwest of the Twin Cities. From I-35W exit 1, go west on CR-42 for nine miles, one mile south on CR-83 —or— From I-494 exit 10, take US-169 south (Townline Road) for 6.5 miles, then CR-18 south for 3.4 miles to CR-42 west for three miles to CR-83 (Mystic Lake Dr.) for one mile.

THIEF RIVER FALLS

Seven Clans Casino – Thief River Falls
20595 Center Street East
Thief River Falls, Minnesota 56701
218-681-4062 • 866-255-7848
www.sevenclanscasino.com

DESCRIPTION: The 24-hour casino has 650 slots and nine gaming tables. The hotel features Native American art in the lobby. There is an indoor water park/pool, arcade and gift shop. The Seven Clans Buffet is open morning to night. A snack bar is at the water park and a 24-hour Triple 7 Malt Shop in the casino. DISCOUNTS: Specials and restaurant discounts every Tuesday for 55+. DIRECTIONS & PARKING: From I-94 exit 50, take US-59 north for 125 miles, then right on CR-3 for .7 mile — or — From I-29 exit 161 in ND, east on SR-1 and cross the Red River into Minnesota; continue east for 28 miles into Thief River Falls, then south on US-50 for eight miles to CR-3 east for .7 mile. Free overnight parking for RVs is available in the east lot.

TOWER

Fortune Bay Resort & Casino & RV Park
1430 Bois Forte Road
Tower, Minnesota 55790
218-753-6400 • 800-992-7529
www.fortunebay.com

DESCRIPTION: The resort has a hotel and 34 RV sites with electric and water and central dump in the parking lot. RVs must register at the hotel and *RVs are required to stay in the RV area*. Rates are $30 for hookups and $20 for dry camping. The resort is on Lake Vermilion with boating and freshwater fishing; boat rentals are available. The resort also has an 18-hole golf course. The 24-hour casino has 750 slots, non-smoking slots area, 12 blackjack tables, video keno, video poker, poker room, two restaurants, sports bar and entertainment. DISCOUNTS: Senior specials are offered weekly for 55 and older. DIRECTIONS: Located about 80 miles northwest of Duluth, from I-35 exit 237, take Hwy-33 north for 19.8 miles, US-53 north for 46.2 miles to Hwy-169 north for 17.7 miles to CR-77 north for 1.8 miles, then east on CR-104 for 1.9 miles. *Free overnight parking is NOT provided*; RVs are required to pull into the fee-pay area.

WALKER

Northern Lights Casino
6800 Y Frontage Road N.W.
Walker, Minnesota 56484
218-547-2744 • 800-252-7529
www.northernlightscasino.com

DESCRIPTION: The casino features 950 slots, 10 gaming tables, poker room, a buffet and snack bar. A 90-foot dome above the casino simulates star constellations. The modern 105-room hotel and conference center also houses the Dancing Fire Restaurant with menu service from morning to night. **DIRECTIONS & PARKING**: The casino is located at the junction of Highways 371 and 200 on the south shore of Lake Leech (175 miles north of the Twin Cities). RVs should park in the parking lot in front of the hotel, walking distance to the casino. Free electric hookups are available on a first-come, first-serve basis.

WELCH

Treasure Island Resort Casino & RV Park
5734 Sturgeon Lake Road
Welch, Minnesota 55089
651-388-6300 • 800-222-7077
www.treasureislandcasino.com

DESCRIPTION: The casino resort is located near the Mississippi River and has an RV Park and a hotel with indoor pool, fitness center and a game room. The RV Park, open April–Oct, has 95 pull-thru sites with full hookups. Last year's RV rates were $20-$22; RV guests are invited to use the pool and other amenities at the hotel. Boating and fishing are available nearby. The 24-hour Caribbean-themed casino features 2,500 slots, video poker, video roulette and 50 gaming tables, four restaurants and fast food. Mississippi River cruises (dinner and sightseeing) are available nearby on weekends in season. **DIRECTIONS**: The resort is located 40 miles southeast of the Twin Cities. From I-35 exit 69 follow MN-19 east 9 miles, north on Northfield Blvd 10.8 miles, east on 240th St 11.6 miles, continue on US-61 south 4 miles, then CR-31 east 1 mile, CR-18 north 2.1 miles and east on Sturgeon Lake Rd 1.3 miles.

Mississippi

City	Casino	🚐	〽	⛨	📄
Bay St. Louis	Hollywood Casino Hotel	✔			131
Bay St. Louis	Silver Slipper Casino	✔			132
Biloxi	Beau Rivage				133
Biloxi	Boomtown Casino			✔	133
Biloxi	Grand Biloxi Casino Hotel				133
Biloxi	Hard Rock Casino				134
Biloxi	IP Casino Resort			✔	134
Biloxi	Isle of Capri Resort				135
Biloxi	The Palace Casino Resort				135
Greenville	Harlow's Casino Resort	✔			135
Greenville	Lighthouse Point & Bayou Caddy's Casinos				136
Gulfport	Island View Casino Resort				136
Lula	Isle of Capri Casino	✔			137
Natchez	Isle of Capri Casino & Hotel				137
Philadelphia	Pearl River Resort				138
Robinsonville	Bally's Casino Tunica				139
Robinsonville	Fitzgerald's Casino / Hotel				139
Robinsonville	Gold Strike Casino				140
Robinsonville	Harrah's Casino Tunica	✔			140
Robinsonville	Hollywood Casino Tunica	✔			141
Robinsonville	Horseshoe Casino & Hotel				141
Robinsonville	Resorts Tunica				142
Robinsonville	Sam's Town Hotel & Gambling Hall	✔			142
Robinsonville	Sheraton Casino & Hotel				142
Vicksburg	Ameristar Casino Hotel	✔		✔	143
Vicksburg	Diamond Jack's Casino			✔	143

MISSISSIPPI

Mississippi is known as the Casino Capitol of the South. All casinos in the state are Vegas-style and open 24/7. Popular casino destinations in the state include:

- The Gulf Coast, with at least a dozen casinos along a 26-mile stretch along the state's scenic southern coastline.

- Tunica County, in the northwestern corner of the state, with 13 casino resorts along the Mississippi River.

- Pearl River Resort in east-central Mississippi owned and operated by the Mississippi Band of Choctow Indians.

- Casinos along the Mississippi River in Lula, Greenville, Natchez, and Vicksburg.

BAY ST. LOUIS

Hollywood Casino Hotel & RV Park
711 Hollywood Boulevard
Bay St. Louis, Mississippi
228-467-9257 • 866-7-LUCKY-1
www.hollywoodcasinobsl.com

DESCRIPTION: Formerly Casino Magic, the Hollywood Casino has a hotel and a 100-site RV Park. The casino has 1,200 slots, 31 pit/table games, poker room on the second floor, buffet and fine dining. The RV Park has modern full-hookup sites and 24-hour shuttle service to the casino. Last year's daily RV rates were from $32. The Bridges 18-hole golf course is unique and challenging. **DISCOUNTS**: Good Sam discount is honored at the RV Park. Points earned in the casino may be applied toward RV Park fees. **DIRECTIONS & PARKING**: From I-10 exit 13, take MS 43/603 toward Bay St. Louis for 6 miles, then left on US-90 east for 2 miles, then left at Blue Meadow for .5 mile, then right at Hollywood

Blvd, follow signs. Free overnight parking is permitted for self-contained vehicles in the parking lot between the casino and the RV Park.

Silver Slipper Casino & RV Park
5000 South Beach Boulevard
Bay St. Louis, Mississippi 39520
228-469-2777 • 866-775-4773
www.silverslipper-ms.com

DESCRIPTION: The casino features 1,000 slots, video poker, video dog and horse racing and 31 table games. The waterfront RV Park adjacent to the casino features 24 full hookup, back-in sites. Last year's rates were $27-$38 per night. Food venues at the casino include a buffet, bar & grille and 24-hour cafe. DISCOUNTS: Players Club members may receive a free night at the RV Park. Call ahead for information. DIRECTIONS & PARKING: From I-10 exit 13, take MS 43/603 south toward Bay St. Louis for 5.4 miles, then west on US-90 for 4.6 miles, then south on Lakeshore Road for 4.5 miles, then west on South Beach Boulevard to the casino. Eastbound travelers on I-10 can use exit 2 and follow signs.

BILOXI

More than a dozen casinos are located along 26 scenic miles of Mississippi's balmy Gulf Coast between Biloxi and Bay St. Louis. The casinos aggressively promote their businesses, offering ongoing discounts as well as seasonal specials designed to attract customers to the gaming floors. Look for casino coupons at the Mississippi Welcome Center on I-10 when you enter the state. Also, pick up a copy of *Jackpot!* for the most timely information about entertainment and current discounts being offered by the Gulf Coast casinos.

RV Parking in Biloxi is more convenient in the Back Bay area. **Note:** Treasure Bay Casino, on Beach Blvd, on the west end of Biloxi does not allow overnight RV parking.

Casino Hopping On Foot: in Biloxi's Back Bay, Boomtown and IP are within walking distance of each other. On Beach Blvd, Beau Rivage and

Hard Rock are next door to one another and The Grand and Isle of Capri are walking distance from each other.

Beau Rivage
875 Beach Boulevard
Biloxi, Mississippi 39530
228-386-7111 • 888-750-7111
www.beaurivageresort.com

DESCRIPTION: The single-level Vegas-style casino features 2,300 slots, 230 video poker machines, 93 pit/gaming tables, 16-table poker room and a non-smoking area. The hotel has 1,740 rooms. The resort includes 7 dining options and retail shops in the atrium lobby. Headline entertainment appears in the Beau Rivage Theater. DIRECTIONS & PARKING: From I-10 exit 46, take I-110 south for 3 miles, then east on Beach Blvd. Beau Rivage has a designated lot for oversize vehicles, but space is limited. Please see Security for space availability, parking permit and directions to the lot for free RV overnight parking.

Boomtown Casino
676 Bayview Avenue
Biloxi, Mississippi 39530
228-435-7000 • 800-627-0777
www.boomtownbiloxi.com

DESCRIPTION: The casino has 1,300 slots, 13 tables, a buffet, cafe and grille. There is no hotel at this location. DISCOUNTS: The Wild Bunch Seniors (50+) receive various discounts and specials every Monday and Wednesday. DIRECTIONS & PARKING: From I-10 exit 46A, go south on I-110 for 2 miles to exit 1D (first exit after the bridge), then east on Bayview Ave. RV parking is available on the west side of the casino.

Grand Biloxi Casino Hotel
280 Beach Boulevard
Biloxi, Mississippi 39530
228-436-2946 • 800-WIN-2-WIN
www.grandbiloxi.com

DESCRIPTION: The resort has a hotel and casino with 800 slots, 35 pit/ table games and live entertainment daily. Dining options include buffet, steakhouse, noodle bar and Starbucks. The Grand Bear golf course is at the resort. **DIRECTIONS & PARKING**: From I-10 exit 46, take I-110 south to exit 1A, then east on US-90 (Beach Blvd) for 2.5 miles; casino is on the left. Check with Security. RV parking is on the gravel lot on the west side of the casino.

Hard Rock Casino

777 Beach Boulevard
Biloxi, Mississippi 39530
228-374-7625
www.hardrockbiloxi.com

DESCRIPTION: The resort located next to Beau Rivage has a hotel, entertainment center and casino featuring 1,500 slots, 50 pit/gaming tables and a poker room. There are five restaurants, including the Hard Rock Café, and retail shops. The Hard Rock Live venue features headline entertainment. **DIRECTIONS & PARKING**: Follow directions to Beau Rivage. RVs may park in the lot directly across the street from the Hard Rock.

IP Casino Resort

850 Bayview Avenue
Biloxi, Mississippi 39530
228-436-3000 • 888-946-2847
www.ipbiloxi.com

DESCRIPTION: The resort includes a hotel and a casino with 1,900 slots, video poker, 84 tables, non-smoking poker room and seven restaurants. Live entertainment is featured in the lounge and there is a 6-movie complex in the resort. **DIRECTIONS & PARKING**: From I-10 exit 46, south on I-110 for 2 miles to exit 1D, then east on Bayview Ave. RVs may park on the level, gravel lot across the street from the IP building (corner of Bayview & Caillavet St). Overnight is OK.

Isle of Capri Resort
151 Beach Boulevard
Biloxi, Mississippi 39530
228-435-5400 • 800-THE-ISLE
www.isleofcapricasino.com

DESCRIPTION: The Caribbean-themed resort has a hotel and casino with 1,300 slots and video poker, 27 table games, poker room and three restaurants, one open 24 hours. DISCOUNTS: The Isle One card can accumulate points earned at Isle of Capri casinos throughout the country. DIRECTIONS & PARKING: From I-10 exit 46, take I-110 south to US-90 (Beach Blvd) then east to the Isle. RV parking is permitted in the outside lot.

The Palace Casino Resort
158 Howard Avenue
Biloxi, Mississippi 39530
228-432-8888 • 800-725-2239
www.palacecasinoresort.com

DESCRIPTION: Located on Cadet Point north of the US-90 bridge, the resort has a hotel and golf course. The casino has over 800 slots, 14 pit/table games, two restaurants and a café. DISCOUNTS: Players Club members receive a discount at restaurants. DIRECTIONS & PARKING: From I-10 exit 46, take I-110 south 3 miles, then US-90 east to Myrtle Ave, then north to the Palace. RV parking is available in the self-park lot west of the casino. Stop at the hotel front desk to obtain a permit for free overnight parking.

GREENVILLE

Harlow's Casino Resort - Greenville
4280 Harlow's Boulevard
Greenville, Mississippi 38701
662-335-9797 • 866-524-5825
www.harlowscasino.com

DESCRIPTION: The resort includes a hotel and casino with 900 slots, 23 tables, poker room, a buffet and café. The arena has entertainment and sporting events. **DIRECTIONS**: From I-20 exit 5A take US-61 north for 40.5 miles, MS-14 north 6.3 miles, then north on MS-1 for 34.4 miles. Turn west on Bowman for one mile & south on Main St. Parking is in the back of the lot close to the levee.

Lighthouse Point and Bayou Caddy Casinos - Greenville
199 North Lakefront Road
Greenville, Mississippi 38701
662-334-7711 • 800-878-1777
www.lighthouse-casino.com

DESCRIPTION: The 24-hour Lighthouse Casino has 650 slots, 9 gaming tables, restaurant and deli. Bayou Caddy's Jubilee Casino, next to Lighthouse, has 626 slots, 13 tables and a snack bar. A shuttle operates between the two. **DISCOUNTS**: Membership in the Wild Bunch Seniors Club gives you a free Hot Seat Thursday entry. **DIRECTIONS & PARKING**: From I-20 exit 5A take US-61 north for 80.5 miles, merge onto US-278/US-82 west for 10.7 miles, then northwest on Main St. RVs should park in the shuttle lot at the corner of Alexander and Walnut and use the shuttle to the casinos.

GULFPORT

Island View Casino Resort
3300 West Beach Boulevard
Gulfport, Mississippi 39501
228-314-2100 • 877-774-8439
www.islandviewcasino.com

DESCRIPTION: Located at the site of the former Grand Casino Gulfport, the resort includes a modern hotel and a casino with 2,100 slots and 56 gaming tables. Food venues include the buffet, Emeril's restaurant and a grille. **DIRECTIONS & PARKING**: From I-10 exit 34, take US-49 south for 4.7 miles to US-90, then west .5 mile to the casino. RV parking is permitted on the southeast corner of the lot, east of the casino. Check in with Security if you plan to stay overnight.

LULA

Isle of Capri Casino – Lula
777 Isle of Capri Parkway
Lula, Mississippi 38644
662-363-4600 • 800-789-LUCK
www.isleofcapricasino.com

DESCRIPTION: The resort includes a hotel, 28 full hookup RV spaces and a casino with 1,350 slots, 21 gaming tables, poker room and the Isle signature restaurants. Last year's RV rate was $15 per night; register at the hotel front desk. **DISCOUNTS**: Ask about specials for seniors 50+ on Wednesdays. **DIRECTIONS & PARKING**: Located on the Mississippi River across from Helena, AR. From I-40 in Arkansas take exit 216 at Brinkley and follow US-49 east to the Helena bridge. From US-61 in Mississippi go west on US-49 to the casino.

NATCHEZ

Isle of Capri Casino & Hotel – Natchez
70 Silver Street
Natchez, Mississippi 39120
601-445-0605 • 800-843-4753
www.isleofcapricasino.com

DESCRIPTION: The riverboat casino has over 500 slots plus pit/gaming tables and the Isle's signature restaurant on the top level. The hotel has 147 rooms. **DIRECTIONS & PARKING**: From junction US-61 and US-84 in Natchez, go west on US-84 for two miles, then north on Canal for .7 mile to the parking lot at D.A. Biglane St. Turn right into the parking lot. Call the casino for a pickup. Overnight parking is permitted in the lot at D.A. Biglane St.

PHILADELPHIA

Pearl River Resort
13541 Highway 16 West
Philadelphia, Mississippi 39350
601-650-1234 • 866-447-3275
www.pearlriverresort.com

DESCRIPTION: Two Las Vegas-style casinos have 5,000 slots, 150 pit/gaming tables and a poker room. There are two hotels at the resort plus 15 restaurants, two golf courses, outdoor and indoor pools, retail shops, a water park, wave pool and water slides. In the evening, there is a free outdoor musical with laser imagery, water screen projections, dancing fountains and fireworks. **DISCOUNTS**: New Players Club members get free slot play. **DIRECTIONS & PARKING**: From I-20 exit 109, north on Rt-15 for 30 miles to Hwy-16, then west for 3.8 miles. The resort is 35 miles northwest of Meridian. Free overnight parking is available for RVs in the Golden Moon east lot.

ROBINSONVILLE / TUNICA RESORTS

Tunica County, in northwest Mississippi, is home to nine casino resorts and ranks as the nation's third most popular destination for gaming. All casino resorts have hotels and three also have RV Parks. The riverfront resorts are nestled near the cotton fields in the fertile Mississippi River Delta, where the weather is mild and pleasant year round. Although the casino resorts are some distance from one another, a shuttle service has three buses circulating from one casino to another continuously from 10am–11pm on weekdays and to 3am on weekends. Popular country and western stars are always among the headliner entertainment featured at virtually all resorts throughout the year. The *Tunica Queen*, a paddlewheeler that day-cruises on the river, is a popular local non-gaming activity.

The largest casino in Tunica County, Harrah's Casino Tunica, is on Old Highway 61 north of the other resorts. It has a modern 200-space RV Park.

On Casino Center Drive, Gold Strike, Horseshoe and Sheraton are clustered together, walking distance from one another. Fitzgerald's and Bally's are a short shuttle hop away.

On Casino Strip Blvd, Sam's Town, Hollywood and Resorts are within walking distance of each other and all are RV-Friendly. Both Sam's and Hollywood have modern RV parks. An 18-hole golf course is located at the Hollywood Resort. Fitzgerald's is a short drive or shuttle hop away.

Directions to the Tunica County Resorts:

* From I-55 in Memphis, TN, take exit 7 to US-61 (a four-lane highway) south for 20 miles.
* From I-55 in MS, take exit 280 (Hernando) to SR 304, then west on 304 (a two-lane scenic route) for 19 miles to US-61.

Bally's Casino Tunica
1450 Bally's Boulevard
Tunica Resorts, Mississippi 38664
662-357-1500 • 800-382-2559
www.casinoms.com

DESCRIPTION: The Western-themed resort has a hotel and casino with 1,200 slots and 17 tables, including $3 blackjack, 50¢ roulette and 25¢ craps. The Maverick Room caters to high stakes players. A reasonably priced 24-hour buffet features five cooking stations. **DISCOUNTS**: Players Club members who are 55 and older receive a discount at the buffet. **DIRECTIONS & PARKING**: From US-61, left on Casino Center Drive and follow signs to Bally's. RVs should park in the east lot. Overnight parking is OK.

Fitzgerald's Casino / Hotel
711 Lucky Lane
Tunica Resorts, Mississippi 38664
662-363-5825 • 800-766-LUCK
www.fitzgeraldstunica.com

DESCRIPTION: The Irish-themed resort has a hotel and casino with 1,300 slots and 34 pit/gaming tables plus a sports pub with multiple TVs. Restaurants include a steakhouse, buffet and 24-hour café. **DISCOUNTS**: The NY Steak and eggs special is on the menu all day at the Shamrock Café. The casino also has a daily breakfast buffet at a discounted price. **DIRECTIONS & PARKING**: From CR-304 (Casino Strip Blvd) follow signs to Fitzgerald's Blvd. RVs should use the south lot. Free overnight parking is permitted.

Gold Strike Casino
1010 Casino Center Drive
Tunica Resorts, Mississippi 38664
662-357-1111
www.goldstrikemississippi.com

DESCRIPTION: The casino includes 1,400 slots, 69 table games, poker room, three restaurants, food court and Starbucks. The hotel has 1,200 rooms/suites. **DIRECTIONS**: From US-61 follow signs to Casino Center Drive. RV parking is at the Horseshoe.

Harrah's Casino Tunica & RV Park
13615 Old Highway 61 North
Robinsonville, Mississippi 38664
662-363-2788 • 800-946-4946
www.harrahstunica.com

DESCRIPTION: Harrah's is the world's largest dockside casino resort. It has a 200-space RV Park and a hotel. The modern RV Park has paved sites with full hookups, cable TV and pool, shuffleboard, horseshoes, a lodge, playground, and laundry. Last year's rates were $18-$20. The casino has 2,400 slots, 94 gaming tables, poker room, six restaurants, and an 18-hole championship golf course. **DISCOUNTS**: Good Sam and AARP discounts are honored. RV rallies are always welcome and a group rate is available for ten or more. **DIRECTIONS**: Located on Old US-61, 2.1 miles north of SR-304.

Hollywood Casino Tunica & RV Park

1150 Casino Strip Resorts Boulevard
Robinsonville, Mississippi 38664
662-357-7700 • 800-871-0711
www.hollywoodcasinotunica.com

DESCRIPTION: Hollywood has a hotel and a modern RV Park that has 123 paved patio sites with full hookups, cable TV and laundry. RV guests are invited to use the heated pool/spa and game room at the hotel. Last year's RV rates were from $18, with a seven-day maximum stay. The Hollywood-themed casino has 1,300 loose slots, 36 pit/gaming tables, poker room, high limits areas. An interesting collection of Hollywood memorabilia is displayed at the casino. Among its three restaurants is the signature Fairbanks Steakhouse. The River Bend Scottish-links golf course is challenging for golfers of all levels. DISCOUNTS: Slot Club members get a discount at the restaurants and gift shop. DIRECTIONS & PARKING: From junction US-61 and SR-304, west on SR-304 for six miles. Dry camping is permitted in the lot behind the hotel.

Horseshoe Casino & Hotel

1021 Casino Center Drive
Robinsonville, Mississippi 38664
662-357-5500 • 800-303-7463
www.horseshoe.com

DESCRIPTION: This upscale resort has a hotel and casino with 1,500 slots and 60 tables. A unique poker room features a striking wall mural depicting a 19th century poker table, flanked by the "Poker Hall of Fame: Legends of the Game" and "World Series of Poker: Gallery of Champions." Notable poker tournaments are held at the Horseshoe. Restaurants include Binion's Steakhouse, Asian, café and buffet. Live entertainment is presented weekly. DIRECTIONS & PARKING: From US-61 follow signs to Casino Center Drive. RVs should park on the east side of the building.

Resorts Tunica

1100 Casino Strip Boulevard
Robinsonville, Mississippi 38664
662-363-7777
www.resortstunica.com

DESCRIPTION: The resort includes a hotel and casino with 1,100 slots, 18 gaming tables poker room, keno and three restaurants. There is free live entertainment on weekends. An 18-hole golf course is adjacent to the resort. DIRECTIONS & PARKING: From junction US-61 & SR-304, go west for six miles on SR-304 (Casino Strip Blvd). RVs may park in the lot behind the casino; follow signs for the dry camping area. A free dump station and fresh water are available on site.

Sam's Town Hotel & Gambling Hall & RV Park

1477 Casino Strip Resorts Boulevard
Robinsonville, Mississippi 38664
662-363-0711 • 800-456-0711
www.samstowntunica.com

DESCRIPTION: Sam's Town has an RV Park and hotel. The modern 100-site RV Park offers full hookups, cable TV, BBQ grill and picnic table at each site and paved park roads with security patrols. RV guests are invited to use the hotel's pool and fitness center. Daily trash pickup and a free courtesy shuttle between the RV Park and the casino are included. Last year's RV rate was $16 per night. The casino has two floors of gaming featuring over 1,500 slots, 47 gaming tables and a separate poker room. Restaurants include the buffet, BBQ buffet, restaurant and fine dining. Live entertainment is featured every weekend. DISCOUNTS: Good Sam discount honored. RV rallies are welcome and should be booked through the convention sales department. DIRECTIONS & PARKING: From junction US-61 and SR-304, west on SR-304 for six miles. Free overnight parking is available on the west side of the main lot.

Sheraton Casino & Hotel

1107 Casino Center Drive
Robinsonville, Mississippi 38664

662-363-4900 • 800-391-3777
www.caesars.com/Sheraton/Tunica

DESCRIPTION: The resort includes a hotel and casino with 1,400 slots and 35 pit/gaming tables. Food venues include a steakhouse, café and buffet. **DIRECTIONS & PARKING**: From US-61, follow signs to Casino Center Drive. RV parking is not allowed.

VICKSBURG

PARKING IN VICKSBURG, MISSISSIPPI: RVs going into Vicksburg are advised to stay at the Ameristar RV Park on Washington Street. Access roads into the parking lots at all casinos have steep grades down and there is the possibility your rig may bottom-out while trying to enter or exit the lots. Because of the steep grades and crowded conditions, parking for RVs or semis is prohibited in casino lots.

Ameristar Casino Hotel & RV Park – Vicksburg
4146 Washington Street
Vicksburg, Mississippi 39180
601-638-1000 • 800-700-7770
www.ameristarcasinos.com

DESCRIPTION: The Ameristar riverboat features over 1,300 slots, 44 gaming tables on two levels, four restaurants and a snack bar. The RV Park has 67 paved patio sites with full hookups, heated pool/spa and laundry. Last year's rates were from $25. Shuttle service is provided. **DISCOUNTS**: Ameristar cardholders receive discounts at the RV Park. **DIRECTIONS**: From I-20 exit 1A exit north onto Washington St. The RV Park is on the east side of Washington St.

Diamond Jack's Casino – Vicksburg
3990 Washington Street
Vicksburg, Mississippi 39182
601-636-5700 • 877-711-0677
www.diamondjacks.com

DESCRIPTION: The resort includes a hotel and casino on the river. The casino has 800 slots, 18 pit/gaming tables, a buffet, steakhouse and deli. **DISCOUNTS**: Ask about current casino discounts for seniors 50+. **DIRECTIONS**: From junction of I-20 and Washington Street (exit 1A), north .3 mile on Washington St. Ameristar RV Park is directly across the street from Diamond Jack's.

Missouri

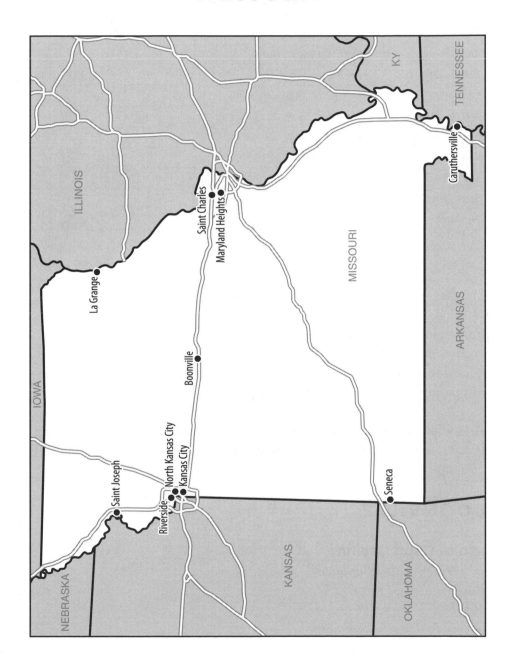

City	Casino	🚐	〽	⛨	🖹
Boonville	Isle of Capri Casino				146
Caruthersville	Lady Luck Casino	✔			147
Kansas City	Ameristar Casino Hotel			✔	147
Kansas City	Isle of Capri			✔	148
La Grange	Terrible's Mark Twain Casino		✔		148
Maryland Heights	Harrah's St. Louis			✔	149
North Kansas City	Harrah's North Kansas City			✔	149
Riverside	Argosy Casino			✔	150
Saint Charles	Ameristar Casino St. Charles			✔	150
Saint Joseph	Terrible's St. Jo Frontier Casino				151
Seneca	Bordertown Casino		✔		151

MISSOURI

Voters in Missouri approved riverboat gambling in 1992. Thus they became the fifth state to have riverboat casinos. All boats must remain dockside. Most casinos in Missouri are not open 24 hours – their hours of operation are noted in each listing.

An Indian casino in Seneca, Missouri, located near the Oklahoma border, is operated by the Eastern Shawnee Tribe. It is open 24/7 and has full-hookup RV spaces.

BOONVILLE

Isle of Capri Casino
100 Isle of Capri Boulevard
Boonville, Missouri 65233
660-882-1200 • 800-843-4753
www.isleofcapricasino.com

DESCRIPTION: The casino features 900 slots, 21 table games and three restaurants. There is a historic display in the pavilion. Hours are: 8am–

5am/24hrs (Fri–Sat). There is a hotel on site. **DISCOUNTS**: The Paradise 50 Club offers benefits for seniors. **DIRECTIONS & PARKING**: From I-70 exit 103 (Hwy-B), go north 2.8 miles and turn left at the 4th traffic light onto Morgan Street, go one-half mile to the casino. RVs are welcome in the west parking lot. Overnight is OK; check in with Security.

CARUTHERSVILLE

Lady Luck Casino & RV Park
777 East Third Street
Caruthersville, Missouri 63830
573-333-6000 • 800-679-4945
800-679-4945 (RV Park)
www.ladyluckcaruthersville.com

DESCRIPTION: The 875-passenger sternwheeler is docked in southeast Missouri. The casino has over 650 slots, 23 pit/table games poker room on the top deck, a restaurant and sports bar.. The first deck is smoke free. Casino hours are 9am–3am/5am (Fri–Sat). There is a 27-space full hookup RV Park with showers, laundry, wi-fi, cable TV and 24-hour security. A nature trail offers great Mississippi River views from dawn to dusk. Last year's rate was $22; RV check-in is at the gift shop in the pavilion between noon and 10pm. Other times, Security will assist with parking. **DISCOUNTS**: RV Park discounts include $2 for Good Sam and $2 off with a Players Club card. Wednesday and Sunday are Senior Days in the casino. **DIRECTIONS & PARKING**: From I-55, exit 19 (Hayti), east on Hwy-84 for 4.4 miles, then continue straight ahead on 3rd Street for .8 mile.

KANSAS CITY

Ameristar Casino Hotel
3200 North Ameristar Drive
Kansas City, Missouri 64161
816-414-7000 • 800-499-4961
www.ameristarcasinos.com

DESCRIPTION: The resort includes a hotel and casino with 3,000 slots, video poker, 105 gaming tables, the largest poker room in the Midwest, three restaurants and fast food court. There is an 18-theater movie complex on site. The casino barge remains dockside on the Missouri River and is open 8am–5am/24 hrs (Fri–Sat). **DISCOUNTS**: A buffet discount is offered for slot club members. **DIRECTIONS & PARKING**: From I-435 in Missouri, exit 55, go east for one mile on Rt-210, then south on Ameristar Dr. Parking spaces are available for RVs. Follow signs to the lot for oversized vehicles. Overnight parking is permitted for self-contained vehicles.

Isle of Capri – Kansas City
1800 East Front Street
Kansas City, Missouri 64120
816-855-7777 • 800-843-4753
www.isleofcapricasino.com

DESCRIPTION: The Caribbean-themed casino aboard a dockside paddlewheeler on the Missouri River has 1,500 slots, 22 pit/table games, poker room and four restaurants. Hours are 8am–5am/24hrs (Fri–Sun). There is no hotel at this location. **DISCOUNTS**: Food discounts are extended on Thursdays to slot club members who are 50 and older. . **DIRECTIONS & PARKING**: From I-35 exit 4B, the casino is on Front St. The casino is situated next to the northbound lanes of the interstate – follow brown riverboat signs. RVs should park in the west lot, which is connected to the casino by a walkway. Check in with Security if you plan to stay overnight.

LA GRANGE

Terrible's Mark Twain Casino & RV Parking
104 Pierce Street
La Grange, Missouri 63448
573-655-4770 • 866-454-5825
www.terribleherbst.com

DESCRIPTION: The casino has 600 slots, 14 pit/table games, a restaurant and deli. The casino is open 8am–2am/4am (Fri–Sat). This RV-friendly casino has seven parking spots with electric and water hookups in an adjacent lot. Last year's fee: $25 per night. A refundable deposit is required. There is no hotel at this location. DISCOUNTS: Senior discount (55+) on food Monday. DIRECTIONS: From I-70 exit 210 take Hwy-61 north for 100 miles to La Grange then east on Hwy B —or— From I-72 take Hwy-61 north 30 miles to La Grange. The casino is located on the south end of La Grange on Old Hwy-61, which is now Hwy B.

MARYLAND HEIGHTS

St. Louis Note: Lumiere Place Casino is located in downtown St. Louis, Missouri. RV parking is not available. But the RV Park at Casino Queen in East St. Louis – just across the river in Illinois – can serve as a good home base for touring downtown St Louis. Public transportation is easy and convenient.

Harrah's St. Louis
777 Casino Drive
Maryland Heights, Missouri 63043
314-770-8100 • 800-HARRAHS
www.harrahs.com

DESCRIPTION: Voted the best casino in St. Louis, Harrah's offers Vegas-style gaming dockside on the Missouri River. Gaming includes over 2,800 slots and 96 table games including a separate poker room. The resort has a hotel and five restaurants including a buffet and steakhouse. Casino hours are 8am–5am/24 hrs (Fri–Sat). DIRECTIONS & PARKING: From I-70 exit 231A, south on Earth City Expressway for 1.5 miles to the fourth stoplight, turn right into Harrah's. Parking for large vehicles is on the south side of the lot. Follow signs to bus parking; overnight is OK. Please check in with Security.

NORTH KANSAS CITY

Harrah's North Kansas City
One Riverboat Drive North
North Kansas City, Missouri 64116

816-472-7777 • 800-427-7247
www.harrahs.com

DESCRIPTION: Docked on the Missouri River, the barge has a hotel and a casino with 1,800 slots, 75 pit/gaming tables including a poker room and five restaurants. Hours are 8am–5am/24hrs (Fri–Sat). **DISCOUNTS**: Buffet discounts for Total Rewards members. **DIRECTIONS & PARKING**: From I-35 exit 6A, go east on Hwy-210 (Armour Road) for 1.1 miles, then south on Chouteau Trafficway to Harrah's on the right —or— From I-435 exit 55A, go to Hwy-210 west for approximately two miles to Chouteau Trafficway, then south for .25 mile. There is a designated parking area for large vehicles; ask Security for directions and notify them if you plan to stay overnight.

RIVERSIDE

Argosy Casino
777 Northwest Argosy Parkway
Riverside, Missouri 64150
816-746-3100 • 800-270-7711
www.argosy.com/kansascity

DESCRIPTION: The casino has 1,900 slot and video poker machines and 47 pit/gaming tables on a single level. It is open daily 8am–5am/24hrs (Fri–Sat). There are four restaurants and a bar. Live entertainment is featured in the Casino Stage Bar. There is a hotel on site. **DISCOUNTS**: Ask about discounts on select days if 55 or older. **DIRECTIONS & PARKING**: From I-29 exit 3B take I-635 to exit 11, then Hwy-9 and follow signs. RVs should use the west end of the lot. Overnight is OK.

SAINT CHARLES

Ameristar Casino St. Charles
1260 South Main Street
St. Charles, Missouri 63301
636-949-7777 • 800-325-7777
www.ameristarcasinos.com

DESCRIPTION: The casino, open 8am–5am/24 hrs (Fri–Sat), has 3,100 slots and video poker machines, 97 pit/gaming tables, poker room and eight food venues. There is a small slots-only non-smoking area on the second floor. There is a hotel and conference center in the resort. DIRECTIONS & PARKING: From I-70 exit 229B, go to the first traffic light, turn right on to Riverbluff Drive for .5 mile to Main St. For RV parking, DO NOT cross the bridge. Turn right on Main Street and go to the first left into the oversize vehicle parking lot under the bridge. The RV parking lot is under the main entrance to the casino. Shuttle service is provided. Please notify Security if you plan to stay overnight.

SAINT JOSEPH

Terrible's St. Jo Frontier Casino
777 Winners Circle
St. Joseph, Missouri 64501
816-279-5514 • 800-888-2946
www.terribleherbst.com

DESCRIPTION: The 600-passenger paddlewheeler docked on the Missouri River has 500 slots and 11 tables plus a restaurant and live entertainment in the Frontier Showroom. It is located 55 miles north of Kansas City. Hours are 8am–2am/4am (Fri–Sat). DISCOUNTS: Senior citizens, 55+, receive discounts at the buffet. DIRECTIONS & PARKING: From I-29 exit 43, take I-229 north for seven miles to Highland Avenue, exit 7, then west. There is a designated parking area for RVs. Check in with Security if you plan to stay overnight.

SENECA

Bordertown Casino
130 West Oneida
Seneca, Missouri 64865
918-309-3111 • 800-957-2435
www.bordertownbingo.com

DESCRIPTION: Owned and operated by the Eastern Shawnee Tribe, the

24-hour casino is near the Missouri/Oklahoma border. It has 1,000 slots, video poker and a card room. There is off track betting of up to 20 pari-mutuel race tracks daily, 10am–12:30am. Bingo is called daily. Dining options include a full service restaurant and fast food concessions open 24 hours. The RV parking area has 30 full-hookup spaces. Last year's rates were $9 for the first night and free for the second and third nights. RV sites are south of the main parking lot. Pull into a space, then register at the gift shop. **DIRECTIONS & PARKING**: In Missouri, from I-44 exit 4, go south on SR-43 for 13 miles. The casino is located at the northwest intersection of SR-43 & US-60. In Oklahoma, from I-44 exit 302 (Afton/Fairland), take US-60 east for 27 miles to SR-43 north for one mile; after crossing the railroad tracks, turn left on Oneida Street and go one-half mile to the casino.

Montana

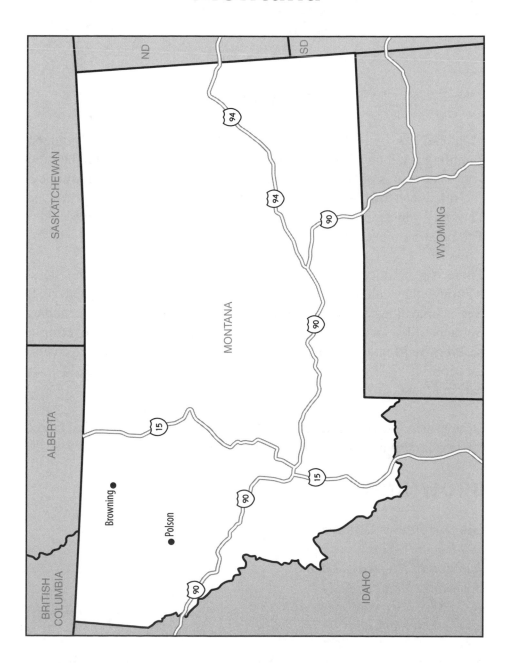

City	Casino	🚐	〰	🛡	📄
Browning	Glacier Peaks Casino				154
Polson	KwaTaqNuk Casino				155

MONTANA

Montana has limited gambling in effect. But this state's legalized gambling is not lavish Vegas-style "gaming." Traveling through the state you'll see scores of "casino" signs. But the typical "casino" in Montana is a relatively small establishment with up to 20 video gaming devices. The only games allowed are video poker, keno, bingo and live poker. The maximum bet is $2.

There are literally hundreds of such locations throughout the state. Although they call themselves casinos, generally, they consist of a small row of machines at a bar, tavern or club. Some have live poker tables frequented by locals. RVers looking for a place to find free overnight parking in Montana should be cautious and selective. Many casino locations have limited hours of operation and do not have 24-hour parking lot security.

Of the casinos owned and operated by Native Americans on tribal lands, the two largest are listed in the following section.

BROWNING

Glacier Peaks Casino
209 North Piegan
Junction of Highways 2 and 89
Browning, Montana 59417
406-338-CASH • 888-848-8188
www.glaciercash.com

DESCRIPTION: The casino has 450 gaming machines, three tables and bingo. Dining options include the buffet, full-service restaurant, fast food and a bingo snack bar. The casino is open 24 hours during the summer season. Located near the entrance of Glacier National Park, it is next to the Museum of the Plains Indians and the Blackfeet Heritage Center and Art Gallery. **DIRECTIONS & PARKING**: The casino is 140 miles northwest of Great Falls. From I-15 exit 363, take US-2 west for approximately 55 miles to the junction of US-89. RVers should call ahead to verify parking availability.

POLSON

KwaTaqNuk Casino
49708 Highway 93 East
Polson, Montana 59860
406-883-3636
www.kwataqnuk.com

DESCRIPTION: The 24-hour casino has 100 gaming machines, live poker and a restaurant. It is connected to a 112-room Best Western hotel. **DIRECTIONS & PARKING**: The casino is located 65 miles north of Missoula directly on US-93. RVers should call ahead to check on availability of parking.

Nevada

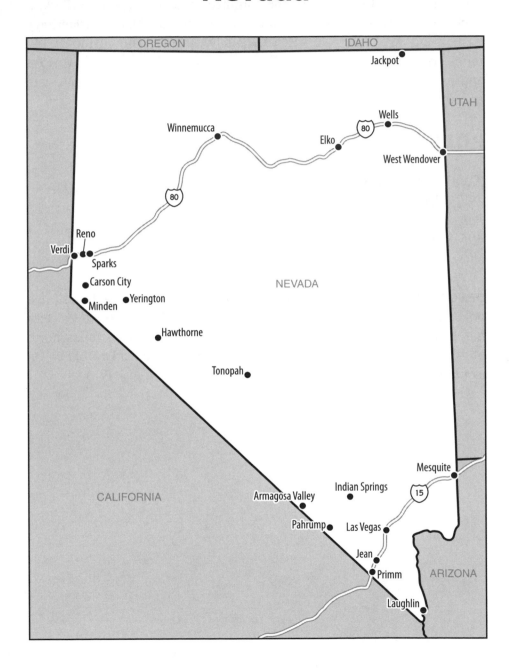

City	Casino	🚐	⚡	🛡	📄
Armagosa Valley	Longstreet Casino	✔			159
Carson City	Carson Nugget				159
Carson City	Gold Dust West Casino	✔			160
Elko	Commercial Casino			✔	161
Elko	Gold Country	✔		✔	161
Elko	Red Lion Inn & Casino			✔	161
Elko	Stockmen's Hotel & Casino			✔	162
Hawthorne	El Capitan Resort Casino				162
Indian Springs	Indian Springs Casino	✔			162
Jackpot	Barton's Club 93				163
Jackpot	Cactus Pete's Casino	✔			163
Jackpot	Horseshu Hotel and Casino				164
Jean	Gold Strike Casino			✔	164
Las Vegas	Arizona Charlie's Casino	✔		✔	169
Las Vegas	California Casino	✔		✔	169
Las Vegas	Circus Circus	✔		✔	170
Las Vegas	Sam's Town Casino	✔		✔	170
Laughlin	Avi Resort & Casino	✔			172
Laughlin	Don Laughlin's	✔			173
Mesquite	CasaBlanca Casino	✔		✔	174
Mesquite	Eureka Casino			✔	175
Mesquite	Virgin River Casino			✔	175
Minden	Carson Valley Inn	✔			175
Pahrump	Saddle West Casino	✔			176
Pahrump	Terrible's Lakeside Casino	✔			176
Primm	Primm Resorts			✔	177
Reno	Bordertown Casino	✔			178
Reno	Grand Sierra Resort Casino	✔		✔	178
Sparks	Sparks Area Casinos			✔	180
Tonopah	Tonopah Station		✔		180
Verdi	Boomtown Casino	✔		✔	181

City	Casino	🚐	🏕	🛡	📄
Verdi	Terrible's Casino	✔		✔	181
Wells	Wells Area Casinos			✔	182
West Wendover	Montego Bay Casino			✔	182
West Wendover	Peppermill Inn & Casino			✔	183
West Wendover	Rainbow Casino Hotel			✔	183
West Wendover	Wendover Nugget Casino	✔		✔	183
Winnemucca	Model T Hotel & Casino	✔		✔	184
Yerington	Casino West		✔		185

NEVADA

The Nevada Legislature legalized most forms of gambling in the state in 1931, and for nearly 50 years afterward, it was the only state where you could go to casinos. The gaming industry in Nevada struggled until after World War II when the prosperity of post-war America started a boom. Then, casinos with lavish hotels, entertainment and restaurants became the norm for Las Vegas, Reno and other locations throughout Nevada.

Today Nevada still reigns as King Casino, with hundreds of casinos throughout the state – all near or adjacent to interstates and major highways. The following section includes three popular "casino hopping" destinations:

- Las Vegas – on I-15 and I-515 in southern Nevada,
- Laughlin – on Highway 95 in southern Nevada at the Arizona border, and
- Reno – on I-80 in western Nevada near the California border.

Also included are casinos along I-15, I-80, US-95 and other major roadways in the state.

ARMAGOSA VALLEY

Longstreet Hotel, Casino & RV Park
4400 South Highway 373
Armagosa Valley, Nevada 89020
775-372-1777 • 800-508-9493
www.longstreetcasino.com

DESCRIPTION: Located 10 miles from Death Valley Junction, the full service resort has a hotel and a 51-space RV Park with full hookups, heated pool/spa, laundry and a 24-hour convenience store. Last year's RV rate was $23; weekly and monthly rates are available. The 24-hour casino features two gaming tables, 69 slots, video poker and two restaurants. **DISCOUNTS**: Seniors, 65 and older, receive 20% off food. Good Sam and Escapees discounts are honored at the RV Park. **DIRECTIONS**: From junction US-95 & SR-373, southwest for 16 miles on SR-373 to California/Nevada border.

CARSON CITY

Carson City, named for adventurer Kit Carson, is Nevada's capital city. The city lies in a beautiful valley at the foot of the Sierras. Among the attractions is the Nevada State Museum, located in the building that once housed the Carson Mint that made over $50 million in silver and gold coins until 1893. It is considered one of the West's top museums. Carson City is also home to the State Railroad Museum, the restored Old Capitol Building and Stewart Indian Museum.

Carson Nugget
507 North Carson Street
Carson City, Nevada 89701
775-882-1626 • 800-426-5239
www.ccnugget.com

DESCRIPTION: The Nugget, in the heart of Carson City, bills itself as the "Happiest Casino In The World." It features a rare collection of natural gold formations. The collection, which took 70 years to accumulate, includes leaf gold, wire gold, thread gold and crystallized gold just as they are found in nature. Its estimated value is over $1 million. The casino has 700 slot and video poker machines, keno, 12 gaming tables, three restaurants and a 24-hour coffee shop. The casino also has a motel and conference center. **DISCOUNTS**: Seniors, 50 and older, receive 10% off food. **DIRECTIONS & PARKING**: From Hwy-395 south exit 57B (Carson City & Virginia City), continue on Hwy-395 to Carson City. In Carson City, Hwy-395 is the same as Carson Street. The free RV parking lot is at Stuart and Robinson, across the street from the back of the Nugget. The parking spots are back-ins and will fit RVs no longer than 38 feet. There are no hookups and the stay limit is 72 hours.

Gold Dust West Casino Resort & RV Park

2171 Highway 50 East
Carson City, Nevada 89701
775-885-9000 • 877-519-5567
www.pinonplaza.com

DESCRIPTION: The RV Park has 30 paved full hookup sites, laundry, and horseshoes. The Best Western hotel has 148 rooms and RV guests are invited to use the pool/spa at the hotel. Daily RV rates last year were from $28-$33. The 24-hour casino has 400 slots, six pit/table games, sports book, three restaurants and a bowling alley. **DISCOUNTS**: Senior citizens, 55 and older, receive 10% off food. Good Sam and AAA discounts are honored. **DIRECTIONS**: From Junction US-395 (Carson Street) and US-50E (center of town), east one mile on US-50E. *Boondocking is not permitted*. RVs planning to stay overnight should pull into the RV Park.

ELKO

Four casinos are located in Elko, where RV Park, hotel and parking accommodations are available. Elko is known as the home of Cowboy Poetry and the Mining Exposition. The oldest continually operating casino in Nevada is also located in Elko.

Commercial Casino

345 4th Street
Elko, Nevada 89801
775-738-3181 • 800-648-2345
www.commercialcasino.com

DESCRIPTION: Over 100 years old, Commercial is the oldest continually operating casino in Nevada. A large gunfighter art collection is on display there. The casino has 185 slots, two restaurants and a bar. **DIRECTIONS & PARKING**: From I-80 exit 301, turn right into downtown. RVs should use the lot at Stockman's Hotel & Casino, across the street; boondocking is OK.

Gold Country Motor Inn & RV Park

2050 Idaho Street
Elko, Nevada 89801
775-738-8421 • 800-621-1332

DESCRIPTION: The RV Park has 26 back-in, full-hookup sites. Last year's RV rate was $25 and major discounts are accepted. RV guests should register at the Best Western front desk. The casino has 150 slots, three gaming tables, a restaurant and lounge. Gold Country is affiliated with Red Lion, Elko's largest casino located just across the street. Both are open 24 hours. **DISCOUNTS**: Good Sam, AAA or AARP discounts honored. **DIRECTIONS**: From I-80 exit 303 (Elko East), Gold Country is visible from the interstate.

Red Lion Inn & Casino

2065 Idaho Street
Elko, Nevada 89801
775-738-2111 • 800-545-0044
www.playelko.com

DESCRIPTION: The casino in downtown Elko has over 100 slots, three gaming tables and two restaurants (one open 24 hours). The hotel has 223 rooms. **DIRECTIONS & PARKING**: From I-80 exit 303, Red Lion is visible from the interstate and an RV Park is located just across the street at Gold Country Motor Inn.

Stockmen's Hotel & Casino
340 Commercial Street
Elko, Nevada 89801
775-738-5141 • 800-648-2345
www.stockmenscasino.com

DESCRIPTION: An Old West themed 24-hour casino, Stockman's has 185 slots and nine table games. The hotel has 141 rooms. It is across the street from the Commercial Casino. DIRECTIONS & PARKING: From I-80 exit 301, turn right into the downtown area. The area for RV parking is across from the rear east corner of Stockman's.

HAWTHORNE

El Capitan Resort Casino
540 F Street (on US-95)
Hawthorne, Nevada 89415
775-945-3321 • 800-922-2311
www.elcapitanresortcasino.com

DESCRIPTION: There is a hotel, casino with 270 slots and five gaming tables and restaurant at the resort. DISCOUNTS: Ask at the front desk about Fun Books. DIRECTIONS & PARKING: The casino is on the northbound side of US-95 at the corner of 6th St. in the center of Hawthorne. RV parking is on the east side of the casino building. Free overnight parking and a free RV dump are available, but there are no electric hookups.

INDIAN SPRINGS

Indian Springs Casino & RV Park
372 Tonopah Highway (US-95)
Indian Springs, Nevada 89018
702-879-3456 • 877-977-7746
702-879-3129 (RV Park)
www.dirtymoe.com

DESCRIPTION: The 59 space RV Park features full hookups at shaded sites, a convenience store and laundry. It is walking distance to the casino. Last year's rate was $22; weekly rates are available. The casino has 60 slots, blackjack tables, a 24-hour restaurant, lounge, video arcade and live music. There is a 45-room hotel on site. **DIRECTIONS**: Indian Springs is 35 miles northwest of Las Vegas; the casino is located on US-95 at mile marker 119 - on Frontage Rd.

JACKPOT

Jackpot, Nevada, a town of 1,500 residents, was the second casino boomtown after Las Vegas. Surrounded by mountain wilderness, Jackpot is a bright cluster of casinos located just south of the Idaho state line. There are also many outdoor recreational activities in and around Jackpot including excellent fishing in the nearby Little Salmon River and its tributaries.

DIRECTIONS TO JACKPOT: From I-84 exit 173 in Idaho, go 42 miles south on US-93 —or— From I-80 exit 352 in Nevada go 68 miles north on US-93.

Barton's Club 93
1002 Highway 93
Jackpot, Nevada 89825
775-755-2341 • 800-258-2937
www.bartonsclub93.com

DESCRIPTION: This friendly casino has 460 slots and 13 gaming tables. There is a 104-room/suite hotel. Food venues include the buffet and a 24 hour full-service restaurant. **DISCOUNTS**: Ask about the Fun Book. **PARKING**: Free overnight parking is permitted in the lot.

Cactus Pete's Resort Casino & RV Park
1385 Highway 93
Jackpot, Nevada 89825
775-755-2321 • 800-821-1103
www.ameristarcasinos.com

DESCRIPTION: The resort has a 91-space RV Park, open year-round, and a hotel. RV guests are invited to use the amenities at the hotel. Last year's RV rates were $17 in season and $13 during winter months (no water in winter). There are four restaurants and a casino at the resort. The casino has 900 slots, 23 pit/table games, live keno and sports book. Headline entertainment is featured weekends in the Gala Showroom. The resort also has an 18-hole golf course.

Horseshu Hotel and Casino

1220 Highway 93
Jackpot, Nevada 89825
775-755-7777
www.ameristarcasinos.com

DESCRIPTION: Located directly across from Cactus Pete's, the resort has a hotel and a casino with 122 slots and six gaming tables. The Frontier Kitchen, open morning to night, specializes in Mexican favorites. Dancing to live Western bands is featured Wednesday through Sunday in the lounge. **PARKING**: Check in with Security for overnight parking in the lot.

JEAN

Gold Strike Casino

I-15 at milepost 12
Jean, Nevada 89019
702-477-5000 • 800-634-1359
www.stopatjean.com

DESCRIPTION: Gold Strike Casino is adjacent to I-15 on the northbound side. It has 850 slots and 10 pit/gaming tables, four restaurants and fast food. **DISCOUNTS**: Discount coupons are available at the hotel. **DIRECTIONS & PARKING**: From I-15 at exit 12. Free overnight parking for self-contained RVs is permitted in the Gold Strike lot.

LAS VEGAS

Even though travelers can now enjoy casinos in many parts of the country, Las Vegas, Nevada remains the premier gaming destination. But the Vegas area can be overwhelming. The sheer volume of casinos, restaurants and entertainment venues make it difficult to decide how to spend your time during your Las Vegas visit.

For RVers going into Las Vegas, it is recommended that you stay at a secure RV Park. As in any large metropolitan area, there will be safety and security concerns when motor homes are left unattended in parking areas generally open to the public. Las Vegas can be crowded and congested and – since 9/11 – security is heightened. The best strategy in Vegas is to check into a full service RV Park and use shuttles, public transportation or your dinghy or tow vehicle to get around town. Although there are lots of fine RV Parks and campgrounds in Las Vegas – consistent with the theme of this book – in the Vegas section we feature only those RV Parks directly connected to and owned by a casino: Las Vegas KOA at Circus Circus (the only RV Park on the Strip); California (downtown) and Arizona Charlie's and Sam's Town (on Boulder Highway). At these four RV Parks, you have the advantage of full hookups in a park that is within walking distance to the casino.

Discounts in Las Vegas

Just as Vegas is the casino capitol of the country, it is also the casino discount capitol. Look for discount coupons in the free visitors' guides found at hotels and RV Parks and on brochure racks all over town. You can even start collecting your Vegas discount coupons by checking out the free guides and brochures on racks at the state welcome center or at other stops along the way into Las Vegas.

Also, be sure to ask about specific casino discounts or coupon books when you join the Players Club at the casinos where you prefer to play.

Some of the free shows/attractions in Las Vegas include:

- *Bellagio*: Synchronized laser lights and music shows at the fountains in front of the casino every half hour during the day and every 15 minutes evenings until midnight.
- *Bellagio*: The Conservatory, open 24 hours daily, features elaborate floral arrangements, crafted by a team of 100 horticulturalists, beneath a 55-foot tall glass ceiling in a bright, airy atrium filled with lovely color and rich fragrance.
- *Caesar's Palace*: Statues come alive during a seven-minute show at the Festival Fountains every hour on the hour in the Forum Shops Mall below the casino.
- *Circus Circus*: Acts featuring clowns, acrobats, jugglers, tightrope walkers and more, perform continuously daily from 11am to midnight.
- *Downtown Area*: The Fremont Street Experience, a one-of-a-kind light & sound computer-generated show 90 feet in the sky over a pedestrian mall stretching four city blocks in downtown Las Vegas. Shows take place five times per night from 7pm.
- *Flamingo*: The Wildlife Habitat is home to more than 300 birds as well as turtles and koi. The habitat is filled with lush foliage imported from around the world. Open 24 hours.
- *M&M World*: Located at the south end of the Strip (near the MGM), check out the 2nd, 3rd and 4th floors that include a 3D movie theater, interesting displays of the sweet treat and a replica of NASCAR's #38. Open daily 9am-11pm/midnight weekends.
- *MGM Grand*: Showcasing the lions at numerous viewing areas in the Grand Lion Habitat located inside the resort's Strip entrance starting at 11am daily.
- *Mirage*: Outside the Mirage Resort, a peaceful waterfall during daylight hours transforms to a volcano once darkness falls. Beginning at 6pm, the volcano erupts every hour on the hour until midnight. Best place to view is from the Strip side.
- *Rio Casino*: Masquerade Show in the Sky is a spectacular high-energy carnival extravaganza. The show plays every hour on the hour, 7pm to midnight. Show viewing is free or $12.95 to get into costume and ride in the show.
- *Sam's Town*: A water and laser show is featured daily at 2, 6, 8 and 10pm in the waterfall area of the indoor park. Sam's Town is

located on Boulder Highway.

- *Silverton*: The Aquarium features 4,000 exotic fish and breathtaking coral in a 117,000-gallon saltwater aquarium. Fish feedings are at 1:30, 4:30 and 7:30pm when a marine biologist is available to answer questions. Silverton is located on Blue Diamond Road (south of the Strip).
- *Treasure Island*: The Sirens of TI live action show takes place in front of the resort four times daily beginning at 7pm.
- *Venetian*: Life-size puppets, magicians, stilt-walkers and living statues vie for your attention all day in St. Mark's Square. Accompanied by musicians, they perform in five shows daily.

"Casino Hopping" On the Strip

The famed Las Vegas "Strip" consists of 3+ miles along Las Vegas Boulevard where you'll find some of the most fabulous casinos in the world showcased in lavish, bigger-than-life themed resorts. There is always something new in Vegas…new shows, new casinos, newly expanded or refurbished facilities. Some you won't want to miss include:

- *At the north end*: Stratosphere, Circus Circus, Sahara, Las Vegas Hilton, Riviera and Echelon,
- *In the heart of the Strip*: Wynn Las Vegas, Treasure Island, Venetian, Mirage, Casino Royale, Harrah's, Imperial Palace, Flamingo, Caesars Palace, Bellagio, Bally's, Paris, Planet Hollywood and Monte Carlo,
- *At the south end*: New York-New York, MGM, Tropicana, Excalibur, Luxor, Mandalay Bay and Four Seasons,
- *Just off the Strip*: Hard Rock, Terrible's, Palms, Rio Palace Station and Silverton.

The Las Vegas Monorail is a convenient way to get from one end of the Strip to the other. There are seven monorail stations (running north to south) at: Sahara Ave & Paradise Road, Las Vegas Hilton, Convention Center, Harrah's/Imperial Palace, Flamingo/Caesars Palace, Paris/Bally's and MGM Grand. The best monorail value is the one-day unlimited pass that allows you to get on and off at each station as many times as you like during a 24-hour period during operational hours (8am–midnight). With your monorail pass and a comfortable pair of walking shoes you can see all the sights on the Strip. Be sure to pick up a copy of the Monorail magazine at the station.

Before venturing out to the Strip, check out the free visitor guides found on brochure racks all over town. These guides feature current shows, special events, dining guides and detailed schedules for the free shows listed above. The *Today in Las Vegas* guide has a handy "easy to locate it" map on the inside of the front cover. Detailed information in the visitor guides will be helpful as you plan your excursions to the Strip. "Casino hopping" adventures in Vegas can take you to more than 30 glitzy casinos along Las Vegas Blvd. So, familiarize yourself with the area beforehand, plan your day and enjoy the Strip!

Downtown Casino Hopping

A dozen casinos are located in the downtown Fremont/ Ogden /Casino Center section of Las Vegas: Jack Binion's Horseshoe, California Hotel, El Cortez, Fitzgerald's, Four Queens, Fremont, Gold Spike, Golden Gate, Golden Nugget, Lady Luck, Vegas Club, Main Street Station and Plaza. Most are located along the pedestrian mall known as "The Fremont Street Experience," offering another opportunity for casino hopping in Vegas. A free computer generated sound and light show takes place each night 90 feet in the sky over Fremont Street.

Boulder Highway - the Other Strip

Another major thoroughfare in Las Vegas is Boulder Highway. But casino hopping on the Boulder Strip is done by car, since casinos there are not within walking distance from one another. Two casinos on the Boulder Strip that have modern RV parks include Arizona Charlie's, and Sam's Town.

Casinos in Las Vegas Suburbs

Casinos in the suburbs tend to be smaller facilities patronized by locals. There are 29 casinos in Henderson, located 15 miles southeast of Las Vegas on Hwy-93 and one in Boulder City, 22 miles from Las Vegas, also on Hwy-93. In North Las Vegas (5 miles northeast of the Strip on Las Vegas Blvd) there are 12 casinos.

The largest of the suburban casinos are: Sunset Station and Fiesta Casino (both can be seen from I-515) in Henderson and Cannery Casino and Fiesta Casino in North Las Vegas.

Arizona Charlie's Casino & RV Park – Boulder

4575 Boulder Highway
Las Vegas, Nevada 89121
702-951-9000 • 800-970-7280 (RV Park)
www.arizonacharliesboulder.com

DESCRIPTION: The RV Park has easy access off the Boulder Strip. It has 239 paved full hookup sites, shuffleboard, horseshoes, a picnic area, dog run, workout facilities and heated pool & spa. Last year's rates were $32.70; weekly and monthly rates available. A walkway leads to the casino that has 1,000 slots and video poker, 16 live pit/table games, 24-hour bingo and three restaurants, including a 24-hour café. The hotel has 300 rooms. DISCOUNTS: Good Sam discount is given at the RV Park. The restaurant features a steak & eggs special. Players Card holders receive a discount on the buffet. DIRECTIONS: From junction I-515/93/95 exit 70, south 1.1 miles on Boulder Hwy.

California Hotel, Casino & RV Park

12 Ogden Avenue
Las Vegas, Nevada 89101
702-385-1222 (Casino) • 800-713-8933 (RV Park)
www.thecal.com

DESCRIPTION: The RV Park located on Main Street, half a block from both California and Main Street Station, has 93 paved full hookup sites and 24-hour security. RV guests may use the pool and other amenities at the California Hotel. Last year's rates were $16–$19 (additional fee for pets.) RV guests should pull into a site, then register at the Main Street Station hotel front desk. The California Casino has 1,100 slots, 28 gaming tables and four restaurants and is walking distance to Fremont Street. Free transportation is provided to the Strip and Sam's Town on Boulder Hwy, 8:30am to 11pm. **DIRECTIONS**: From I-15 exit 42B, go east for .5 mile to I-515 exit 75B, two blocks west on Stewart, then one block north on Main St. Register at the Main Street hotel desk.

Circus Circus & Las Vegas KOA at Circus Circus

2880 Las Vegas Boulevard
Las Vegas, Nevada 89109
702-734-0410
www.circuscircus.com

Las Vegas KOA at Circus Circus
500 Circus Circus Dr
Las Vegas, Nevada 89109
702-733-9707 (RV Reservations)
www.circuscircuskoa.com

DESCRIPTION: The KOA RV Park, on the north end of the Strip, has 399 paved full service sites, swimming pool & jacuzzi/sauna, playground, laundry facilities, pet runs and convenience store. Free circus acts run daily from 11am–midnight. Seasonally adjusted rates range from $30 to $77. The adjacent 24-hour Circus Circus casino has over 1,700 slots, 70 pit/table games, eight restaurants, live circus acts and a carnival midway. Also featured is Adventuredome, an indoor themed amusement park with roller coaster, motion machines, log flume ride and children's rides and amusements. **DISCOUNTS**: The KOA Value Kard Rewards card is the only discount honored at the RV park. **DIRECTIONS**: From I-15 exit 40, east .2 mile on Sahara, cross the overpass, to South Bridge Lane, then south .1 mile to the rear entrance.

Sam's Town Casino Resort & RV Park

5111 Boulder Highway
Las Vegas, Nevada 89122
702-456-7777 (Casino) • 702-454-8055 (RV Park)

800-634-6371 (RV Park reservations)
www.samstownlv.com

DESCRIPTION: The modern RV Park on Boulder Highway has 287 full service sites, heated pool/spa, cable TV and laundry facilities. Free shuttle service to the Strip and downtown casinos operates from 10am–11pm daily. Last year's RV rate range was $21-$37. Casino gaming includes 3,000 slots, 51 pit/table games, poker room, sports book, keno and bingo. The Sam's Town complex includes a 646 room/suite hotel, 56-lane bowling center, movie complex and six restaurants. A free laser light and water show is presented nightly. **DISCOUNTS**: Good Sam discount honored. **DIRECTIONS & PARKING**: From I-515 (93/95S), exit 68, go east on Tropicana Avenue for 1.5 miles, then north on Boulder Highway for .7 mile to Sam's Town RV Park. Free dry camping is not permitted. RV guests should check into the RV Park.

LAUGHLIN

Laughlin is nestled in the Colorado River Valley where Nevada, Arizona and California meet. The City by the River has a special appeal…in Laughlin visitors can enjoy a slower-paced, pleasant casino hopping hiatus. There are 11 Vegas-style casinos, ongoing live entertainment, more than 60 restaurants, museum, bowling center, boutiques, spas, salons plus many water sports and activities. Sightseeing on the Colorado River aboard the USS Riverside tour boat is a popular non-gaming activity. When you arrive in Laughlin, pick up a copy of *Laughlin Entertainer*, a free weekly publication that will give you information about current happenings and discounts around town. More than five million people visit Laughlin annually.

People who enjoy casino-hopping on foot will welcome the pretty walkway along the river where they can stroll along the picturesque river and stop at nine casinos along the way. For those who prefer to ride, there is a water taxi that goes from casino to casino on the river side and a city bus that runs along Casino Drive. Both are fee-pay transportation.

Accommodations in Laughlin: All casinos in town have hotels. There are two full-hookup RV Resorts in Laughlin: Riverside is the only RV Resort on Casino Drive and Avi Resort is located several miles south of town.

For RVers looking to boondock, many of the casinos permit free overnight parking for self-contained RVs. Specifically, Harrah's (at the end of the Laughlin Strip) has two lots across the street where RVs can park free for up to three days. Please register at the gas station. There is a dump at the gas station ($3 fee). The River Palms has parking on the hill above the Strip for a nominal fee. Present your vehicle registration at the River Palms to get a pass for dry camping. For other casinos, check with Security regarding their overnight parking policy.

Avi Resort & Casino
10000 Aha Macav Parkway
Laughlin, Nevada 89029
702-535-5555 • 800-430-0721 • 800-284-2946 (Reservations)
www.avicasino.com

DESCRIPTION: Avi is known for its spectacular beach, the largest along the banks of the Colorado River with views of the Mohave Valley. The hotel has 455 rooms. The KOA RV Park has 260 full service sites, pool, laundry, pavilion, lounge, beach and boat launch. Shuttle service is provided to the casino. Last year's RV rates were $24-$26 ($40 on holidays.) Weekly rates are available. Recreation at the resort includes swimming, boating, canoeing, kayaking, fishing and an 18-hole golf course. The casino has 1,200 slots and 34 live table games. Also included at the resort are kids quest and eight movie theaters. DISCOUNTS: KOA Value Card, Good Sam, AAA and AARP honored at the RV Park. DIRECTIONS: The Avi is south of the rest of the Casino Drive casinos. From I-40, River Road cutoff, which becomes Needles Highway, north for 14 miles to Aha Macav Pkwy. Follow Avi signs.

Don Laughlin's Riverside Resort & RV Park
1650 South Casino Drive
Laughlin, Nevada 89029
702-298-2535 • 800-227-3849
www.riversideresort.com

DESCRIPTION: The city itself is named after Don Laughlin, owner of the Riverside Resort, who settled there in 1966. His terraced RV Park has a lovely view of the mountains. It features 840 full hookup spaces, laundry and showers. RV guests may use the two swimming pools and other amenities at the hotel. A climate controlled enclosed walkway connects the RV Park with the casino; 24-hour shuttle service is provided. Last year's rates were from $25-$27. The casino has 1,500 slots, 44 gaming tables and bingo. Dozens of rare antique slot machines from Don Laughlin's private collection are on display in the casino. Also included at the resort are a 34-lane bowling center and a Western Dance Hall featuring live country bands. There is river access for boating and fishing from the resort. DISCOUNTS: AAA and AARP discounts honored. DIRECTIONS: Laughlin is located 100 miles south of Las Vegas. From junction of US-95 & SR-163, east for 19.9 miles on SR-163 to Casino Drive, then south for .4 mile.

Other casinos (listed from north to south) on Casino Drive include:

Flamingo Hilton Laughlin
1900 South Casino Drive — 702-298-5111 • 800-352-6464

Edgewater Hotel & Casino
2020 Casino Drive — 702-298-2453 • 800-677-4837

Colorado Belle Hotel/Casino & Microbrewery
2100 South Casino Drive — 702-298-4000 • 800-477-4837

Ramada Express Hotel Casino
2121 South Casino Drive — 702-298-4200 • 800-243-6846

Pioneer Hotel & Gambling Hall
2200 South Casino Drive — 702-298-2442 • 800-634-3469

Golden Nugget Laughlin
2300 South Casino Drive — 702-298-7111 • 800-950-7700

River Palms Resort Casino
2700 South Casino Drive — 702-298-2242 • 800-835-7904

Harrah's Laughlin Casino
2900 South Casino Drive — 702-298-4600 • 800-427-7247

MESQUITE

Three casino resorts are located within a mile of the interstate in Mesquite – two at exit 120 and two at exit 122. They offer a variety of gaming and non-gaming activities. In addition to Vegas-style casinos, there are two 18-hole golf courses, health spas, a bowling center, movie theaters, live entertainment nightly and ten restaurants (some open 24 hours). Mesquite is 77 miles northeast of Las Vegas at the Arizona border. There are hotels and RV Resorts in Mesquite. In addition, there are provisions for free RV parking at Mesquite's casinos.

CasaBlanca Hotel, Casino, Golf, Spa & RV Park
950 West Mesquite Boulevard
Mesquite, Nevada 89027
702-346-7259 • 800-459-7529
800-896-4567 (RV Park)
www.casablancaresort.com

DESCRIPTION: The resort includes an RV Park with 45 paved sites with full hookups and patios, pool/spa and phones at the sites. Last year's RV rate was $19 with a 30-day maximum stay. There is a 500-room hotel on site. The 24-hour casino has 700 slots and 26 pit/gaming tables. There are three restaurants, one open 24 hours. The resort also includes an 18-hole championship golf course and a world-class co-ed health spa offering massages, facials and mud treatments. Live lounge entertainment is featured nightly. DIRECTIONS & PARKING: From I-15 exit 120, east for .1 mile. The resort is visible from the interstate. The parking lot for RV dry camping is east of the hotel building.

Eureka Casino & Hotel
275 Mesa Boulevard
Mesquite, Nevada 89027
702-346-4646 • 800-346-4611
www.eurekamesquite.com

DESCRIPTION: Open 24 hours, the casino has 1,200 slots, 30 live gaming tables, race and sports book and three restaurants. **DIRECTIONS & PARKING**: From I-15 exit 122, Eureka is visible from the north side of the interstate. The large parking lot behind the 76 Gas Station is designated for trucks and RVs and is walking distance to both Virgin River and Eureka casinos. Boondocking is permitted for self-contained RVs.

Virgin River Hotel, Casino & Bingo
100 North Pioneer Boulevard
Mesquite, Nevada 89027
702-346-7777 • 800-346-7721
www.virginriver.com

DESCRIPTION: The resort has a hotel and a 24-hour casino with 700 slots, 21 gaming tables, race and sports book, bingo daily, live keno, 24-lane bowling center and four movie theaters. There are two restaurants and a snack bar on site. **DIRECTIONS & PARKING**: From I-15 exit 122, north for .25 mile on the exit road. The casino is visible from the interstate. Free overnight parking is permitted for self-contained vehicles.

MINDEN

Carson Valley Inn & RV Park
1627 Highway 395 North
Minden, Nevada 89423
775-782-9711 • 800-321-6983
www.cvinn.com

DESCRIPTION: The resort is situated in a valley at the foot of the mountains surrounding Lake Tahoe. It includes the Carson Valley Inn and an RV Park with 60 full hookup sites, pool/spa, game room and laundry. There is a 14-day maximum RV stay. Last year's RV rates were from $30-$34. The casino has 650 slots, 14 pit/table games and three restaurants (one is open 24 hours). DISCOUNTS: Membership in the Senior Inn Club offers various discounts. RV guests receive a fun book at check-in. Good Sam discount is honored. DIRECTIONS: From junction US-395 & SR-88, south one mile on US-395.

PAHRUMP

Saddle West Casino & RV Park
1220 South Highway 160
Pahrump, Nevada 89048
775-727-1111 • 800-433-3987
www.saddlewest.com

DESCRIPTION: There is an RV Park and a hotel at Saddle West. The RV Park has 80 full service hookups, laundry, pool/spa and gift shop. Last year's RV rates were from $20. Weekly and monthly rates are also available. The casino features 340 slots, video poker, six gaming tables and the Silver Spur restaurant. It is the closest RV Park/casino to Death Valley National Park. DISCOUNTS: Good Sam and Escapee discounts are honored at the RV Park. There is a special senior citizen menu at the restaurant. DIRECTIONS: From junction of SR-160 & SR-372, south on SR-160 for .5 mile.

Terrible's Lakeside Casino & RV Park
5870 South Homestead Road
Pahrump, Nevada 89048
775-751-7770 • 888-558-5253
www.terribleherbst.com

DESCRIPTION: The RV Park has 160 sites on a seven-acre lake offering fishing, swimming, peddle boats, kayaks, pool/spa, laundry and a 24-hour general store. Last year's rates were $29–$39. Weekly and monthly rates are also available. The casino has 320 slots, video poker, 3 gaming tables and bingo every day in winter (five days in summer) plus a restaurant with buffet and menu service. DISCOUNTS: Good Sam, AAA, AARP and FMCA discounts are honored at the RV Park. Seniors, 55 and older, receive a buffet discount. DIRECTIONS: From junction SR-160 & SR-372, go six miles southeast on SR-160, then south on Homestead Road for 3.5 miles.

PRIMM

Primm Resorts
I-15 at milepost 1
Primm, Nevada 89019
702-386-7867 • 800-386-7867
www.primmvalleyresorts.com

DESCRIPTION: Three separate casino resorts are located in Primm Valley; all have affordable luxury hotels. Casino hopping among the facilities is made easy by train shuttles that run from Buffalo Bill's to Primm Valley Resort to Whiskey Pete's. Buffalo Bill's has the rides: roller coaster, water slides and log flume and a movie theater. Al Capone's car and Bonnie & Clyde's "death" car are on display at Whiskey Pete's. All casinos are open 24 hours daily and have the full range of slots and pit/gaming tables plus more than a dozen food venues from fast food to full service restaurants. DISCOUNTS: Discount coupons are available in all brochure racks. DIRECTIONS & PARKING: The resorts are located on both sides of I-15 at the California/Nevada state line, 35 miles south of Las Vegas. RVs are welcome to park in any of the lots. Overnight parking is permitted for self-contained vehicles. *Note*: The Primm Resorts RV Park is permanently closed.

RENO

Reno's famed landmark is the glitzy arch over Virginia Street proclaiming, "Reno – The Biggest Little City in the World." The arch was first built in 1899 and it was illuminated in 1928. The town of Reno was founded as a station on the Central Pacific Railroad in 1868 and was incorporated in 1903, named for General Jesse Reno, a Union general who was killed in the Civil War. An auto museum and the national bowling center are popular stops for visitors. Reno is located near the California border along I-80. Bordertown Casino in North Reno has a pretty high desert RV Park with a small casino. The largest casino resort in Reno, the Grand Sierra, has an RV Park and is a short drive to the casinos in downtown Reno. RV overnight parking is not permitted at most downtown Reno casino parking lots.

Bordertown Casino RV Resort
19575 Highway 395 North
Reno, Nevada 89506
775-972-1309 • 800-443-4383
800-218-9339 (RV Park)
www.bordertowncasinorv.com

DESCRIPTION: The high desert mountain resort has 50 paved and grassy sites with water, electric, dump station, and laundry. It is open all year and there is a gas station on site. Last year's daily RV rate was $25. Maximum RV stay is 21 days. The casino has video poker, 200 slots, restaurant, deli and gift shop. Gaming time is 6am to midnight daily. DISCOUNTS: FMCA discount is honored at the RV Park. Ask at the casino about a free Fun Book. DIRECTIONS: From I-80 & US-395, north on US-395 for 17.5 miles to the CA/NV border, exit 83. Go a quarter mile on Frontage Road. Located 15 miles north of downtown Reno.

Grand Sierra Resort Casino & RV Park
2500 East Second Street
Reno, Nevada 89595
775-789-2000 • 800-648-5080
www.grandsierraresort.com

DESCRIPTION: The resort features a hotel, modern RV Park, 50-lane bowling center, health club, shopping mall, golf driving range and ten restaurants. The RV Park has 178 full hookup sites and laundry. RV guests have access to the amenities at the hotel. Last year's RV rates were $36. The casino, the largest in Reno, has 975 slots, 55 gaming tables, keno and race & sports book. DISCOUNTS: AAA and AARP discounts honored. DIRECTIONS & PARKING: From junction I-80 (exit

15) & US-395, south on US-395 for one mile to Glendale Avenue (exit 67), then east on Glendale.

Downtown Reno Casinos

Downtown Reno Casinos include many within Reno's "Gaming Strip," on or near Virginia Street.

Circus Circus — Free circus acts. More than 1,500 slots from 1¢ to $5. Pit/table games, hotel.

Silver Legacy — Hotel, casino, automated mining machine above casino floor. Over 2,000 slots, table games on 85,000 square feet. On Virginia Street.

Eldorado — Hotel, casino, ten restaurants, eight themed bars, microbrewery, in-house coffee roasting. 76,000 square feet of gaming. On Virginia Street.

Club Cal-Neva — Hotel, multiple gaming floors, $1 minimum bet on craps and roulette, five restaurants.

Harrah's — Hotel, casino, 1,300 slots and table games on 53,000 square feet, seven restaurants.

Siena — On the banks of the Truckee River. Hotel, casino, spa. Tuscan village atmosphere, wine cellar.

Sands Regency — Hotel, casino, 800 slots, 10X craps odds, live entertainment nightly.

Peppermill — Hotel, casino on South Virginia St, voted by MSN one of the top ten casinos in country.

Atlantis — On South Virginia St across from convention center. Seven restaurants, 24/7 gaming. One of three best poker rooms in U.S.

SPARKS

Six casinos are located in Sparks, a suburb that is known as Reno's sister city. Located one mile east of Reno on I-80, the casino district and the festival marketplace called Victorian Square have a turn-of-the-century theme. The square hosts special events throughout the year including summer concerts and the annual Victorian Christmas parade. Sparks casinos have the highest slots returns of any gaming city in the country. Casinos in Sparks include:

Alamo Travel Center, Casino, Super 8 Motel, 1959 East Greg Street
Baldini's Sports Casino, 865 South Rock Boulevard
John Ascuaga's Nugget, 1100 Nugget Avenue (the largest casino in Sparks), hotel, 8 restaurants.
Rail City Casino, 2121 Victorian Avenue
Western Village Inn & Casino, 815 Nicholas Boulevard

DISCOUNTS: Ask about senior citizen discounts at restaurants.

RV PARKING is permitted at most Sparks casinos, but authorization should be obtained from Security. John Ascuaga's Nugget parking area can be seen from the eastbound lanes of I-80; use exit 17 and follow signs to the Nugget. RV parking is permitted on the northwest corner of 14th and Victorian Avenue.

TONOPAH

Tonopah Station & RV Spaces
1137 Main Street
Tonopah, Nevada 89049
775-482-9777
www.tonopahstation.com

DESCRIPTION: There are 20 full hookup spaces located behind the 103-room Ramada Hotel. Last year's RV rates were $18.50-$21.50 Pull into a site, then register at the hotel. There is a laundry room at the hotel. The sites are walking distance to the casino. The small Old West style casino, open 24 hours, has 90 slots in all denominations and a 24-hour restaurant and bar. **DISCOUNTS**: AARP, AAA or GoodSam discount lowers the daily RV rate to $15. **DIRECTIONS**: Located directly on US-95 at the south end of Tonopah.

VERDI

Two RV resorts at casinos are located in Verdi, four miles west of Reno (on I-80 at the California border): Boomtown and Terrible's.

Boomtown Hotel, Casino & RV Park
I-80 at Exit 4
Verdi, Nevada 89439
775-345-6000 • 800-648-3790
877-626-6686 (RV Park)
www.boomtownreno.com

DESCRIPTION: The resort in the rolling hills of the Sierras has a hotel and a KOA RV Park with 203 scenic full hookup sites. The RV Park has an outdoor pool, two spas, family fun center with rides and arcade games, miniature golf, 24-hour mini-mart and free popcorn and coffee. Last year's rates were $24–$27. The 24-hour casino features 950 slots and table games including #1 rated blackjack. There are 3 restaurants on site. A free shuttle runs to/from Reno. **DIRECTIONS & PARKING**: From I-80 exit 4 (Boomtown/Garson Road) north for .25 mile to the resort. Free overnight parking is permitted for self-contained RVs in the lot behind the mini mart.

Terrible's Casino & RV Resort
I-80 at Exit 2
Verdi, Nevada 89439
775-345-6789 • 877-912-6789 (RV Resort)
www.goldranchrvcasino.com

DESCRIPTION: The modern resort has 105 paved, full hookup RV sites in the scenic Sierra Nevada locale that straddles the CA/NV border. Amenities include heated pool/spa, horseshoes, laundry, showers and a 24-hour general store. Last year's daily RV rates were $41–$44 (higher rates for holidays and special events.) A casino and full service travel center are in walking distance. The casino features 230 slots, the Sierra Café and fast food. **DISCOUNTS**: Good Sam, AAA and AARP discounts honored. **DIRECTIONS & PARKING**: From I-80 exit 2 (Gold Ranch Road) on the north side of the interstate. Free overnight parking for self-contained RVs is available in the parking lot behind the casino building.

WELLS

Two small casinos are located at I-80 exit 352 (Jct. US-93). They are:

Four Way Bar/Café & Casino (775-752-3344), 4,500 square feet of gaming with a restaurant,

Lucky J's Casino (775-752-2252), in the Flying J, 900 square feet of gaming and a restaurant.

WEST WENDOVER

The West Wendover casinos are located along Wendover Blvd, parallel to Interstate 80 near the Nevada/Utah state line. Montego Bay and Wendover Nugget Casinos are nearest the state line, across the boulevard from one another and connected by a skyway. Traveling west on the boulevard are the Peppermill and Rainbow Casinos.

ACCOMMODATIONS: All casinos have hotels and there is a 50-space RV Park at the Wendover Nugget. There is a large lot designated for free overnight parking for large vehicles at the far west end of the boulevard.

Montego Bay Hotel & Casino
100 Wendover Boulevard
West Wendover, Nevada 89883
775-664-9100
www.montegobaywendover.com

DESCRIPTION: The complex includes a hotel and casino with 990 slots and 46 tables. Restaurants include the buffet and two cafes. The casino is connected by a skyway to the Wendover Nugget Casino on the other side of Wendover Blvd. DIRECTIONS: From I-80 Utah exit 2, go west for two miles on Wendover Boulevard to First Street, then south for 200 feet.

Peppermill Inn & Casino
680 Wendover Boulevard
West Wendover, Nevada 89883
775-664-2255 • 800-648-9660
www.peppermillwendover.com

DESCRIPTION: The casino has 900 slots, 24 tables and four restaurants. The hotel has 300 rooms. DIRECTIONS & PARKING: From I-80 exit 410, the casino is visible from the interstate. RVs should use the designated RV/truck lot just west of the Peppermill. Overnight is OK.

Rainbow Hotel Casino
1045 Wendover Boulevard
West Wendover, Nevada 89883
775-664-4000 • 800-217-0049
www.rainbowwendover.com

DESCRIPTION: The casino features 950 slots, 33 gaming tables, poker room and five restaurants. DISCOUNTS: Seniors, 65 and older, receive discounts at the buffet. DIRECTIONS & PARKING: From I-80 exit 410, turn left at the stop sign and right on to Wendover Blvd. A parking lot for large vehicles is directly across the street from the casino. Overnight is permitted for self-contained RVs.

Wendover Nugget Casino & RV Park
101 Wendover Boulevard
West Wendover, Nevada 89883
775-664-2221 • 800-848-7300 (RV Park)
www.wendovernugget.com

DESCRIPTION: The resort includes a 50-space RV Park and 500-room hotel. The casino has 800 slots, 52 pit/table games, keno, sports book and poker room. It is connected by a sky bridge to Montego Bay Casino. The RV Park has paved sites with full hookups, heated pool/spa, pavilion, horseshoes, game room and laundry. Last year's rates were $25. Food venues at the casino include a steakhouse, buffet, café and Starbucks. **DISCOUNTS**: Senior discounts are given at the restaurants. **DIRECTIONS**: From I-80 exit 410 take US-93 south .5 mile then east on Wendover Blvd .8 mile.

WINNEMUCCA

Note: The Red Lion Casino and Winners Casino are also located on West Winnemucca Blvd, but parking is tight and generally not recommended for large vehicles.

Model T Hotel, Casino & RV Park
1130 West Winnemucca Boulevard
Winnemucca, Nevada 89446
775-623-2588 • 800-645-5658
www.modelt.com

DESCRIPTION: The hotel has 75 rooms and the RV Park (on the west side of the casino) has 58 level, paved pull-thru sites with full hookup, swimming pool, game room and laundry. Last year's RV rates were from $22; dry camping is $10. The Park is a short walk to the casino, but shuttle service is also provided. The casino features 24 hour Nevada-style gaming: slots, table games and live keno plus a food court, 24-hour café and country store. Live entertainment is featured on weekends. **DISCOUNTS**: AAA, Good Sam and FMCA discounts honored. Fun Book with valuable casino coupons is given to all RV guests. **DIRECTIONS**: From I-80 exit 176, go .5 mile east on Winnemucca Blvd. A lot for free parking for large vehicles is behind the hotel; enter via the driveway at the east end of the hotel. Notify Security if you plan to stay overnight.

YERINGTON

Casino West & RV Spaces
11 North Main Street
Yerington, Nevada 89447
775-463-2481 • 800-227-4661
www.casino-west.net

DESCRIPTION: The resort includes a motel, casino and 5 back-in RV spaces with water and electric in the parking lot. Last year's RV rate was $15. The 24-hour casino has 190 slots, 3 tables, restaurant and coffee shop. **DIRECTIONS:** From I-80 exit 46 go south on US-95ALT for 45.8 miles then east on Main St/NV-208 for one-half mile.

New Jersey

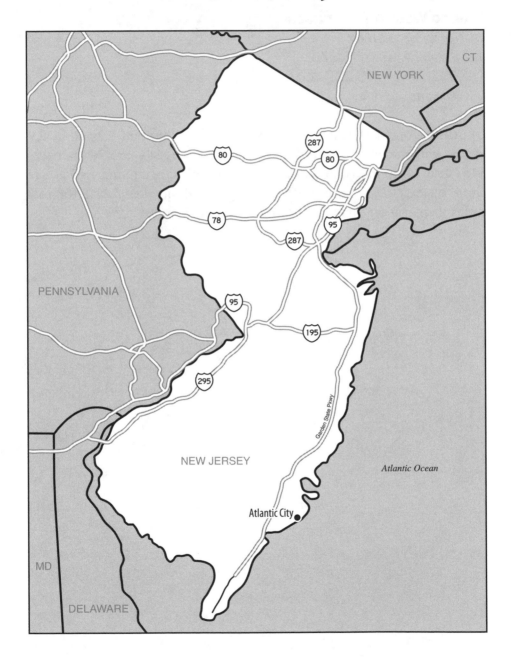

City	Casino	🚐	〰	⛊	📄
Atlantic City	Atlantic City Casinos				187

NEW JERSEY

In 1977 when voters in New Jersey approved casino gambling, the state became the second in the U.S. to legalize gambling. The legislation was designed to revitalize Atlantic City, formerly the Queen of Resorts at the Jersey Shore. A trip to Atlantic City gives you an opportunity to see the nation's only seaside casino strip and experience the world-famous boardwalk.

ATLANTIC CITY

Nine casinos positioned along about 26 blocks of the Boardwalk overlooking the Atlantic Ocean and three in the marina area include:

- *On the Boardwalk's north end*: Showboat, Trump Taj Mahal & Resorts between Maryland and North Carolina Avenues;
- *Clustered in the center*: Bally's and Wild Wild West (connected by walkways), Caesars and Trump Plaza, located between Illinois and Mississippi Avenues;
- *On the south end*: Tropicana at Brighton Avenue and Atlantic City Hilton at Boston Ave.
- *Casinos in the Marina area* include: Borgata, Harrah's and Trump Marina.

Note: A new Sands Casino Resort currently under construction on the Boardwalk is expected to open in 2012.

Atlantic City casinos all have hotel accommodations, varied dining options and many luxurious amenities. There are **no overnight parking accommodations for RVs**. A city ordinance specifically prohibits overnight camping in Atlantic City.

PARKING: "Daytime only" parking is available for RVs in several locations. Harrah's at the Marina has a parking lot designated for large vehicles. The Convention and Visitors Authority notes that the following Boardwalk casinos have lots that can accommodate oversized vehicles: the Trump Taj Mahal at Virginia Avenue, Showboat at Delaware Avenue or the Hilton at Boston Ave. Parking garages for cars can be found at all casinos for fees of $3 to $5 for 24-hour parking.

TRANSPORTATION: An efficient jitney service operates 24 hours among the casinos for $2 per ride, with frequent ride discounted tickets also available. The famous rolling chairs on the Boardwalk are a popular form of transportation, especially during warm weather months. The two-seater wicker chairs are pushed along the Boardwalk by an attendant who walks you to your destination.

DIRECTIONS: Use exit 38 from the Garden State Parkway to the Atlantic City Expressway that leads directly to the casino areas.

New Mexico

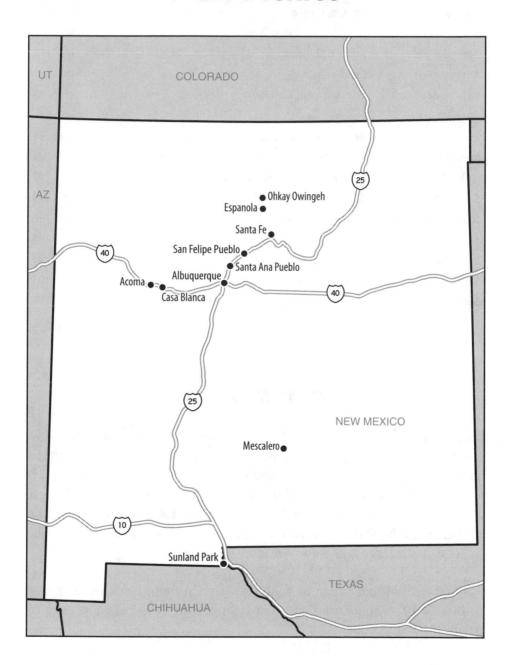

City	Casino	🚐	〽	🌰	📄
Acoma	Sky City Casino	✔		✔	191
Albuquerque	Isleta Casino & Resort			✔	191
Albuquerque	Route 66 Casino			✔	192
Albuquerque	Sandia Casino			✔	192
Casa Blanca	Dancing Eagle Casino	✔		✔	193
Church Rock	Fire Rock Casino			✔	193
Espanola	Big Rock Casino Bowl				194
Mescalero	Casino Apache / Inn of the Mountain Gods				194
Ohkay Owingeh	Ohkay Casino Resort & Hotel				195
San Felipe Pueblo	San Felipe Casino Hollywood	✔		✔	195
Santa Ana Pueblo	Santa Ana Star Casino			✔	196
Santa Fe	Buffalo Thunder Casino Resort				196
Santa Fe	Camel Rock Casino				196
Santa Fe	Cities of Gold Casino Hotel				197
Sunland Park	Sunland Park Racetrack & Casino		✔	✔	197

NEW MEXICO

Various Indian tribes own and operate New Mexico's casinos. Most casinos are located in the north central part of the state – the Santa Fe and Albuquerque areas. The Apache casino in southern New Mexico is a popular resort destination. Sunland Park, in southern New Mexico, is located near I-10 (just outside of El Paso, TX.) Casino expansion continues in the state. The Buffalo Thunder Casino Resort that opened in 2008 is the largest in New Mexico.

Full-service RV parks can be found at Sky City and Dancing Eagle on I-40 west of Albuquerque and San Felipe Hollywood Casino on I-25 north of Albuquerque.

ACOMA

Sky City Casino Hotel & RV Park
I-40 exit 102- Acoma Pueblo
Acoma, New Mexico 87034
505-552-6017 • 888-759-2489
www.skycitycasino.com

DESCRIPTION: Owned and operated by the Acoma Pueblo, the resort includes a hotel, RV Park and casino with 800 slots, nine gaming tables and bingo. The RV Park, located northwest of the casino building (within walking distance), has 42 modern full hookup sites. Last year's rate was $26. The Huwaka restaurant and buffet features Native, New Mexican and American cuisine. There is also a coffee bar and fast food. Hours are 8am–4am/24hrs (Thu–Sat). The adjacent Sky City Travel Center is a popular stop for truckers. It has fuel services, a convenience store, laundry and a small non-smoking slots-only casino. DISCOUNTS: Good Sam discount honored at the RV Park. Seniors, 55+ get a discount at the buffet. DIRECTIONS & PARKING: From I-40 exit 102, the casino can be seen from the westbound lanes. Free overnight parking is also permitted in the lot east of the hotel.

ALBUQUERQUE

Isleta Casino & Resort
11000 Broadway S.E.
Albuquerque, New Mexico 87105
505-724-3800 • 877-747-5382
www.isletacasinoresort.com

DESCRIPTION: The resort has a hotel and casino with 1,700 slots, 28 gaming tables, poker room and five dining choices, including a 24-hour café. There is a showroom with Vegas-style entertainment. Casino hours are 8am–4am/24hrs (Fri–Sat). The 27-hole Isleta Eagle golf course is nearby. DISCOUNTS: Seniors 55+ receive discounts at the buffet. DIRECTIONS & PARKING: From I-25 exit 215, south on Hwy-47 for .5

mile. Parking for large vehicles is in the east lot (level gravel surface). Free overnight parking is permitted for RVs.

Route 66 Casino
I-40, exit 140
Albuquerque, New Mexico
505-352-7866 • 866-352-7866
www.rt66casino.com

DESCRIPTION: The 50's-themed resort has a hotel and casino with 1,600 slots, 41 tables, poker room, bingo daily, three restaurants and fast food. Cabaret Dell Rhea features live entertainment on weekends. The Route 66 store has a wide variety of logo merchandise. Casino hours: 8am– 4am/24hrs (Fri–Sat). The adjacent travel center caters to truckers and RVers with fuel services, a diner, convenience store, gift shop, snack bar and slots-only casino. DISCOUNTS: Late night specials at the restaurant. DIRECTIONS & PARKING: The casino complex is visible from I-40 eastbound lanes at exit 140. RV parking areas are behind the casino building and at the travel center; overnight parking is permitted. Shuttle service is provided.

Sandia Casino
30 Rainbow Road Northeast
Albuquerque, New Mexico 87113
505-796-7500 • 800-526-9366
www.sandiacasino.com

DESCRIPTION: The modern casino with the majestic Sandia Mountains as a backdrop, has 2,000 slots, 33 table games, the largest poker room in New Mexico, separate non-smoking area, high limits area and five restaurants. The resort includes hotel, conference center and 18-hole golf course. Restaurants include: fine dining, buffet and sandwich shop. Live entertainment is featured nightly in the lounge. Casino hours are 8am–4am/24hrs (Thu–Sun). DIRECTIONS & PARKING: From I-25 exit 234, east on Tramway Road and turn left into the casino's main entrance. Overnight RV parking is permitted.

CASA BLANCA

Dancing Eagle Casino & RV Park
I-40 exit 108
Casa Blanca, New Mexico 87007
505-552-7777 • 877-440-9969
505-552-7730 (RV Park)
www.dancingeaglecasino.com

DESCRIPTION: The RV Park, casino and travel center are located in an adobe-type village owned and operated by the Pueblo of Laguna tribe. The RV Park has 35 level gravel sites (some pull thrus) with water and electric, central dump, pet run, showers and laundry. Last year's daily RV rate was $20 ($10 if you have a casino Player's Card). The travel center includes a supermarket, fast food, gas station, bakery and hair salon. The casino, walking distance from the RV Park, features 500 slots, six tables, a restaurant and gift shop. Casino hours are 8am–4am/24hrs (Thu–Sat).
DIRECTIONS & PARKING: From I-40 exit 108, the village is visible from the eastbound side of the interstate. RV parking is also permitted on any of the gravel areas adjacent to the paved casino parking lot.

CHURCH ROCK

Fire Rock Casino
149 Route 118 East
Church Rock, New Mexico 87311
505-905-7100 • 866-941-2444
www.firerocknavajocasino.com

The first Navajo casino opened in 2009 in Church Rock, just off I-40 near Gallup. It includes 800 slots, 15 gaming tables, bingo, a restaurant and food court. Hours: 8am–4am/24hrs (Fri–Sat). DIRECTIONS & PARKING: From I-40 exit 26 (Old Route 66), go east on SR-118N. The casino is located 2.5 miles east of Gallup, NM. There is ample space for RVs in the parking lot and overnight parking is permitted.

ESPANOLA

Big Rock Casino Bowl
460 North Riverside Drive
Espanola, New Mexico 87532
505-367-4500 • 866-244-7625
www.bigrockcasino.com

DESCRIPTION: This casino is located in the heart of downtown Espanola, 25 miles north of Santa Fe. It has 800 slots, 8 gaming tables bowling alley and three restaurants. Casino hours: 8am–4am/24hrs (Fri–Sat). DISCOUNT: The restaurant features breakfast specials. DIRECTIONS & PARKING: From US-84/285 in Espanola, east on Fairview Drive (Rt-584) for 1.2 miles, south on Riverside Drive for one mile. Use the east end of the lot, next to the gas station. Overnight parking is allowed, but the parking lot is small and in a busy downtown area.

MESCALERO

Casino Apache / Inn of the Mountain Gods Resort
276 Carrizo Canyon Road
Mescalero, New Mexico 88340
505-464-7777 • 877-277-5677
www.innofthemountaingods.com

DESCRIPTION: The Mescalero Apache Tribe owns and operates two casinos on tribal land in rural southern New Mexico. A Travel Center casino is located convenient for travelers on Highway 70, one mile west of Ruidoso. With over 500 slots and ten gaming tables, the casino is open 24/7. There is also a convenience store, laundry and plenty of parking for large vehicles. The Inn of the Mountain Gods resort has a hotel, four restaurants, 1,400 slots and 45 gaming tables in the casino. DISCOUNTS: Seniors, 62 and older, get discounts at the buffet at the Inn. Tobacco products are sold at discounted prices in the smoke shop. DIRECTIONS & PARKING: From I-25 exit 6, follow US-70 for about 105 miles. The travel center is on US-70, before you get to the road to the Inn. There is ample space for RV parking at the travel center, overnight parking is

OK and shuttle service is provided to the larger casino 4 miles west of the travel center.

OHKAY OWINGEH

Ohkay Casino Resort & Hotel
Hwy-68 / Riverside Drive
Ohkay Owingeh, New Mexico 87566
505-747-1668 • 877-829-2865

DESCRIPTION: The casino, just north of Espanola, has 690 slots, 7 pit/ gaming tables, bingo, snack bar, buffet and lounge. There is a hotel on site. **DIRECTIONS & PARKING**: From downtown Espanola take Riverside Dr (Hwy-68) north for 4 miles. Free overnight parking is permitted for self-contained RVs. The resort is 24 miles north of Santa Fe. RV parking is on the lot south of the casino.

SAN FELIPE PUEBLO

San Felipe Casino Hollywood & RV Park
25 Hagan Road
San Felipe Pueblo, New Mexico 87001
505-867-6700 • 877-529-2946
www.sanfelipecasino.com

DESCRIPTION: Next to I-25, the complex includes an RV Park, travel center and convenience store. The RV Park has 50 sites with water and electric and a central dump station. Last year's rates were $10 per night. RVers should check in and pay at the casino before pulling in to a site. Security will assist with parking. The casino has 700 slots, 15 tables, a buffet restaurant, high rollers grill and gift shop. Casino hours are 8am–4am/24hrs (Fri–Sat). An amphitheater and the Hollywood Hills Raceway (Sprint Car Racing) are located in the complex. **DISCOUNT**: Ask about special offers for new Players Club members. **DIRECTIONS**: I-25 at exit 252. The casino can be seen from the northbound side of the interstate. Free overnight parking is permitted in the travel plaza parking lot for RV dry camping. All parking areas are walking distance to the casino.

SANTA ANA PUEBLO

Santa Ana Star Casino
54 Jemez Canyon Dam Road
Santa Ana Pueblo, New Mexico 87004
505-867-0000
www.santaanastar.com

DESCRIPTION: The Vegas-style casino has 1,300 slots, 35 pit/gaming tables, poker room, four restaurants and a 36-lane bowling alley. It is open 8am–4am/24 hrs (Fri–Sat). DISCOUNTS: Senior Citizen Day discounts offered on Mondays. DIRECTIONS & PARKING: From I-25 exit 242, west on Hwy-550 for two miles. RV parking is in the lot west of the casino; shuttle service is provided to the casino.

SANTA FE

Buffalo Thunder Casino Resort
30 Buffalo Thunder Trail
Santa Fe, New Mexico 87506
505-455-5555
www.buffalothunderresort.com

DESCRIPTION: The resort has a casino with 1,200 slots, 22 gaming tables, poker room, Hilton hotel, golf course, retail shopping area and seven restaurants. The resort is owned by the Pueblo of Pojuaque. Casino hours are 8am-4am/24hrs (Fri-Sat). DIRECTIONS & PARKING: From I-25 exit 282B go north on Hwy-84/285 for 17.7 miles to exit 177. RV parking is available in a designated area in the northwest section of the parking lot; overnight parking is permitted.

Camel Rock Casino
17486-A Highway 84/285
Santa Fe, New Mexico 87504

505-984-8414 • 800-GO-CAMEL
www.camelrockcasino.com

DESCRIPTION: The Las Vegas-style casino has 600 slots, 10 gaming tables, snack bar and buffet. It is owned by the Pueblo of Tesuque. Casino hours: 8am–4am/24 hrs (Fri–Sat). **DISCOUNTS**: A Fun Book with valuable coupons is given to new Players Club members. Senior discounts are offered for those 55 and older. **DIRECTIONS & PARKING**: From I-25 exit 282-B, north on Hwy-84/285 for 13.6 miles to exit 175 (Camel Rock Road). The casino is located next to the northbound side of 84/285. RV parking is in the large gravel lot north of the casino building. Overnight parking is permitted.

Cities of Gold Casino Hotel
10-B Cities of Gold Road
Santa Fe, New Mexico 87506
505-455-3313 • 800-455-3313
www.citiesofgold.com

DESCRIPTION: The casino features 600 slots, 14 gaming tables, bingo, poker room, race book, a buffet and snack bar. It is open 8am–4am/24hrs (Fri–Sun). The hotel has a restaurant serving Southwestern and American cuisine. **DISCOUNTS**: Coupons are given to new Players Club members. **DIRECTIONS & PARKING**: From I-25 exit 282-B (St. Francis Dr exit), north on Hwy-84/285 for 19 miles to Cities of Gold Road exit at SR-502. The casino is visible from the northbound side of the highway. RV parking is at the east end; follow signs for RV/truck parking. Overnight parking is permitted.

SUNLAND PARK

Sunland Park Racetrack, Casino & RV Spaces
1200 Futurity Drive
Sunland Park, New Mexico 88063
575-874-5200
www.sunland-park.com

DESCRIPTION: The casino at the racetrack features 700 slots plus blackjack and 3-card poker machines with five individual player stations. Casino hours: 9:30-1am/2am (Fri-Sat.) Thoroughbred quarter horse racing is held Dec-April. Admission to the races is free. Simulcast wagering is year-round. Live music is featured on weekends in the lounge. Dining options include the buffet, a full-service restaurant and two snack bars. **DIRECTIONS & PARKING**: Sunland is just off I-10 at exit 13 (5 miles west of El Paso, TX). Follow signs. There are 8 RV spaces with electric; the fee is $10 per night, with a maximum stay of 30 days. RV dry camping is free.

New York

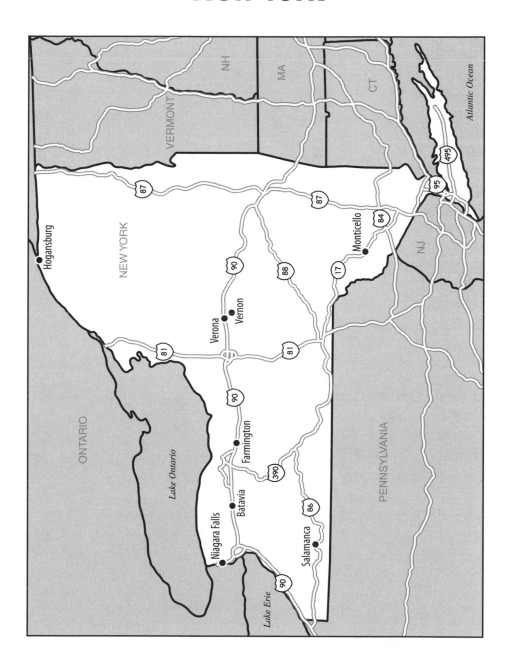

City	Casino	🚐	〽	⛺	📄
Batavia	Batavia Downs Gaming			✔	200
Farmington	Finger Lakes Gaming & Racetrack			✔	201
Hogansburg	Akwesasne Mohawk Casino				201
Monticello	Monticello Gaming and Raceway				202
Niagara Falls	Seneca Niagara Casino				202
Salamanca	Seneca Allegany Casino			✔	203
Vernon	Vernon Downs				203
Verona	Turning Stone Casino Resort	✔		✔	204

NEW YORK

New York State's gaming consists of Indian casinos (open 24 hours) and "racinos," casinos at horse and harness race tracks (open daily until 2am.)

BATAVIA

Batavia Downs Gaming
8315 Park Road
Batavia, New York 14020
585-343-3750 • 800-724-2000
www.bataviadownsgaming.com

DESCRIPTION: The oldest lighted harness track in the country features live harness racing Aug–Dec, Wed–Sat. The racino has 600 slots and daily simulcasting of thoroughbred and harness racing. Dining options include two restaurants and a café. Casino hours are 10am-2am.
DIRECTIONS & PARKING: From I-90, exit 48, go through the toll booth and proceed straight through on to Veterans Memorial Dr for .2 mile to Park Rd for .3 mile to Batavia Downs. Check in with Security to verify where they want large vehicles to park.

FARMINGTON

Finger Lakes Gaming & Racetrack
5857 Route 96
Farmington, New York 14425
585-924-3232
www.fingerlakesracetrack.com

DESCRIPTION: This non-smoking racino features 1,200 slots and four restaurants. Live thoroughbred racing is held Fri–Tue from mid-April to late Nov. Simulcasting is offered every day. DIRECTIONS & PARKING: From NY State Thruway I-90, exit 44 take Rt-332 south for one mile to Rt-96, then left on Rt-96 for one-half mile. Check in with Security for parking directions.

HOGANSBURG

Akwesasne Mohawk Casino
837 State Route 37
Hogansburg, New York 13655
518-358-2222 • 888-622-1155
www.mohawkcasino.com

DESCRIPTION: The 24-hour casino has 1,600 slots and video poker machines, 20 gaming tables and poker room. Food venues include the buffet, pub and fast food. The gift shop features Native American art. DIRECTIONS & PARKING: From I-81 exit 49 go north on Rt-411 for 3 miles, then follow Rt-37 north for about 80 miles. The casino is located just eight miles south of the US/Canada border in Hogansburg. After entering the casino property take the first driveway on the left to the large vehicle lot; 24-hour security is provided. Free overnight parking is permitted for self-contained RVs.

MONTICELLO

Monticello Gaming and Raceway

204 Route 17B
Monticello, New York 12701
845-794-4100 • 866-777-4263
www.monticelloraceway.com

DESCRIPTION: The raceway has live harness racing year-round, Sun–Wed. The racino has 1,500 slots, race book and four restaurants. There is a high limits area. Daily simulcasting features thoroughbreds and harness racing. Nightly entertainment is featured in the Lava Lounge.
DIRECTIONS & PARKING: From I-87 exit 16, merge onto Rt-17 west to exit 104 and merge onto Rt-17B west for 1.3 miles. The raceway is located directly on Rt-17B, 50 miles west of Newburgh. Please check with Security if you plan to park overnight.

NIAGARA FALLS

Seneca Niagara Casino

310 Fourth Street
Niagara Falls, New York 14303
716-299-1100 • 877-873-6322
www.senecaniagaracasino.com

DESCRIPTION: The resort has a hotel, casino, seven restaurants and retail shopping. The casino features 4,200 slots, 125 gaming tables and poker room. Live entertainment is featured in the casino; headliners are scheduled at the events center and free concerts take place in summer.
DIRECTIONS & PARKING: From I-90 exit 53 merge onto I-190 to exit 21, then merge onto Moses Pkwy north 3.1 miles, continue on Park entrance for .4 mile, then north at Fourth St. RVs should park in the self-park lot on Falls St. Parking in this area is first-come, first-serve and RVs are asked to park near the back fence.

SALAMANCA

Seneca Allegany Casino
777 Seneca Allegany Boulevard
Salamanca, New York 14779
716-945-3200 • 877-553-9500
www.senecaalleganycasino.com

DESCRIPTION: The 24-hour casino has 2,300 gaming machines, 56 gaming tables and five restaurants. There is a separate non-smoking casino. The resort includes a hotel, entertainment center and retail shops. DIRECTIONS & PARKING: The casino is located in Erie County, southwestern New York State, 65 miles south of Buffalo. From I-86 take exit 20. The casino can be seen on the south side of the interstate. There is ample parking lot space for large vehicles. Please check in with Security if you plan to stay overnight.

VERNON

Vernon Downs
4229 Stuhlman Road
Vernon, New York 13476
315-829-2201 • 877-777-8559
www.vernondowns.com

DESCRIPTION: The casino, located at a harness track, features 777 slots and simulcasting daily. Casino hours are 10am-2am. Live racing is held Thurs-Sat, Aug-Nov. There are seven restaurants and a hotel at the resort. DIRECTIONS & PARKING: From I-90 exit 33 take Rt-365E for 1 mile then south on Rt-31 for 1.3 miles. Free parking is permitted for self-contained RVs. Please check in with Security.

VERONA

Turning Stone Casino Resort & RV Park

5218 Patrick Road
Verona, New York 13478
315-361-7711 • 800-771-7711
www.turning-stone.com

DESCRIPTION: Owned by the Oneida Nation, casino has 2,400 slots with PIN-controlled account cards that track the account balance, 162 table games and keno. The resort includes an RV Park, inn, lodge and hotel, nine restaurants, five golf courses, a showroom and a discount smoke shop. The Villages at Turning Stone RV Park features 175 full-hookup, paved sites, including 50 pull thrus. The park has a heated pool and jacuzzi, nature trails and a wide variety of recreational activities including tennis, bocce ball, volleyball, basketball and horseshoes. The RV Park, open April-Oct, provides shuttle service to the casino. Last year's rates were $45-$55. DISCOUNTS: Good Sam and AARP discounts are honored. DIRECTIONS & PARKING: The casino resort is located in central New York. From I-90 exit 33 follow Rt-365W for 1.6 miles. Free overnight parking is permitted for self-contained RVs at the casino parking lot.

North Carolina

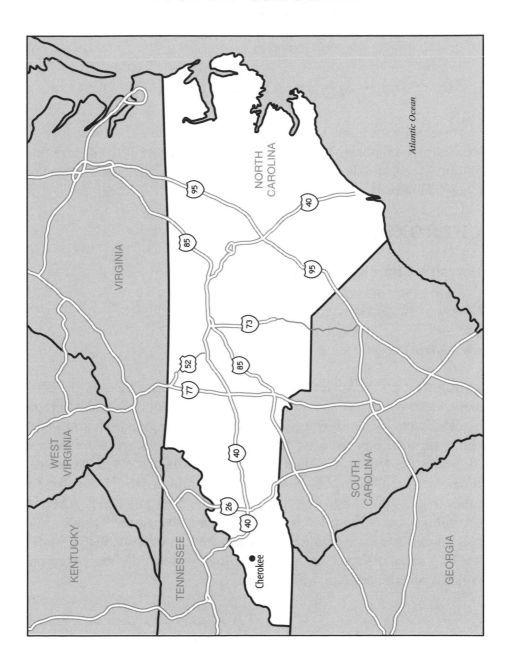

City	Casino	🚐	⚡	⛑	📄
Cherokee	Harrah's Cherokee Casino				206

NORTH CAROLINA

North Carolina is home to a single casino – Harrah's Cherokee Casino located in the Smokey Mountains in the western part of the state, some 55 miles west of Ashville. The facility is owned by the Eastern Band of Cherokee Indians.

CHEROKEE

Harrah's Cherokee Casino
777 Casino Drive
Cherokee, North Carolina 28719
828-497-7777 • 800-427-7247
www.harrahs.com

DESCRIPTION: The resort has a hotel and 24-hour casino with 3,400 slots, video poker machines and 40 digital table games including craps, blackjack and baccarat. The casino floor also includes a high limits area and a separate non-smoking slots area. There are seven food venues including the buffet, steakhouse and café. DIRECTIONS & PARKING: From Ashville, NC, take I-40 to exit 27, then follow US-74 west for 3.3 miles to exit 103, merge onto US-19 west for 23.1 miles then north on Casino Dr. – or – From Knoxville, TN take I-40 east for 93 miles into NC. At exit 20 merge onto US-276 south for 5.9 miles then US-19 west for 19.3 miles. RVs should park at the lower end of the lot. Overnight parking is permitted for casino patrons.

North Dakota

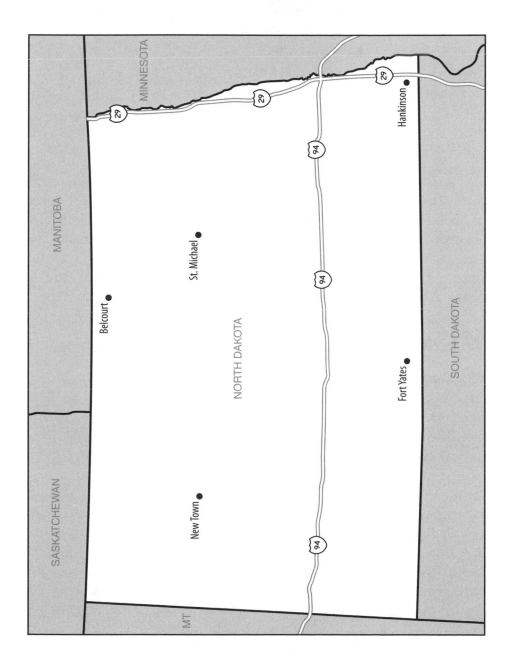

City	Casino	🚐	𝈆	⛰	📄
Belcourt	Sky Dancer Hotel & Casino		✔		208
Fort Yates	Prairie Knights Casino Resort		✔		209
Hankinson	Dakota Magic Casino		✔	✔	209
New Town	Four Bears Casino & Lodge	✔			210
St. Michael	Spirit Lake Casino Resort		✔		211

NORTH DAKOTA

North Dakota's casino resorts have hotels and most have campgrounds or hookups available for RV travelers. Although the casinos and hotels are open all year, some campgrounds close during winter months. North Dakota, known as the state "Where The West Begins," offers scenic beauty, lots of outdoor non-gaming activities and a strong influence of Native American heritage.

BELCOURT

Sky Dancer Hotel & Casino
Highway 5 West
Belcourt, North Dakota 58316
701-244-2400 • 866-244-9467
www.skydancercasino.com

DESCRIPTION: The 24-hour casino has over 500 slots, 14 gaming tables, poker room, simulcast racing and a restaurant/snack bar. There is a hotel and gift shop. A Mini-Casino is located four miles east of the Sky Dancer on Hwy-5 West. It is a slots-only facility, no table games.
DIRECTIONS & PARKING: From I-29 exit 203 go west on US-81 for 95.7 miles, continue west on US-281 for 27.2 miles and south on County Rd for 1.2 miles. RV parking with free electric hookups is available in the casino parking lot and overnight is OK. The casino is ten miles south of the Canada border. RV parking is also permitted at the mini-casino.

FORT YATES

Prairie Knights Casino Resort & RV Spaces
7932 Highway 24
Fort Yates, North Dakota 58538
701-854-7777 • 800-425-8277
www.prairieknights.com

DESCRIPTION: The resort, owned and operated by the Standing Rock Sioux Indian Community, has a lodge, casino and 12 RV (electric only) spaces within walking distance of the casino. Last year's daily rate for RV sites was $5. Pull into a site first, then register at the hotel desk. A 24-hour gas station and Quik Mart, bait and tackle shop and central dump are near the RV sites at the casino. The casino has 600 slots, nine gaming tables and keno. There are two restaurants at the casino. Headline entertainment is featured on weekends at the pavilion. The Marina at Prairie Knights is a few miles down the hill from the casino/lodge. It has 32 sites with electric and fire rings at a daily rate of $10. A central dump and fresh water supply are available for campers at the marina. There is a boat ramp with access to the 231-mile long Lake Oahe reservoir on the Missouri River where anglers can hook walleye, northern pike, Chinook salmon, perch and bass. Shuttle service is provided between the marina and the casino. There is 24-hour security throughout the resort. DISCOUNTS: Seniors, 55 and older, get discounts at the buffet weekdays. Buffet specials are also offered on concert days. DIRECTIONS: From I-94 exit 152 follow ND-6 south for 62.8 miles, then east on ND-24 for 1.3 miles.

HANKINSON

Dakota Magic Casino & RV Spaces
16849 102nd Street SE
Hankinson, North Dakota 58041
701-634-3000 • 800-325-6825
www.dakotanationgaming.com

DESCRIPTION: The casino complex, owned and operated by the Sisseton-Wahpeton Sioux Tribe, includes a hotel, entertainment center and 25 RV spaces with full hookups on the north side of the casino (electric only during winter months). Last year's daily rate was $10.50. RV guests should register at the hotel front desk. The casino has 800 slots, 18 gaming tables, high limits area, poker room, live keno and a pari-mutuel betting parlor. Restaurants include the buffet and restaurant with menu service. The Dakota Winds Golf Course is adjacent. **DISCOUNTS**: Ask about senior citizen discounts. Stay and Play golf packages are also available from the hotel. **DIRECTIONS**: The casino is just off I-29 at exit 1 at the ND/SD state line.

NEW TOWN

Four Bears Casino & Lodge & RV Park
202 Frontage Road
New Town, North Dakota 58763
701-627-4018 • 800-294-5454
www.4bearscasino.com

DESCRIPTION: Located on the shores of Lake Sakakawee, the third largest man-made lake in the U.S. with 1,500 miles of shoreline, Four Bears is a popular fishing destination. The lodge has 97 rooms. There are 85 RV spaces about one-quarter mile behind the casino. Most sites are occupied seasonally; it is advisable to call ahead to check on availability. Last year's daily rates were $7 for dry camping and $13 for full hookups. The campground closes for the winter season. The casino has 600 slots, 17 pit/gaming tables, poker room and a restaurant/snack bar. **DIRECTIONS**: From I-94 exit 159 follow US-83 north for 90.3 miles, then 55 miles west on ND-23.

ST. MICHAEL

Spirit Lake Casino Resort & RV Spaces
7889 Highway 57
St. Michael, North Dakota 58370
701-766-4747 • 800-946-8238
www.spiritlakecasino.com

DESCRIPTION: Located on the scenic shores of Devil's Lake in the central region of the state, the resort has a casino, hotel, RV sites and a marina. There are 15 RV sites with electric (open all year) around the back perimeter of the fully paved parking lot. Last year's daily rate was $18. RV guests are invited to use the hotel amenities that include indoor pool/spa, water slide and fitness room. RV reservations are suggested during warm weather months. Boat rentals and fishing services are available at the marina. The 24-hour casino has 600 slots, 11 gaming tables, poker room and three restaurants. DISCOUNTS: There is a discount smoke shop on the premises. DIRECTIONS: From I-29 exit 141, west on Hwy-2 for 86 miles to Devil's Lake, then south on ND-20 for five miles and continue on ND-57 for another 1.5 miles.

Oklahoma

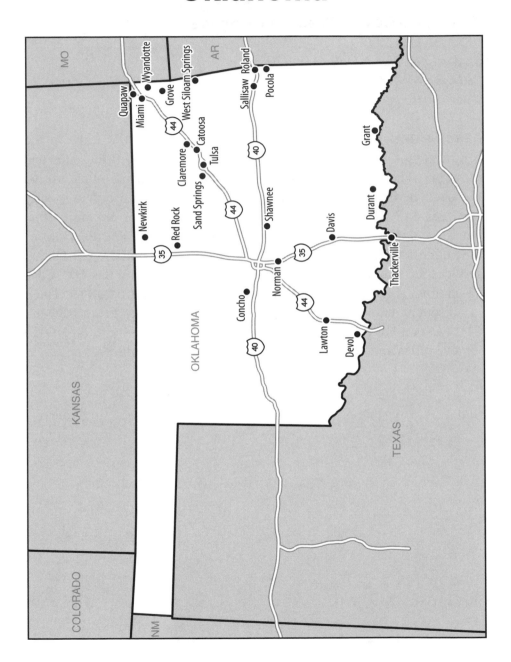

City	Casino	🚐	〰	🛡	📄
Catoosa	Hard Rock Hotel & Casino			✔	214
Claremore	Cherokee Casino/Will Rogers Downs	✔			214
Concho	Lucky Star Casino		✔		215
Davis	Treasure Valley Casino			✔	215
Devol	Comanche Red River Casino		✔		216
Devol	Kiowa Casino			✔	216
Durant	Choctaw Casino Resort	✔			216
Grant	Choctaw Casino - Grant				217
Grove	Grand Lake Casino				217
Lawton	Comanche Nation Casino		✔	✔	218
Miami	Buffalo Run Casino			✔	218
Miami	High Winds Casino				218
Miami	Quapaw Casino		✔		219
Newkirk	First Council Casino				219
Newkirk	Kaw SouthWind Casino		✔		220
Newkirk	Native Lights Casino		✔		220
Norman	Riverwind Casino			✔	220
Norman	Thunderbird Wild Wild West Casino				221
Pocola	Choctaw Casino - Pocola				221
Quapaw	Downstream Casino Resort	✔		✔	221
Red Rock	7 Clans Paradise Casino		✔		222
Roland	Cherokee Casino			✔	222
Sallisaw	Blue Ribbon Downs Racino			✔	223
Sand Springs	Osage Million Dollar Elm Casino				223
Shawnee	Fire Lake Grand Casino		✔	✔	224
Thackerville	WinStar World Casino	✔		✔	224
Tulsa	River Spirit Casino				225
West Siloam Springs	Cherokee Casino				225
Wyandotte	Wyandotte Nation Casino				225

OKLAHOMA

Oklahoma has more Native American tribes and more Indian gaming than any other state. There are over 100 Indian gaming locations throughout Oklahoma. This book includes the RV-Friendly 24-hour facilities that are accessible, near major highways and secure for RV overnight parking. Oklahoma's three horse racing tracks also have casinos.

CATOOSA

Hard Rock Hotel and Casino
777 West Cherokee Street
Catoosa, Oklahoma 74015
918-384-7800 • 800-760-6700
www.hardrockcasinotulsa.com

DESCRIPTION: The resort includes a hotel, inn, golf course and casino with 2,200 slots, 70 gaming tables, poker room and six restaurants. The poker room hosts qualifying rounds for the World Poker Tour. DISCOUNTS: Senior Day features discounts and specials for those 50 and older. DIRECTIONS & PARKING: From I-40 exit 240A (193rd East Ave) turn right, stay in the left lane and turn left at the light. Parking for RVs and motor coaches is north of the casino building. Follow signs and check in with Security if you plan to stay overnight.

CLAREMORE

Cherokee Casino/Will Rogers Downs & RV Park
20900 South 4200 Road
Claremore, Oklahoma 74017
918-283-8800 • 918-283-8876 (RV Park)
www.cherokeecasino.com

DESCRIPTION: The Cherokee Nation owns and operates Will Rogers Downs. There is a full-service KOA RV Park at the facility. The casino has 250 slots and video poker machines, race simulcasting, restaurant and sidewalk cafe. Thoroughbred racing takes place Feb-May. Hours of operation are 11am-1am/4am(Fri-Sat.) The RV Park has 400 full hookup sites and is open year round. Last year's rates were $32-$38; $10 for dry camping. Weekly and monthly rates are also available. **DIRECTIONS & PARKING**: The racino is located directly on Hwy-20 east of Claremore. From I-44 (Will Rogers Turnpike) take exit 255, then east on Hwy-20 for four miles. Overnight RV parking is NOT permitted in the casino lot. If staying overnight, please check into the RV Park. Dry camping rates are available.

CONCHO

Lucky Star Casino & RV Spaces
7777 North Highway 81
Concho, Oklahoma 73022
405-262-7612
www.luckystarcasino.org

DESCRIPTION: The casino, open 24/7, has 900 slots, 24 gaming tables, poker room and a restaurant and bar. A separate smoke shop is on the property. There are 10 RV spaces with free full hookups. **DIRECTIONS & PARKING**: From I-40 exit 125, take US-81 north for eight miles to the casino. The casino complex is located on the southbound side of US-81. RV spaces with hookups are on the east side of the casino building. Please sign in and register at the security desk in the casino before hooking up.

DAVIS

Treasure Valley Casino
I-35 Exit 55
Davis, Oklahoma 73030
580-369-2895
www.chickasaw.net

DESCRIPTION: The casino has 400 slots, 8 live action gaming tables, buffet restaurant and snack bar. The casino is open 24 hours, OTB is available and there is a Microtel motel on site. **DIRECTIONS & PARKING**:

From I-35 exit 55, follow signs to the casino. Free RV parking is available on the east side of the casino building. Please notify Security if you plan to stay overnight.

DEVOL

Comanche Red River Casino & RV Spaces
Highway 36 and Highway 70
Devol, Oklahoma 73531
580-299-3370 • 866-280-3261
www.crrcasino.com

DESCRIPTION: The casino has 1,200 slots, 34 pit/gaming tables, poker room concession stand and lounge. Spaces with free RV electric hookups are available for RVers playing in the casino. DIRECTIONS & PARKING: From I-44 exit 4, take US-70 west for about seven miles to the casino. RV spaces are at the south side of the parking lot. Register at the front desk.

Kiowa Casino
36 East County Road 1980
Devol, Oklahoma 73531
580-299-3333 • 866-370-4077
www.kiowacasino

DESCRIPTION: The casino has over 900 slots, 30 gaming tables, poker room, buffet, steakhouse and sports bar. DIRECTIONS & PARKING: From I-44 exit 1 take OK-36 north for 1.1 miles. RV parking is on the south side of the parking lot.

DURANT

Choctaw Casino Resort
3735 Choctaw Road, Highway 69/75
Durant, Oklahoma 74701
580-920-0160 • 800-788-2464
www.choctawcasinos.com

DESCRIPTION: The resort has a KOA RV Park, inn, casino and event center. The RV Park has 77 modern pull-thru sites. Last year's rates were $30-$50. The 24/7 casino has 1,400 slots, 42 gaming tables, poker room, OTB/race book, bingo and three restaurants. Headline entertainment is featured on weekends. There are two adjacent travel plazas with smoke shops. There is also gaming at the Travel Plaza. DISCOUNTS: The KOA Value card gives a 10% discount. DIRECTIONS & PARKING: The casino is located just north of the Texas state line on the northbound side of Hwy-69/75. Security will assist with RV parking.

GRANT

Choctaw Casino - Grant
US Highway 271 South
Grant, Oklahoma 74738
580-326-8397
www.choctawcasinos.com

DESCRIPTION: Located on Hwy-271 north of Paris, Texas, the 24-hour casino has over 1,200 slots, three gaming tables and three restaurants. There is a smoke shop in the travel plaza. DIRECTIONS & PARKING: The casino is located just north of the Texas/Oklahoma state line, directly on US-271 in Grant. RVs should park in the lot north of the casino building; overnight is OK.

GROVE

Grand Lake Casino
24701 South 655th Road
Grove, Oklahoma 74344
918-786-8528 • 800-426-4640
www.grandlakecasino.com

DESCRIPTION: Located 90 miles east of Tulsa near a popular fishing lake, the casino is open 24/7 and has 900 slots, 10 live gaming tables, poker room and race book. Live bingo is held every day. There is a sports bar & grille deli at the casino. DIRECTIONS & PARKING: From

I-44 exit 302 (Fairland/Grove/Afton), follow US-59 south for 14.7 miles, continue on OK-25/OK-10 for 3.3 miles, then north on OK-10 for 4 miles. RVs should park on the north side of the lot. Check in with Security if you plan to stay overnight.

LAWTON

Comanche Nation Casino & RV Spaces
402 South Interstate Drive
Lawton, OK 73501
580-354-2000 • 866-354-2500
www.comanchenationcasino.com

DESCRIPTION: Open 24/7, the casino features over 700 slots, 15 gaming tables, bingo, a restaurant and snack bar. The casino offers free electric hookups for RVs. DIRECTIONS & PARKING: From I-44 exit 37 (Gore Blvd), the casino can be seen from the eastbound lanes of the interstate. RV spaces with electric hookups are located behind the bingo hall. Check in with Security if you plan to stay overnight.

MIAMI

Buffalo Run Casino
1000 Buffalo Run Boulevard
Miami, Oklahoma 74354
918-542-7140
www.buffalorun.com

DESCRIPTION: The casino, open 24 hours, has over 900 slots, sports simulcasting, poker room, 24 gaming tables and two restaurants. Live entertainment is featured on weekends. DISCOUNTS: Ask about Senior discounts on weekdays. DIRECTIONS & PARKING: From I-44 exit 313 (Miami), after the toll booth, continue straight on US-69A for 1.5 miles. If playing at the casino, free overnight parking is available for RVs.

High Winds Casino
61475 East 100 Road

Miami, Oklahoma74354
918-541-9463
www.highwindscasino.net

DESCRIPTION: The casino features 500 slots, 8 gaming tables, restaurant and lounge. It is open 24 hours daily. **DIRECTIONS & PARKING**: From I-44 exit 313 (Miami) turn right (east) at the stoplight. The casino is 3 miles ahead on the right. Parking is available for RVs and overnight is permitted.

Quapaw Casino
58100 E 64th Rd
Miami, Oklahoma 74355
918-540-9100
www.quapawcasino.com

DESCRIPTION: The 24-hour casino has 400 slots, video poker, nine tables and a non-smoking poker room. Live entertainment is featured on weekends in the sports bar. There are several pull-thru RV spaces with water and electric and a central dump on the east side of the parking lot. Please sign in and register at the front desk of the casino to use an RV site. There is no charge for the first three days and $10 per day afterward. **DIRECTIONS & PARKING**: From I-44 exit 313, after going through the toll booth, continue straight on US-69A north for 3.5 miles and turn right into the casino.

NEWKIRK

First Council Casino
12175 North US-77
Newkirk, Oklahoma 74647
580-448-3015
www.myfirstwin.com

DESCRIPTION: The casino has 700 slots, 18 gaming tables including a poker room, buffet, fast food and sports bar. There is a travel center on site. **DIRECTIONS & PARKING**: The casino is located 2 miles south of

Arkansas City on US-77 just south of the KS/OK border. Check in with Security if you plan to stay overnight.

Kaw SouthWind Casino & RV Spaces
5640 North LaCann Drive
Newkirk, Oklahoma 74647
580-362-2578 • 866-529-2464
www.southwindcasino.com

DESCRIPTION: The 24-hour casino has 800 slots, live action gaming tables, poker room, bingo, two restaurants and a café. DIRECTIONS & PARKING: From I-35 exit 222 take OK-11 east toward Blackwell for 15 miles, then US-77 north for six miles to Newkirk. The casino is 1.2 miles east of the traffic light in Newkirk. RV spaces with free electric hookups are available in the east lot.

Native Lights Casino
12375 North Highway 77
Newkirk, Oklahoma 74647
580-448-3100
www.nativelightscasino.com

DESCRIPTION: Owned and operated by the Tonkawa Tribe of Oklahoma, the 24-hour casino has over 600 Vegas-style slots, six gaming tables and a café. Free RV spaces are available. DIRECTIONS & PARKING: The casino is located on US-77, just south of Arkansas City, Kansas. Free RV spaces with full hookup, located south of the casino building, are first-come, first-serve. Check in with Security.

NORMAN

Riverwind Casino
1544 West State Highway 9
Norman, Oklahoma 73072
405-322-6000
www.riverwind.com

DESCRIPTION: The 24-hour casino features 2,300 slots, 55 gaming tables, three restaurants, fast food and lounge. Headline entertainment is featured in the Showplace Theater. Local and regional acts perform free. **DIRECTIONS & PARKING**: From I-35 exit 106, the casino is located on the west side of the interstate. Parking is available for self-contained RVs at the south end of the lot.

Thunderbird Wild Wild West Casino
15100 East Highway 9
Norman, Oklahoma 73026
405-360-9270 • 800-259-LUCK
www.shawneecasinos.com

DESCRIPTION: The 24-hour, western-themed Vegas-style casino features 600 gaming machines, 6 tables, restaurant and snack bar. **DIRECTIONS & PARKING**: From I-35 exit 108, take Hwy-9 east toward Tecumsah for 17.5 miles. RV parking spaces are behind the casino building and overnight is OK for self-contained vehicles.

POCOLA

Choctaw Casino - Pocola
3400 Choctaw Road
Pocola, Oklahoma 74902
918-436-7761 • 800-590-5825
www.choctawcasinos.com

DESCRIPTION: The casino has 1,400 slots, 19 gaming tables, race book, bingo and three restaurants. **DIRECTIONS & PARKING**: From I-40 exit 325 follow US-64E for 6.3 miles, then south on AR-255 for 2 miles, west on Schulter St for .4 mile and continue on OK-9A for .7 mile. RV parking is available at the back of the casino building; overnight is OK.

QUAPAW

Downstream Casino Resort
69300 East Nee Road

Quapaw, Oklahoma 74363
918-919-6000
www.downstreamcasino.com

DESCRIPTION: The resort is located in the northeastern corner of Oklahoma on the Kansas state line and 7 miles west of Joplin, Missouri. It includes a hotel, RV spaces, casino and two golf courses. The 22 RV spaces in the parking area have water and electric hookups and a central dump. There is no charge for the space, just pull in and hook up. The casino has 2,000 slots, a variety of table games, non-smoking section and four restaurants. DIRECTIONS & PARKING: From I-44 exit 1 (in Missouri) take Hwy 166 north to the roundabout and follow signs.

RED ROCK

7 Clans Paradise Casino & RV Spaces
7500 Highway 177
Red Rock, Oklahoma 74651
580-723-4005 • 866-723-4005

DESCRIPTION: The 24-hour casino has over 600 slots, 14 live action tables including a poker room and a buffet restaurant. Live entertainment is featured in the casino on weekends. Seven RV spaces (back-in) with electric and water are available; first night is free and subsequent nights are $10. DISCOUNTS: Ask about Senior Day discounts. DIRECTIONS & PARKING: From I-35 exit 194 take US-412 east for about 12 miles to the Stillwater/Ponca City exit / US-177. Go north on US-177 for seven miles to the casino. RVs should register at the Players Club desk.

ROLAND

Cherokee Casino
205 Cherokee Boulevard
Roland, Oklahoma 74954
918-427-7491 • 800-256-2338
www.cherokeecasino.com

DESCRIPTION: The 24/7 casino has over 600 slots, 12 gaming tables, poker room, bingo and a sidewalk café with deli menu. **DIRECTIONS & PARKING**: From I-40 exit 325 take US-64W for .4 mile, then right at Paw Paw Rd and immediate right on Cherokee Blvd for .3 mile. RVs should use the large lot behind the casino building. Overnight parking is permitted for self-contained RVs.

SALLISAW

Blue Ribbon Downs Racino
3700 West Cherokee Street
Sallisaw, Oklahoma 74955
918-775-7771
www.blueribbondowns.net

DESCRIPTION: Blue Ribbon Downs is Oklahoma's oldest racing facility and its first pari-mutuel race track. Owned and operated by the Choctaw Nation, the racino has 250 slots and a snack bar. Hours are 10am-midnight/4am (Fri-Sat.) Live racing of thoroughbreds, quarter horses, paint and appaloosas are held in season (May–Sept) and there is daily simulcasting. **DIRECTIONS & PARKING**: Fom I-40 exit 308, follow I-40BL/US-59 north for 1 mile then east on Cherokee Ave. There is ample parking for large vehicles; check-in with Security is required if you want to stay overnight.

SAND SPRINGS

Osage Million Dollar Elm Casino
301 Blackjack Drive
Sand Springs, Oklahoma 74063
918-699-7777 • 877-246-8777
www.milliondollarelm.com

DESCRIPTION: The casino has 500 slots, six gaming tables, food court, bar, lounge and live entertainment. The casino is open 24/7. **DIRECTIONS & PARKING**: From I-44 exit 231, take US-64 west/SR-51 west toward Sand Springs for 15.5 miles to the 129th West Avenue exit. At the end of the exit ramp, turn left, then turn right and go north up the long hill for 1.5 miles and turn left into the casino. RVs should park on the west side of the parking lot. Free overnight parking is permitted.

SHAWNEE

Fire Lake Grand Casino & RV Parking
777 Grand Casino Boulevard
Shawnee, Oklahoma 74804
405-964-7263
www.firelakegrand.com

DESCRIPTION: The 24-hour Vegas-style casino has 1,800 slots, 45 gaming tables, the largest poker room in OK and four restaurants. There are 20 back-in spaces next to the casino with electric & water and a central dump. RV sites are free for the first three days with a players card. Register in the gift shop. There is a travel center on site. DIRECTIONS & PARKING: The casino is located just off I-40 at exit 178 on the north side of the interstate. The RV spaces are on the north side of the lot.

THACKERVILLE

WinStar World Casino
I-35 Exit 1
Thackerville, Oklahoma 73459
580-276-4229 • 800-622-6317
580-276-8900 (RV Reservations)
www.winstarcasinos.com

DESCRIPTION: The resort has a hotel, RV Park, golf course, entertainment center and the fifth largest casino in the world. The RV Park has 200 sites, pavilion and 24/7 shuttle service to the casino. Last year's rates were $25-$35. The Vegas-style casino has 5,700 slots, 40 blackjack tables, 46 poker tables, bingo, OTB, three restaurants and fast food. The showplace theater features headline entertainment. The nearby travel plaza has gas, 96 slots and fast food. DISCOUNTS: Ask about discounts for seniors 55+. **DIRECTIONS & PARKING**: Located on I-35 at exit 1, one mile north of the Red River TX/OK border.

TULSA

River Spirit Casino
1616 East 81st Street
Tulsa, Oklahoma 74137
918-299-8518

DESCRIPTION: The 24-hour casino has 2,800 slots, 39 gaming tables and three restaurants. **DIRECTIONS & PARKING**: From I-44 exit 226A, go south on Riverside Dr for 2 miles. Continue 1.6 miles on Riverside Pkwy. Parking is available in the north or the south lot. Call the casino for shuttle service.

WEST SILOAM SPRINGS

Cherokee Casino
2416 Route 412
West Siloam Springs, Oklahoma 74338
918-422-5100 • 800-754-4111
www.cherokeecasino.com

DESCRIPTION: The 24-hour casino, has over 1,200 slots, 14 gaming tables, poker room, bingo and three restaurants. **DIRECTIONS & PARKING**: The casino is located directly at the junction of US-412 and Hwy-59 near the Arkansas border. RVs should park in the west lot. Overnight parking is permitted for self-contained vehicles.

WYANDOTTE

Wyandotte Nation Casino
100 Jackpot Place
Wyandotte, OK 74370
918-678-4946 • 866-447-4946
www.wyandottecasinos.com

DESCRIPTION: The 24-hour casino has 500 slots, 8 gaming tables, poker room, snack bar, restaurant and lounge. **DIRECTIONS & PARKING**: From I-44 exit 302, take US-60 east for 15 miles, then south on OK-10 for 2.1 miles.

Oregon

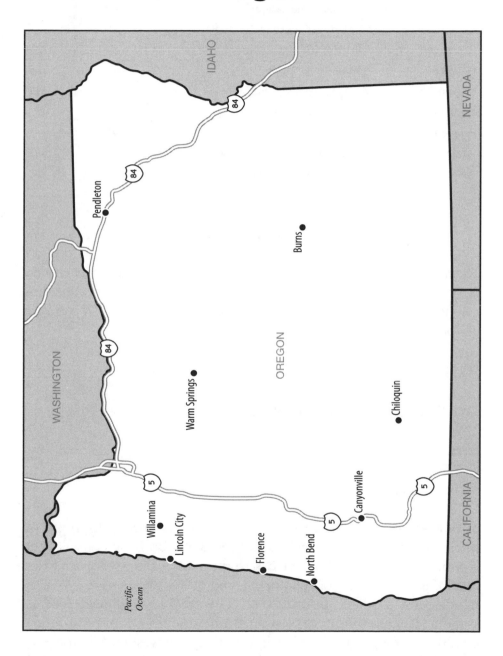

City	Casino	🚐	〰	⬯	📄
Burns	The Old Camp Casino	✔			228
Canyonville	Seven Feathers Hotel Casino Resort	✔		✔	229
Chiloquin	Kla-Mo-Ya Casino				229
Florence	Three Rivers Casino				230
Lincoln City	Chinook Winds Casino Resort	✔			230
North Bend	The Mill Casino Resort	✔			231
Pendleton	Wildhorse Resort Casino	✔		✔	231
Warm Springs	Kah-Nee-Ta High Desert Resort	✔			232
Willamina	Spirit Mountain Casino				232

OREGON

The nine Indian casinos in Oregon listed here are located within an easy drive of an interstate or major highway. Some of the casino resorts rank among the top Oregon attractions according to the State's Department of Tourism.

BURNS

The Old Camp Casino & RV Park
2205 W. Monroe
Burns, Oregon 97720
541-573-1500 • 888-343-7568
www.oldcampcasino.com

DESCRIPTION: The casino has 140 slots and is open until 10pm on weekdays and midnight weekends. The Sa-Wa-Be Restaurant is open morning till night. The RV Park has 15 spaces in walking distance to the casino. Rates are $22 for full hookup and $6 for dry camping. Weekly rates are also available. DISCOUNTS: Daily breakfast and lunch specials at the restaurant. DIRECTIONS & PARKING: From I-84 exit 374 follow US-20 west for about 130 miles into Burns, then west on Monroe St .6 mile. If dry camping, do not use the parking lot, pull into the RV Park where there is 24-hour security.

CANYONVILLE

Seven Feathers Hotel Casino Resort & RV Park
146 Chief Miwaleta Lane
Canyonville, Oregon 97417
541-839-1111 • 800-548-8461
www.sevenfeathers.com

DESCRIPTION: The resort located next to I-5 at exit 99, has a casino, hotel and a modern RV Park. The casino is on the east side of the interstate while the RV park is west of the interstate. The RV Park has 191 full hookup sites, many pull thrus, pool/spa, fitness center and laundry. Last year's rates were $40-$44. Shuttle service is provided to the 24-hour casino that has 1,300 slots, 26 pit/table games, live keno, poker room, non-smoking gaming area, bingo six days a week, two restaurants and sports bar. Headline entertainment is featured at the convention center. There is an 18-hole golf course at the resort. DISCOUNTS: The RV Park honors Good Sam, FMCA, AAA or AARP discounts. A Players Club discount can be added. DIRECTIONS & PARKING: From junction I-5 and Canyonville/Crater Lake (exit 99), the resort is visible from the roadway. Seven Feathers is 80 miles south of Eugene, Oregon. There are 51 designated RV spaces in the dry camping area of the casino parking lot where free overnight parking is permitted; shuttle service is provided.

CHILOQUIN

Kla-Mo-Ya Casino
3433 Highway 97 North
Chiloquin, Oregon 97624
541-783-7529 • 888-552-6692
www.klamoyacasino.com

DESCRIPTION: The 24/7 casino has 380 slots, 6 gaming tables, keno, a buffet restaurant and deli. DISCOUNTS: Senior citizen discount is given at the buffet and there are promotions on Senior Day, every Monday. DIRECTIONS & PARKING: Located on US-97, 22 miles north of Klamath Falls. Parking is available for RVs; please check in with Security if you plan to stay overnight.

FLORENCE

Three Rivers Casino
5647 US Highway 126
Florence, Oregon 97439
541-997-7529
www.threeriverscasino.com

DESCRIPTION: The casino has 650 slots, 16 live action gaming tables, five restaurants and a bar. The casino is open 24/7 and there is a 93-room hotel on site. **DIRECTIONS & PARKING**: From I-5 exit 195 go west on Beltline Hwy 9.7 miles, then OR-126 west for 54.6 miles. The casino is on SR-126 just east of Florence. Free overnight parking is available on leveled gravel.

LINCOLN CITY

Chinook Winds Casino Resort & RV Park
1777 NW 44th Street
Lincoln City, Oregon 97367
541-996-5825 • 877-564-2678 (RV Park)
www.chinookwindscasino.com

DESCRIPTION: The 24-hour casino on the beach has a 225-room/suite hotel and an RV Park with 51 full-hookup spaces close to the beach. Last year's rates were $28-$32. Shuttle service is provided. The casino features 1,100 slots, 33 pit/gaming tables, poker room, live keno, bingo, smoke-free area, a buffet, full-service restaurant and deli. The resort has an 18-hole golf course. **DISCOUNTS**: Seniors, 55 and older, receive a buffet discount. Match play is given to new Players Club members. Ask about discounts at the RV Park. **DIRECTIONS & PARKING**: From I-5 exit 253 follow OR-22 west for 30 miles then OR-18 west for 27 miles to US-101 south for 2.3 miles, then north on Logan Rd for .3 mile and west on 44th St. There are 30 spaces in the casino lot designated for RVs on a first-come, first-serve basis. Overnight parking is allowed, but generators may not be used.

NORTH BEND

The Mill Casino Resort & RV Park
3201 Tremont Avenue (Highway 101)
North Bend, Oregon 97459
541-756-8800 • 800-953-4800
www.themillcasino.com

DESCRIPTION: On the Oregon coast, the resort has a hotel and a 102-space full hookup RV Park (many pull thrus). The RV Park has a stunning waterfront location and last year's rate range was $21-$32. Shuttle service is provided. The casino has 700 slots, 13 pit/gaming tables, smoke-free area, bingo four days a week, waterfront restaurant, café and two buffets. There is an espresso bar, lounge, gift shop and live music nightly. DISCOUNTS: A buffet discount is extended to club members and seniors 55 and older. Good Sam and AAA discounts are honored at the RV Park. New Millionaires Club members receive a free Fun Book. DIRECTIONS & PARKING: The Mill is on US-101 in North Bend. From I-5 exit 162 follow OR-38 west for 56.8 miles, then south on US-101 for 24.7 miles. Free overnight parking is also permitted, but must sign in at the RV Park. A pet area is provided.

PENDLETON

Wildhorse Resort, Casino & RV Park
72777 Highway 331
Pendleton, Oregon 97801
541-278-2274 • 800-654-9453
www.wildhorseresort.com

DESCRIPTION: The resort has a hotel and RV Park with 100 full-hookup sites (walking distance to the casino), a heated pool, spa and laundry. Free continental breakfast is served to RV guests. Last year's RV rates were $22–$25. The casino has 850 slots, 16 pit/gaming tables, poker room, off track betting, live keno and four restaurants (one is open 24 hours.) There is an 18-hole championship golf course with clubhouse, grill café, cultural museum, teepee village plus indoor and outdoor pools. DIRECTIONS: From I-84 exit 216, the resort entrance is .8 mile north of the interstate. The resort is four miles east of Pendleton, Oregon in the northeastern part of the state.

WARM SPRINGS

Kah-Nee-Ta High Desert Resort, Casino & RV Park
6823 Highway 8
Warm Springs, Oregon 97761
541-553-1112 • 800-554-4786
www.kahneeta.com

DESCRIPTION: The unique resort in the high desert features a 139-room rustic lodge, RV Park, casino, restaurant, golf course and a variety of outdoor activities. The RV Park has 51 spaces with a daily rate of $53 (no discounts.) Winter rates are $28. Shuttle service is provided throughout the resort. The 25,000 square-foot casino has 350 slots, live action at the 9 gaming tables and five food venues. DIRECTIONS & PARKING: Located at the beginning of the high desert region of Central Oregon 100 miles east of Portland. From I-84 exit 16 (Woodvillage), follow 238th (turns into 242nd) through 6 stoplights. At the 7th stoplight turn left on to Burnside (turns into Hwy-26 East), then continue to follow US-26 southeast for 84.4 miles. Free overnight parking is permitted for RVs in the casino lot (up the hill from the RV Park).

WILLAMINA

Spirit Mountain Casino
27100 SW Salmon River Highway
Willamina, Oregon 97396
503-879-2350 • 800-760-7977
www.spiritmountain.com

DESCRIPTION: The 24/7 casino has 2,000 slots, 46 gaming tables, poker room, non-smoking gaming area, bingo, keno and six restaurants, including a 24-hour café. There is a hotel and video arcade on site. DISCOUNTS: Ask about Fun Books at the Players Services desk.

DIRECTIONS & PARKING: The resort is 60 miles southwest of Portland on Hwy-18. From I-5 exit 253 follow OR-22 west for about 30 miles then OR-18 west for 4.5 miles. There is a designated lot for RV parking and overnight is OK.

Pennsylvania

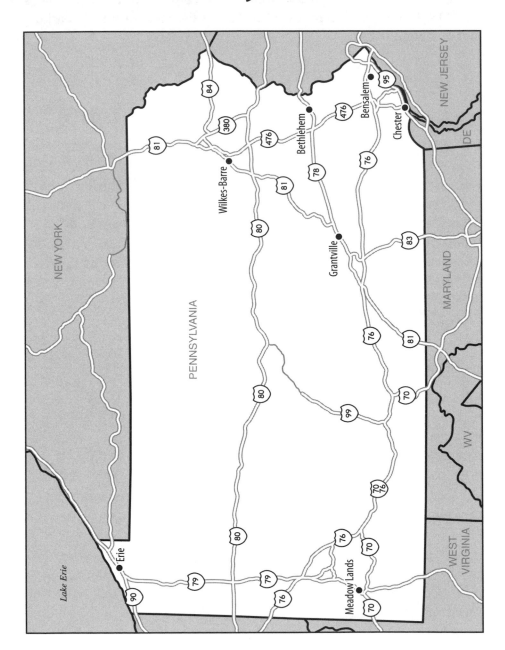

City	Casino	🚐	🎣	🛡	📄
Bensalem	Philadelphia Park Casino & Racetrack				235
Bethlehem	Sands Casino Resort			✔	236
Chester	Harrah's Chester Casino & Racetrack				236
Erie	Presque Isle Downs & Casino			✔	236
Grantville	Penn National Race Course			✔	237
Meadow Lands	Meadows Racetrack & Casino			✔	237
Wilkes-Barre	Mohegan Sun at Pocono Downs				238

PENNSYLVANIA

Pennsylvania legalized gambling in 2004 and eleven applications for permanent slots-only casinos were approved in 2006. Six of the state's racetracks were also authorized to install slots; up to 3,000 machines were initially authorized for each. Subsequently, live pit and table games were approved as casino expansion continues in the state.

Note: **Mt. Airy Casino Resort**, located in the Pocono Mountains, does NOT allow overnight parking for RVs.

BENSALEM

Philadelphia Park Casino & Racetrack
3001 Street Road
Bensalem, Pennsylvania 19020
215-639-9000 • 800-523-6886
www.philadelphiapark.com

DESCRIPTION: The 24-hour casino features 2,200 slots, 11 table games, smoke-free slots area and three restaurants. Live racing is year round, Sat-Mon, on the all-weather thoroughbred track, with the first post at 12:05pm. Simulcast events daily. A live band entertains every night at the Circle Bar. DIRECTIONS & PARKING: From I-95 exit 37 (Street Rd/Rt-132W), then west on SR-132 for 3 miles. RVs should check with Security to find out where to park.

BETHLEHEM

Sands Casino Resort

77 Sands Boulevard
Bethlehem, Pennsylvania 18015
877-726-3777
www.sandsbethworks.com

DESCRIPTION: The casino includes 3,000 slots, table games, non-smoking gaming area, three restaurants and a food court. DIRECTIONS & PARKING: From I-78 exit 67 take SR-412 north for .8 mile, then left at East 4th St for .7 mile, then right at Daly Ave. RV parking is in the employee lot behind the casino building, for players in the casino. Overnight parking is NOT permitted.

CHESTER

Harrah's Chester Casino & Racetrack

777 Harrah's Boulevard
Chester, Pennsylvania 19013
800-480-8020
www.harrahs.com

DESCRIPTION: The 24-hour casino has 2,750 slots, race book and five restaurants. Live harness racing is three days a week July-Dec. There is a 1,500-seat outdoor grandstand, indoor wagering area with seating and simulcast video options. A large outdoor deck offers a sweeping panoramic view of the Delaware River and a bird's eye view of the homestretch of the track. DIRECTIONS & PARKING: From I-95 exit 8 (Ridley Park/Chester), take SR-291 west toward Chester, about 2.5 miles. Harrah's is located on the Delaware River waterfront. Follow signs. RV parking is on the far side of the self-park lot.

ERIE

Presque Isle Downs & Casino

8199 Perry Highway

Erie, Pennsylvania 16509
814-860-8999 • 866-374-3386
www.presqueisledowns.com

DESCRIPTION: The casino/racing complex in the northwest corner of the state includes a casino with 2,000 machines, electronic blackjack and roulette, three restaurants and a lounge. Live thoroughbred racing May-Sept five days a week; post time is 5:30pm. **DIRECTIONS & PARKING**: From I-94 exit 27 take SR-97 south for .2 mile then left into the complex. RVs should park in the lower lot. Shuttle service is provided. Overnight stays are restricted to one night.

GRANTVILLE

Penn National Race Course
777 Hollywood Blvd – I-81 at Exit 80
Grantville, Pennsylvania 17028
717-469-2211
www.pennnational.com

DESCRIPTION: The Hollywood Casino at Penn National is a state-of-the-art integrated racing and gaming complex with live thoroughbred racing and full-card simulcasting; the 24-hour casino has 2,000 slots, six restaurants (including trackside dining) and lounge. Entertainment areas are on the gaming level and another entertainment venue features headline artists. **DIRECTIONS & PARKING**: From I-81 exit 80, the track is just north of the exit ramp. RV parking is available in the lot north of the casino building near the red barn (walking distance).

MEADOW LANDS

Meadows Racetrack & Casino
Racetrack Road
Meadow Lands, Pennsylvania 15347
724-225-9300
www.themeadowsracing.com

DESCRIPTION: The 24-hour racing and gaming complex includes harness racing five evenings a week, 6pm. The casino has 3,700 slots, gaming tables, race book, five restaurants and live entertainment. **DIRECTIONS & PARKING**: Meadow is located 25 miles southwest of Pittsburgh. From I-79 exit 41 go east on Racetrack Rd for .3 mile then left into the complex. RVs should park in the lower lot; call 724-503-1295 for shuttle pickup. Overnight parking is permitted.

WILKES-BARRE

Mohegan Sun at Pocono Downs
1280 Highway 315
Wilkes-Barre, Pennsylvania 18702
570-831-2100
www.mohegansunpocono.com

DESCRIPTION: The 24-hour complex has 1,200 slots including a non-smoking slots area, three restaurants, food court and several lounges. Live harness racing is April-Nov four days a week; Post time 2pm. Simulcasting is available every day. **DIRECTIONS & PARKING**: From I-81 southbound take exit 175A then follow SR-315 south for 4 miles. From I-81 northbound use exit 170B, the Cross Valley Expressway to exit 1, then left on SR-315 north for 1 mile. Parking is provided for RVs toward the back of the parking lot. Shuttle service is available.

South Dakota

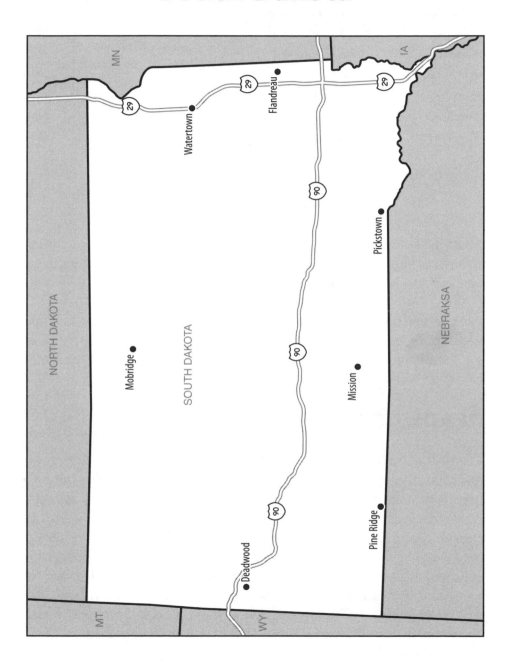

City	Casino	🚐	〰	⛊	📄
Deadwood	Historic Deadwood Casinos				240
Flandreau	Royal River Casino	✔			244
Mission	Rosebud Casino				244
Mobridge	Grand River Casino	✔			245
Pickstown	Fort Randall Casino Hotel			✔	245
Pine Ridge	Prairie Wind Casino				246
Watertown	Dakota Sioux Casino			✔	246

SOUTH DAKOTA

South Dakota's casinos can be found at six Indian operated facilities (many convenient to interstates) and in historic Deadwood where there are dozens of small gaming halls.

Also, as you travel this state you'll notice "casino" signs at bars, taverns, gas stations, even laundromats. Up to ten video lottery terminals (VLT's) are permitted at some locations. The machines, regulated by the state, are poker, keno, blackjack or bingo.

DEADWOOD

The historic mining town of Deadwood, South Dakota, is an interesting and unique gaming destination. Deadwood's long history of gambling began when the gold rush of 1876 ushered in the now legendary saloons, dance hall girls and notorious gamblers such as Poker Alice and Wild Bill Hickok. Gambling was officially banned in 1905 but kept going strong until 1947 when it was eliminated. In 1989, voters of South Dakota approved legislation to once again open the gaming halls in Deadwood as part of a massive historic preservation project. Today visitors can enjoy Deadwood's brick streets, period lighting, old-time trolleys and Victorian facades. Proceeds from Deadwood gaming benefit historic preservation.

Deadwood is a designated historic landmark and all buildings in the downtown area conform to authentic 1800's architecture. Tours are available in the downtown area. Deadwood is famous as the place where Wild Bill Hickok was shot to death while playing cards in a saloon. It is said the hand Wild Bill held when he was shot contained two pair, aces and eights, known thereafter as "the dead man's hand." Visitors can actually go to the Old Style Saloon #10 and see the place where Wild Bill met his fate. Wild Bill's chair and other Old West artifacts are on display. During the summer, reenactments are held at 1, 3, 5 and 7pm. A variety of hotel/motel accommodations can be found in the historic buildings of Deadwood.

For more information, log on to www.deadwood.com or call the History & Information Center at 605-578-2507.

RV PARKING: RVers should note that in recent years Deadwood has become a very popular tourist destination. Consequently, **overnight RV parking is no longer permitted in the public parking lots**. Hotel and casino parking lots are designated for guest cars only. The Days of 76 RV Park (605-578-2872) is located close to downtown Deadwood and is on the city trolley route. It is moderately priced and proceeds benefit the 76 Historic Museum.

DIRECTIONS TO DEADWOOD: From I-90 Exit 30, follow Highway 14A west into Deadwood for 10.9 scenic miles to the 76 Museum & RV Park (across from First Gold Hotel). Continue on into Deadwood to find parking *for cars only* at the various downtown locations.

The 1800's style Deadwood Restoration includes:

Bourbon Street, 671 Main Street, Mardi Gras theme, 63 slots, free beads, music.

B.B. Cody's, 681 Main Street, family fun stop. 57 slots plus three blackjack tables. Steakhouse.

Best Western Hickok House, 137 Charles Street, nickel to $5 slots and cozy lounge with beer and wine.

Bodega Bar, 662 Main Street, built in 1879, one of Deadwood's landmarks, oldest bar, open 24 hours, slots and tables.

Buffalo Saloon, 658 Main Street, where Buffalo Bill Cody ate and drank; 6,900 buffalo nickels on display. 40 slots.

Bullock Express, 68 Main Street, hotel, casino, 25 slots, '76 Restaurant.

Bullock Hotel & Casino, 633 Main Street, 24 hour gaming on two floors. Bully's Restaurant features steak and seafood. Deluxe historic accommodations.

Cadillac Jack's Gaming Resort, 360 Main Street, newest slots and friendly dealers. Hotel with indoor pool, free breakfast, 24-hour gaming, 24-hour restaurant.

Celebrity Hotel & Casino, 629 Main Street, open 24/7 with 74 slots. Continental breakfast for hotel guests. Historic hotel, movie memorabilia.

Deadwood Dick's Suites, Saloon & Gaming Hall, 51 Sherman Street, historic building, continental breakfast, slots, blackjack tables, outdoor patio and antique mall.

Deadwood Gulch Resort, Hwy 85 South, 24 hour gaming. 100 slots, blackjack, video poker. Complimentary drinks to players. Hotel, pool, restaurant, convention center.

Main Street Deadwood Gulch, 560 Main Street, saloon open 9am-2am, 80 slots and lottery tickets. In historic "Chinese Badlands" district.

Fairmont Hotel & Oyster Bar Restaurant, 628 Main Street, World-Famous Oyster Bar and Italian restaurant, casino. Site over 100 years old.

First Gold Hotel & Gaming, 270 Main Street, blackjack, three-card poker, 24 hour slots. Complimentary beer and wine to players. Horseshoe Restaurant & Bar.

Four Aces, 531 Main Street, 240 slots, table games. Home of the famous Wild Bill statue. Open 24 hours. Casino in Hampton Inn.

Gold Country Inn Casino, 801 Main Street. Casino. Free drinks to all players. Friendly service.

Gold Dust Gaming, 688 Main Street, open 24/7. Poker, blackjack, 300 slots. Complimentary drinks to players. Casino adjacent to Holiday Inn Express.

Comfort Inn at Gulches of Fun Casino, 225 Cliff Street, relaxed gaming atmosphere, NASCAR lounge, slots, video poker.

Hickok's Saloon, 685 Main Street, 89 slots, blackjack, three-card poker. Historic rooms & suites.

Historic Franklin Hotel, 700 Main Street, landmark hotel & casino, 172 slots, tables.

Lady Luck, 660 Main Street, loose slots, complimentary drinks to players. Located in the same building as Buffalo Saloon.

Lucky 8 Gaming, 196 Cliff Street, open 24 hours, high percentage payback slots. Super 8 motel has indoor pool.

Midnight Star, 677 Main Street, 52 slots, 6 tables, casual and fine dining.

Mineral Palace, 605 Main Street, blackjack, poker, 100 slots, open 24 hours. Hotel, restaurant.

Miss Kitty's, 649 Main Street, in the heart of Deadwood's Main St, live action games and 100 slots. Two restaurants.

Mustang Sally's, 634 Main Street, antique slot display. Nickel, quarter, dollar & five-dollar slots.

Old Style Saloon #10, 657 Main Street, where Wild Bill was shot; reenactments four times daily. Single deck blackjack & poker, slots.

Silverado Gaming, 709 Main Street, open 24 hours. 225 slots, 16 tables. Grand Buffet at Silverado Restaurant. Largest blackjack area in town.

Tin Lizzie Gaming, 555 Main Street, gaming in the heart of Deadwood, 100 slots, open 24/7. Lizzies Restaurant.

FLANDREAU

Royal River Casino & RV Spaces
607 South Veterans Street
Flandreau, South Dakota 57028
605-997-3746 • 800-833-8666
www.royalrivercasino.com

DESCRIPTION: The casino complex includes a motel and RV Park. The motel has an indoor pool/spa. The RV area is located on the south side of the motel and has 20 sites with electric and cable TV plus a central dump and fresh water supply. RV guests are invited to use the motel pool and showers. Last year's RV rate was $10. Check in at the motel. The casino has over 200 slots, 11 gaming tables, race book, restaurant and snack bar. The entertainment center features live concerts on weekends. There are also free shows in the Royal Room. **DIRECTIONS & PARKING**: From I-29 exit 114 go east into Flandreau for 7.6 miles, then right on Veterans Street for .4 mile. Free overnight RV parking is also permitted in the casino lot.

MISSION

Rosebud Casino
US Highway 83 (on the SD/NE state line)
Mission, South Dakota 69201

605-378-3800 • 800-786-7673
www.rosebudcasino.com

DESCRIPTION: Located at the state line, the 24-hour casino has 250 slots, 8 gaming tables, poker room, bingo every day, a restaurant, deli and gift shop. The modern Quality Inn hotel is on site. **DIRECTIONS & PARKING:** From I-90 exit 192, follow US-83 south for 95 miles to the Nebraska state line. The casino is 22 miles south of the city of Mission, SD and is on the southbound side of US-83. The parking area for large vehicles in on the east side of the lot; overnight RV parking is OK.

MOBRIDGE

Grand River Casino & RV Park
27903 US Highway 12
Mobridge, South Dakota 57601
605-845-7104 • 800-475-3321
www.grandrivercasino.com

DESCRIPTION: Owned by the Standing Rock Sioux Tribe, the gaming facility has a lodge and RV sites with electric hookups next to the casino. The sites are $10 per night ($7 for senior citizens.) There are 250 slots, nine blackjack and poker tables, restaurant and sandwich bar in the casino. The Bay at Grand River Casino, located east of the casino, has a campground with over 70 sites (with electric hookups) and six rental cabins. There is fresh water, a dump station and a convenience store where bait, tackle and sundries are available. **DISCOUNTS:** From I-29 exit 207 go west on US-12 for 172 miles. (Located directly on US-12, two miles west of Mobridge.)

PICKSTOWN

Fort Randall Casino Hotel & RV Spaces
East Highway 46
Pickstown, South Dakota 57380
605-487-7871 • 800-362-6333
www.fortrandall.com

DESCRIPTION: Owned and operated by the Yankton Sioux Tribe, the 24-hour casino has 250 slots, 10 gaming tables and a restaurant. There are ten free back-in RV spaces with electric hookups on the west side of the hotel. **DIRECTIONS & PARKING**: From I-90 exit 310 go south on US-281 for 41.6 miles, then south on SD-50 for 4 miles, then west on Hwy-46 for 3.4 miles.

PINE RIDGE

Prairie Wind Casino
Highway 18
Pine Ridge, South Dakota 57770
605-867-6300 • 800-705-9463
www.prairiewindcasino.com

DESCRIPTION: The 24-hour casino, located in a hotel, has 300 slots, 8 gaming tables, bingo and a restaurant. The facility is owned and operated by the Oglala Sioux Tribe on the Pine Ridge Indian Reservation just north of the Nebraska state line. **DIRECTIONS & PARKING**: The casino is 12 miles east of Oelrichs on US-18, about 12 miles west of Oglala. Free overnight parking is permitted for self-contained RVs.

WATERTOWN

Dakota Sioux Casino & RV Spaces
16415 Sioux Conifer Road
Watertown, South Dakota 57201
605-882-2051 • 800-658-4717
www.dakotanationgaming.com

DESCRIPTION: The 24-hour casino features 395 slots, 16 gaming tables, poker room, a buffet and 24-hour deli. There are 9 RV spaces in the paved parking lot with electric hookups plus a central dump and fresh water supply. These spaces are free on a first-come, first-serve basis. Register at the guest services desk. There is a hotel on site. **DISCOUNTS**: Monday is Senior Day with match play and other incentives offered. Daily promotions and drawings are featured for Players Club members. Gifts are given during players' birthday and anniversary months. **DIRECTIONS & PARKING**: From I-29 exit 180 take US-81 west 2.6 miles, CR-11 north 4 miles, 165th St west 2 miles and north on CR-13.

Washington

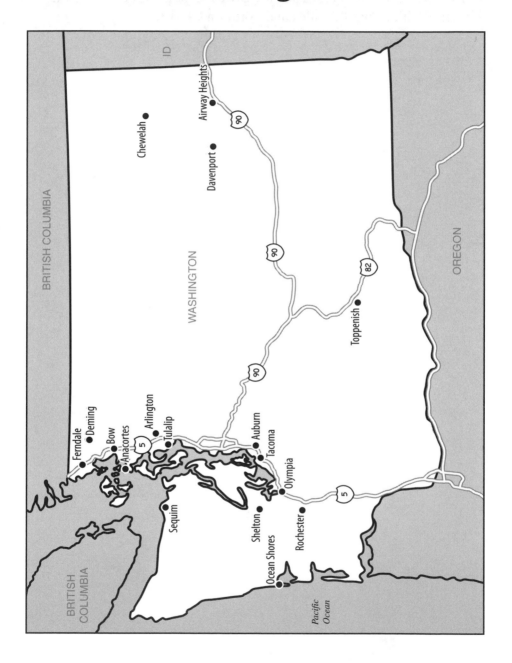

City	Casino	🚐	〽	⛉	📄
Airway Heights	Northern Quest Casino				250
Anacortes	Swinomish Northern Lights Casino	✔			250
Arlington	Angel of the Winds Casino	✔		✔	251
Auburn	Muckleshoot Casino				251
Bow	Skagit Valley Casino Resort			✔	252
Chewelah	Chewelah Casino				252
Davenport	Two Rivers Casino	✔			252
Deming	Nooksack River Casino		✔		253
Ferndale	Silver Reef Casino				254
Ocean Shores	Quinault Beach Resort & Casino				254
Olympia	Red Wind Casino				255
Rochester	Lucky Eagle Casino		✔		255
Sequim	7 Cedars Casino				256
Shelton	Little Creek Casino				256
Tacoma	Emerald Queen Casino at I-5			✔	257
Toppenish	Yakama Nation Legends Casino	✔			257
Tulalip	Tulalip Casino			✔	258

WASHINGTON

The State of Washington is home to 17 Indian gaming facilities:

- 13 casinos in Western Washington, all accessible from I-5,
- One casino in South-Central Washington accessible from I-82,
- Three casinos in Eastern Washington convenient to I-90.

Most gaming machines in Washington are cashless; players must buy slot tickets from the cashier or from machines located around the gaming floor.

AIRWAY HEIGHTS

Northern Quest Casino
100 North Hayford Road
Airway Heights, Washington 99001
509-242-7000 • 888-603-7051
www.northernquest.com

DESCRIPTION: Located near Spokane, the casino is open daily 9am–5am/24hrs(Fri-Sat.) It has 1,600 slots, 46 pit/table games, keno, race book, non-smoking poker room and separate non-smoking gaming area with slots and tables. Food venues include a buffet restaurant, coffee shop, a noodle bar and 24-hour deli. There is also a lounge with a large screen TV. DISCOUNTS: Buffet discounts on designated Senior Days. DIRECTIONS & PARKING: From I-90 exit 277, west on Hwy-2 for four miles, right on Hayford Road for one mile to the casino on the left. RVs should follow signs to the designated area. Overnight parking is permitted for self-contained RVs.

ANACORTES

Swinomish Northern Lights Casino & RV Park
12885 Casino Drive
Anacortes, Washington 98221
360-293-2691 • 888-288-8883
www.swinomishcasino.com

DESCRIPTION: The RV Park next to the casino has 32 full hookup sites with cable TV. Last year's rates were $22-$25. RV guests should register in the casino gift shop. The casino has 700 slots, 18 gaming tables, poker room, separate keno area, OTB in the summer and bingo every day. Food venues include a café and a deli. The Starlight Lounge has entertainment (including standup comics) on Fridays and live music on Saturdays. Casino hours are: 11am–4am/24hrs (Fri–Sat). DISCOUNTS: Senior Appreciation Day is every Tuesday. DIRECTIONS & PARKING: From I-5 exit 230, take Hwy-20 west for 8.5 miles. The casino can be seen on the north side of the highway as you cross the bridge from the mainland to Fidalgo Island at the Swinomish Channel.

ARLINGTON

Angel of the Winds Casino & RV Park
3438 Stoluckquamish Lane
Arlington, Washington 98223
360-474-9740 • 877-394-8210
www.angelofthewinds.com

DESCRIPTION: Located 50 miles north of Seattle, there is a casino and RV Park on site. The casino, open daily 8am-4am, has 1,000 slots, 22 gaming tables, two restaurants and bar. The RV Park has 20 full hookup sites; last year's rate was $10 per night. DIRECTIONS & PARKING: From I-5 exit 210 follow 236th St/Kackman Rd east for 1.5 miles, then north on 35th Ave for .3 mile and west in Stoluckquamish Lane to the casino.

AUBURN

Muckleshoot Casino
2402 Auburn Way South
Auburn, Washington 98002
253-804-4444 • 800-804-4944
www.muckleshootcasino.com

DESCRIPTION: Owned and operated by the Muckleshoot Indian Tribe, the casino has 2,600 slots, 136 pit/gaming tables, poker room, non-smoking section with slots and tables, keno, bingo every day and five restaurants. Live entertainment is featured nightly in Club Galaxy. DIRECTIONS & PARKING: From I-5 exit 142 (Auburn), Hwy-18 east for 4.2 miles to Auburn Way exit, then Hwy-164 east for 1.8 miles to the casino on the left. RV parking is in the southeast corner of the lot. Please check in with Security if you plan to stay overnight.

BOW

Skagit Valley Casino Resort

5984 North Darrk Lane
Bow, Washington 98232
360-724-7777 • 877-275-2448
www.theskagit.com

DESCRIPTION: The casino features 700 slots, 10 gaming tables, keno lounge and three restaurants. Hours are: 9am–3am/5am(Fri–Sat). A hotel is connected to the casino. An outdoor concert series every summer features headline entertainment. DISCOUNTS: Senior discounts are given on Mondays. DIRECTIONS & PARKING: From I-5 exit 236, take Bow Hill Road to Darrk Lane. The casino can be seen from the interstate. RVs should park in the lot designated for oversized vehicles if staying for a short time, but overnight parking is NOT permitted.

CHEWELAH

Chewelah Casino

2555 Smith Road / Highway 395 South
Chewelah, Washington 99109
509-935-6167 • 800-322-2788
www.chewelahcasino.com

DESCRIPTION: The casino has 450 slots and 6 pit/table games, a café and lounge. Casino hours are 7am–2am/24hrs(Fri-Sat.) *Note*: The smaller Double Eagle Casino is next to the main casino; it has additional slots and a deli. DISCOUNTS: Senior discounts are offered on Wednesdays. DIRECTIONS & PARKING: From I-90 exit 281, go north on US-395 for approximately 46.3 miles. The casino can be seen on the east side of the highway. Free overnight parking is also permitted for RVs.

DAVENPORT

Two Rivers Casino & RV Resort

6828-B Highway 25 South

Davenport, Washington 99122
509-722-4000 • 800-722-4031
509-722-4029 (RV Park reservations)
www.tworiverscasinoandresort.com

DESCRIPTION: Owned and operated by the Spokane Tribe, the casino resort has an RV Park that offers beautiful views from 100 sites with full hookups. The park has a swimming beach at Lake Roosevelt, laundry, convenience store and deli. There is also a 260-slip marina. Last year's RV rates were $28–$35/$38 on holidays; the park is open all year. Early reservations are suggested during warm weather months. The casino is walking distance and has 300 slots, six tables and a restaurant. Casino hours are 9am–11pm/midnight (Fri–Sat). There is no hotel at this location. **DISCOUNTS**: The RV Park gives casino match play coupons. Good Sam discount is honored. Special rates are in effect in December and January. **DIRECTIONS**: From I-90 exit 277B, west on US-2 for 31.3 miles, then north on WA-25 for 9.5 miles (some steep grades and a narrow bridge). RVs that want to boondock in the casino lot must check with Security. There is a $5 fee for use of the dump station by those not staying in the RV Park.

DEMING

Nooksack River Casino

5048 Mt. Baker Highway
Deming, Washington 98244
360-592-5472 • 877-935-9300
www.nooksackcasino.com

DESCRIPTION: The casino has over 400 slots, 15 gaming tables, poker room and separate keno area. Five RV back-in spaces with electric are on the south side of the parking lot. Last year's charge was $10; register and pay the cashier in the casino. Dining options include a buffet, grille and coffee house. Live entertainment is featured in the lounge, Fridays and Saturdays. Casino hours are: 8am–3am/24hrs (Fri–Sat). The Nooksack Market Center with a deli, pizza and full service bakery is located next door to the casino. **DIRECTIONS & PARKING**: From I-5 exit 255, go east on Hwy-542 (Sunset Drive - turns into Mt. Baker Hwy) for 13 miles to the casino on the right. Nine free RV spaces (no electric) are on the east side of the casino and free overnight parking is OK.

FERNDALE

Silver Reef Casino
4876 Haxton Way
Ferndale, Washington 98248
360-383-0777 • 866-383-0777
www.silverreefcasino.com

DESCRIPTION: Located seven miles north of Bellingham and just below the Canadian border, the casino has 975 slots, 20 pit/gaming tables, race book, three restaurants and a lounge. There is a hotel on site. Live entertainment appears in the pavilion. Hours are: 9am–4am/6am (Fri–Sat). DIRECTIONS & PARKING: From I-5 exit 260, go west on Slater Road for 3.7 miles, then turn left on Haxton Way into the casino. RVs should park in the south lot; overnight parking is permitted.

OCEAN SHORES

Quinault Beach Resort and Casino
78 State Road 115
Ocean Shores, Washington 98569
360-289-9466 • 888-461-2214
www.quinaultbeachresort.com

DESCRIPTION: The casino has over 400 slots, 15 pit/gaming tables, a sidewalk bistro, fine dining and a sushi bar. DISCOUNTS: Wednesday is Senior Day. DIRECTIONS & PARKING: From I-5 exit 88B go west on US-12 for 46.3 miles, then US-101N for 3.7 miles, turn right at Levee St then left on Emerson St for 1.5 miles. Continue on WA-109 for 14.6 miles, then left at WA-115. Free overnight parking is available for self-contained RVs in the designated area.

OLYMPIA

Red Wind Casino
12819 Yelm Highway
Olympia, Washington 98513
360-412-5000 • 866-946-2444
www.redwindcasino.com

DESCRIPTION: Located on the Nisqually Reservation, the casino has 850 slots, 19 gaming tables, keno, three restaurants and a bar. Hours are: Mon-Wed, 8am–5am/24 hrs (Thu-Sun). **DISCOUNTS**: Fun books are available at the promotions booth. Senior discounts for 55 and older are given on weekdays. **DIRECTIONS & PARKING**: From I-5 exit 111, go east on Hwy-510 (Marvin Road) for 1.7 miles. At the roundabout, turn left to continue on Hwy-510 east for six miles. RV parking is across from the casino building. Overnight parking is permitted.

ROCHESTER

Lucky Eagle Casino & RV Spaces
12888 188th Avenue SW
Rochester, Washington 98579
360-273-2000 • 800-720-1788
www.luckyeagle.com

DESCRIPTION: The casino has 775 slots, 26 pit/table games, keno area, bingo, non-smoking slots in a separate clean-air room, three restaurants and a bar. There are 20 RV sites with electric hookups available on a first-come, first-serve basis. Last year's charge was $14 per night for those with a players card (free hookups for qualified players). Live entertainment is featured in the Cabaret Room on Friday and Saturday nights. Casino hours are 10am–4am/6am (Fri–Sat). **DIRECTIONS & PARKING**: The casino is located 26 miles south of Olympia. From I-5 exit 88, go west on Hwy-12 for 7.7 miles, then left on Anderson Road for .8 mile, then left on 188th Avenue for .2 mile. RV sites are located in the parking area; register at the casino.

SEQUIM

7 Cedars Casino
270756 Highway 101
Sequim, Washington 98382
360-683-7777 • 800-458-2597
www.7cedarscasino.com

DESCRIPTION: The casino, located on the north side of the Olympic Peninsula directly on US-101 in Sequim, is open daily from 10am–1am/3am (Fri–Sat). It has 500 slots, 26 gaming tables, a separate clean-air non smoking section, bingo, keno and three restaurants. Live entertainment is featured in the Cabaret Room. **DISCOUNTS**: Restaurant specials are offered throughout the week. **DIRECTIONS & PARKING**: The casino can be reached by ferry from Seattle, or by driving on US-101 north into Sequim from the Olympia area. Free overnight parking is available for RVs. Please check in at the casino if you plan to stay overnight.

SHELTON

Little Creek Casino
West 91 Highway 108
Shelton, Washington 98584
360-427-7711 • 800-667-7711
www.little-creek.com

DESCRIPTION: The casino has over 800 cashless slots, 28 gaming tables, bingo, keno, three restaurants, deli and lounge. There is a non-smoking section in the casino. Casino hours are 10am–4am/5am (Fri–Sat). There is a hotel at the casino and a gas station/convenience store is across the street. **DISCOUNTS**: Ask about senior specials on weekdays. **DIRECTIONS & PARKING**: From I-5 in Olympia, exit 104, north on US-101 for five miles (follow signs to Port Angeles/Shelton) and continue north on US-101 for another 7.5 miles. Exit US-101 between mileposts 353 & 354 (at Hwy-108). The casino is next to the southbound lanes of the highway and can be seen from both sides. The designated parking area for RVs is on the west side of the parking lot. Overnight is OK.

TACOMA

Emerald Queen Casino at I-5
2024 East 29th Street
Tacoma, Washington 98404
253-594-7777 • 888-831-7655
www.emeraldqueen.com

DESCRIPTION: The casino features 3,000 slots, 57 pit/gaming tables, a clean-air separate non-smoking area, keno lounge, 5 restaurants and a sports bar. Headline entertainment is featured at the EQC I-5 Showroom. Casino hours are: Tue-Thur, 10am-6am/24 hrs (Fri-Mon). **DIRECTIONS & PARKING**: The casino can be seen from the northbound lanes of I-5 at exit 135. From southbound: exit at #135, turn left at the first light, drive under the interstate and make an immediate left. Stay in the right lane for about a mile and watch for the casino entrance on your right. From northbound: exit at #135 and go straight through the traffic light. Bear right at the Puyallup sign, go about one mile and look for the casino entrance on the right. RVs should park in the overflow area or on the perimeter of the main lot. Overnight RV parking is permitted for self-contained vehicles.

TOPPENISH

Yakama Nation Legends Casino
580 Fort Road
Toppenish, Washington 98948
509-865-8800 • 877-726-6311
www.yakamalegends.com

DESCRIPTION: Owned and operated by the Yakama Nation, the casino in south-central Washington has 1,000 slots, 38 pit/gaming tables, poker room, live keno, bingo six days a week and three restaurants. Hours are 9am-4am/5am (Fri–Sat). Special outdoor events (concerts, rodeos, pow-wows) are held during the summer. The Yakama Nation's modern RV Park is located a short distance from the casino and is next to the Yakama National Heritage Center. **DISCOUNTS**: New Players Club members receive a Fun Book. **DIRECTIONS & PARKING**: From I-82 exit 50, take WA-22E (through the town of Toppenish) for 2.8 miles, continue straight on to Washington St and Elm St for .4 mile, turn right at W 1st Ave for .5 mile and continue on Fort Rd/WA-220 for .7 mile. Ample free RV parking is available in the casino lot. Please notify Security if you are staying overnight.

TULALIP

Tulalip Casino
10200 Quil Ceda Boulevard
Tulalip, Washington 98271
360-716-6000 • 888-272-1111
www.tulalipcasino.com

DESCRIPTION: The casino, located in the resort hotel, has 2,000 video slots, 71 tables, High Roller Room with ten tables, keno, bingo, separate non-smoking area and four restaurants. The casino has a vaulted ceiling over the 100-foot entryway with a hand painted mural depicting the life of the salmon. The main casino floor has a spectacular center dome. Casino hours are: 10am–6am/24hours (Fri–Sun). **DIRECTIONS & PARKING**: From I-5 exit 200, follow casino signs. The resort complex is visible from the southbound lanes of the interstate. RV parking is on the west side of the casino and overnight parking is permitted.

West Virginia

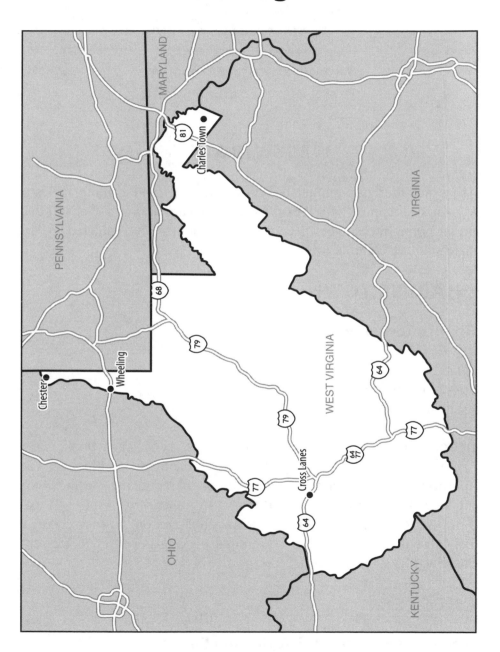

City	Casino	🚐	🏕	🛡	📄
Charles Town	Charles Town Races & Slots				260
Chester	Mountaineer Race Track & Gaming Resort				260
Cross Lanes	Tri State Racetrack & Gaming Center			✔	261
Wheeling	Wheeling Island Racetrack & Gaming Center			✔	261

WEST VIRGINIA

There are four pari-mutuel facilities with slots and gaming tables – known as "racinos" – in West Virginia. Two are at dog tracks and two are at horse tracks. The machines at the racinos are regulated by the state's lottery commission.

CHARLES TOWN

Charles Town Races & Slots
608 East Washington Street
Charles Town, West Virginia 25414
304-725-7001 • 800-795-7001
www.ctownraces.com

DESCRIPTION: The casino has 5,000 slots, keno, race book, daily simulcasting of horse and dog racing, five restaurants and lounge. The six-furlongs horse track features live thoroughbred racing. Casino hours are 7am–4am/24hrs (Fri-Sat). DIRECTIONS & PARKING: From I-81 exit 5, follow Rt-51 east for 12 miles. RVs should park on the back end of F Lot (near the railroad tracks). Overnight parking is permitted for self-contained RVs.

CHESTER

Mountaineer Race Track & Gaming Resort
State Route 2

Chester, West Virginia 26034
304-387-8300 • 800-804-0468
www.mtrgaming.com

DESCRIPTION: The resort includes a 24-hour casino with 3,200 slots, 87 gaming tables, race book, bingo, 12 restaurants, a hotel and golf course. Live thoroughbred racing is held year-round. DIRECTIONS & PARKING: From Weirton, West Virginia, follow US-2 north for 15 miles to Mountaineer. The south lot (trackside) is designated for large vehicles. Overnight parking is OK for RVs.

CROSS LANES

Tri State Racetrack & Gaming Center
1 Greyhound Lane
Cross Lanes, West Virginia 25356
304-776-1000 • 800-224-9683
www.tristateracetrack.com

DESCRIPTION: The gaming complex includes a hotel, casino and live greyhound racing. The casino has 1,800 slots, live table games, race book, bingo, daily racing simulcasting, three restaurants and lounge. Live racing takes place daily, year-round except Tuesday and Sunday. Casino hours are 11am–3am\5am (Fri-Sat.) DIRECTIONS & PARKING: From I-64 use exit 47 or 47A. Tri-State can be seen from the eastbound lanes of the interstate. RVs should park on the perimeter of the lot across from the casino building. Check in with Security if you plan to stay overnight.

WHEELING

Wheeling Island Racetrack & Gaming Center
1 South Stone Street
Wheeling, West Virginia 26003
304-232-5050 • 877-946-4373
www.wheelingisland.com

DESCRIPTION: The casino features 2,400 gaming machines, 73 gaming tables, race book, daily simulcasting of dog and horse racing, bingo and six restaurants. Live greyhound racing takes place year-round. Resort hours are 7am-4am daily. There is a hotel at the resort. **DIRECTIONS& PARKING**: <u>From I-70 eastbound</u>, take exit 225. Turn left at the end of the ramp, then right at the first light. At the next light continue straight and cross the bridge onto Wheeling Island. At the second light after the bridge turn right onto South York Street and follow to Wheeling Island. <u>From I-70 westbound</u>, after passing through Wheeling tunnel, in the left lane, use exit 0 (Wheeling Island). At the first light turn left onto South York Street and follow to Wheeling Island. Parking for RVs is in Lot H.

Wisconsin

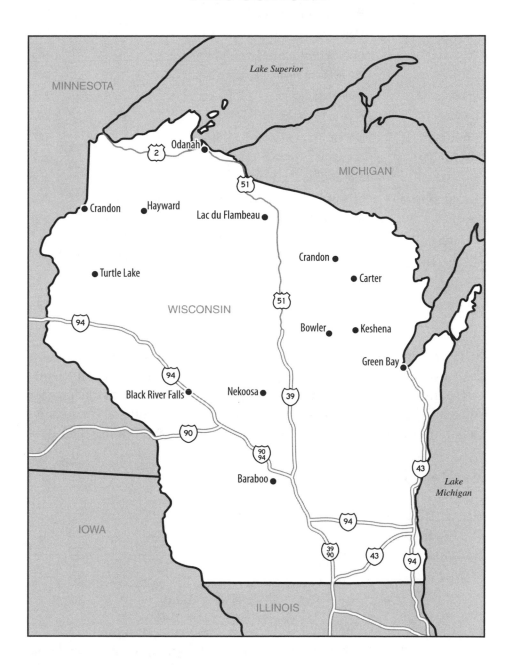

City	Casino	🚐	〽	⬭	📄
Baraboo	Ho-Chunk Casino Hotel				264
Black River Falls	Majestic Pines Hotel & Casino & RV Spaces		✔		265
Bowler	Mohican North Star Casino & RV Park	✔			265
Carter	Potawatomi Bingo / Northern Lights Casino				266
Crandon	Mole Lake Casino				266
Danbury	Hole In The Wall Casino				267
Green Bay	Oneida Bingo & Casino & RV Spaces		✔		267
Hayward	LCO Casino, Lodge & RV Spaces		✔		267
Keshena	Menominee Casino, Hotel & RV Park	✔			268
Lac du Flambeau	Lake of the Torches Resort Casino & RV Park	✔			268
Nekoosa	Rainbow Casino & RV Spaces		✔		269
Odanah	Bad River Lodge & Casino & RV Spaces		✔		269
Turtle Lake	St. Croix Casino & RV Park	✔			270

WISCONSIN

In 1987, when Wisconsin voters approved the creation of a state lottery, they also gave Wisconsin's Indian Tribes the right to establish casino-type gambling. Since then, a number of tribes opened casinos that provide substantial economic benefits to reservation communities. Wisconsin's Indian tribes offer casino gaming in locations throughout the state.

BARABOO

Ho-Chunk Casino Hotel
S3214 Highway 12
Baraboo, Wisconsin 53913
608-356-6210 • 800-746-2486
www.ho-chunk.com

DESCRIPTION: Located in The Dells, a popular vacation area, the 24-hour casino features 2,400 slot machines, 49 gaming tables, race book, bingo, three restaurants, fast food and a bar. There is a hotel on site. Live entertainment is featured on weekends. **DISCOUNTS**: Discount smoke shop at the resort. **DIRECTIONS & PARKING**: From I-90/94 exit 92, follow US-12E for 3 miles. RVs should park in the back lot. Free overnight parking is available; check in with Security.

BLACK RIVER FALLS

Majestic Pines Hotel & Casino & RV Spaces
W9010 State Road 54 East
Black River Falls, Wisconsin 54615
715-284-9098 • 800-657-4621
www.mpcwin.com

DESCRIPTION: The casino has 600 slots, 9 pit/gaming tables, bingo, a buffet restaurant and snack bar. The casino is open 24 hours during the summer season with modified hours in winter. There is a hotel with an indoor pool on site. **DISCOUNTS**: Players Club card holders get buffet discounts. **DIRECTIONS & PARKING**: From I-94 exit 116, take WI-54 south for 2.6 miles. RV parking is in the east parking lot. There are a few spaces with free electric hookups at the northeast end of the lot. Overnight RV parking is OK.

BOWLER

Mohican North Star Casino & RV Park
W12180 County Road A
Bowler, Wisconsin 54416
715-793-4090 • 800-952-0195
715-787-2751 (RV Park)
www.mohicannorthstar.com

DESCRIPTION: Owned and operated by the Mohican Nation, the facility has a casino and RV Park with 57 full hookup, wooded sites. It is walking distance to the casino. Last year's camping fees were $25-$28 per night. The casino has 1,200 slots, 14 pit/gaming tables and two restaurants. Hours are 8am–2am/24hrs (Fri–Sat). The RV Park and casino are open all year. There is a convenience store on site. **DIRECTIONS**: Located 50 miles northwest of Green Bay. From US-41 exit 169 take WI-29 west for 41.6 miles to mile post 217, then north on CR-U for 2 miles, continue north on CR-A for 1.9 miles and continue to follow CR-A northwest for 7.5 miles.

CARTER

Potawatomi Bingo / Northern Lights Casino
618 State Highway 32
Carter, Wisconsin 54566
715-473-2021 • 800-487-9522
www.cartercasino.com

DESCRIPTION: The 24-hour casino has 500 slots, 8 pit/gaming tables, bingo (Wed–Sun), two restaurants and sports bar. There is a lodge, 24-hour gas station and convenience store on site. DISCOUNTS: Weekly specials on Senior Day. DIRECTIONS & PARKING: Located 85 miles north of Green Bay, take US-141 north for 23.7 miles, then WI-64 west for 20.1 miles and WI-32 north for 23.4 miles. There is ample parking space for RVs. Please check in with Security if you plan to stay overnight.

CRANDON

Mole Lake Casino
3084 Highway 55
Crandon, Wisconsin 54520
715-478-7557 • 800-236-9466
www.molelake.com

DESCRIPTION: The casino has 500 slots, 7 gaming tables, bingo, keno, a café, bistro and lounge. There is a lodge on the property. Casino hours are 10am–2am/3am (Fri–Sat). DISCOUNTS: Senior Day on Wednesdays features match play for those 50 and older. DIRECTIONS & PARKING: The casino is located about 30 miles southeast of Rhinelander. From US-51 follow US-8 east for 39.1 miles, then south on CR-S for 2 miles and continue south on WI-55 for 4.5 miles. Free overnight parking is permitted for self-contained RVs.

DANBURY

Hole In The Wall Casino
30222 State Road 35
Danbury, Wisconsin 54830
715-656-3444 • 800-238-8946
www.stcroixcasino.com

DESCRIPTION: The Western-themed casino has 340 slots, 12 pit/table games and a restaurant. Hours are 9am-2am/4am (Fri-Sat.) There is a hotel on site. **DIRECTIONS & PARKING**: From I-35 exit 183 in Minnesota, go east on SR-48 for 23.4 miles (crossing into Wisconsin); continue on WI-77 for 4 miles. RVs should park in the bus parking area.

GREEN BAY

Oneida Bingo & Casino & RV Spaces
2020/2100 Airport Drive
Green Bay, Wisconsin 54313
920-494-4500 • 800-238-4263
www.oneidabingoandcasino.net

DESCRIPTION: Two 24-hour casinos and a hotel are located on the property. The casinos have 1,000 slots, 34 pit/gaming tables, bingo, high stakes area in the main casino and four restaurants. **DIRECTIONS & PARKING**: From I-43 exit 180 take SR-172 west 8 miles to Airport Rd. Several RV parking spaces with free electric hookups can be found along the road near the smaller casino at the back of the property. The spaces are first come, first served; no water or dump.

HAYWARD

LCO Casino, Lodge & RV Spaces
13767 West County Road B
Hayward, Wisconsin 54843
715-634-5643 • 800-526-2274
www.lcocasino.com

DESCRIPTION: Located in northwestern Wisconsin, the resort has a lodge and a casino with 640 slots, 18 pit/gaming tables, poker room, bingo six days a week, keno, two restaurants, and sports bar. Eight RV spaces with water and electric hookups are available May-Sept; last year's rates were $15 per night with weekly rates available. Register at the hotel. DIRECTIONS & PARKING: From jct US-53 & US-63 go east on US 63 to Hayward, then Hwy-27 south for .5 mile to CR-B, then east for 5 miles to the casino.

KESHENA

Menominee Casino, Hotel & RV Spaces
Highway 47/55
Keshena, Wisconsin 54135
715-799-3600 • 800-343-7778
www.menomineecasinoresort.com

DESCRIPTION: Located on the Menominee Indian Reservation, the 24-hour casino has over 800 slots, 15 pit/gaming tables, poker room, bingo, live entertainment in the lounge and two restaurants. RV spaces are available for $16 per night; register at the hotel DISCOUNTS: Seniors 55+ receive discounts on Tuesdays. DIRECTIONS: Located 40 miles northwest of Green Bay. From US-41 exit 169 go west on WI-29 for 32.2 miles, take exit 225 for WI-22 north for 2 miles then north on WI-47/55 for 7.8 miles.

LAC DU FLAMBEAU

Lake of the Torches Resort Casino & RV Park
510 Old Abe Road
Lac du Flambeau, Wisconsin 54538
715-588-7070 • 800-25-TORCH
www.lakeofthetorches.com

DESCRIPTION: The resort includes a casino, hotel and RV Park that is a mile north of the casino building. Open May-Sept, the RV Park has 72 sites, central dump, showers and laundry. All sites are lakefront. On-call shuttle service is available to the casino. Last year's daily rates were $28-$31. The resort is situated near a ten-lake chain with boating and fishing at lakes that have trophy size muskies, walleyes and bass. Canoe rental with guide service is available. The unique 24-hour casino-in-the-round features Native American-themed murals on the rounded walls. It has 900 slots, 15 pit/gaming tables and two restaurants. **DIRECTIONS & PARKING**: From I-39 in Wausau, continue north on US-51 for 73 miles to the town of Woodruff (Jct WI-47). Go west on US-47 for 12 miles to the casino. Free overnight parking for RVs is available on the level gravel lot across the street from the casino next to the gas station.

NEKOOSA

Rainbow Casino & RV Spaces
949 County Road G
Nekoosa, Wisconsin 54457
715-886-4560 • 800-782-4560
www.rbcwin.com

DESCRIPTION: The casino has 660 slots, 11 tables, bingo, grille and snack bar. There is a smoke and gift shop featuring Native American gifts. Casino hours are 8am–2am/24hrs (Fri–Sat). **DISCOUNTS**: Senior citizen specials on Thursdays if 55+. **DIRECTIONS & PARKING**: From I-39 exit 136, follow WI-73 west for 20.8 miles, continue on WI-173 for 2.2 miles, then west on County Rd G for 3.7 miles. The casino is about four miles south of Nekoosa. There are eight RV spaces in the parking lot with free electric hookups, first-come first-serve. Maximum stay is 3 days.

ODANAH

Bad River Lodge & Casino & RV Spaces
73370 US Highway 2
Odanah, Wisconsin 54861
715-682-7121 • 800-777-7449
www.badriver.com

DESCRIPTION: Owned and operated by the Bad River Band of the Lake Superior Tribe of Chippewa Indians, the resort offers 20 free RV spaces with electric and water and a dump station. There is a gas station, IGA market, post office and mini casino at the convenience store. The hotel has 50 rooms. The main casino has 500 slots, 8 gaming tables, keno, restaurant and snack bar. RV spaces are walking distance to the casino and the store. Casino hours are 8am–2am daily. DISCOUNTS: First time visitors get casino cash tokens. A discounted breakfast is offered daily at the restaurant. Ask about discounts at the gas station. DIRECTIONS & PARKING: Located near Lake Superior ten miles east of Ashland on US-2. The RV spaces are first-come, first-serve.

TURTLE LAKE

St. Croix Casino & RV Park
777 U.S. Highway 8 West
Turtle Lake, Wisconsin 54889
715-986-4777 • 800-846-8946
www.stcroixcasino.com

DESCRIPTION: Located in northwestern Wisconsin, the resort includes a casino, hotel and RV Park. The RV Park, open May-Oct, has 18 sites with water and electric, laundry and shower facilities. Last year's rate was $20 per night; weekly rates are available. The Vegas-style casino has 1,300 slots, 36 pit/gaming tables, poker room, non-smoking slots area, high stakes area and three restaurants. DIRECTIONS & PARKING: The resort is 65 miles northwest of Eau Claire, WI. From US-53 exit 135 go west on US-8 for 20 miles. Free RV parking is available across from the casino in the Barn Lot, where there is a heated bus waiting area. Shuttle service is provided.

Wyoming

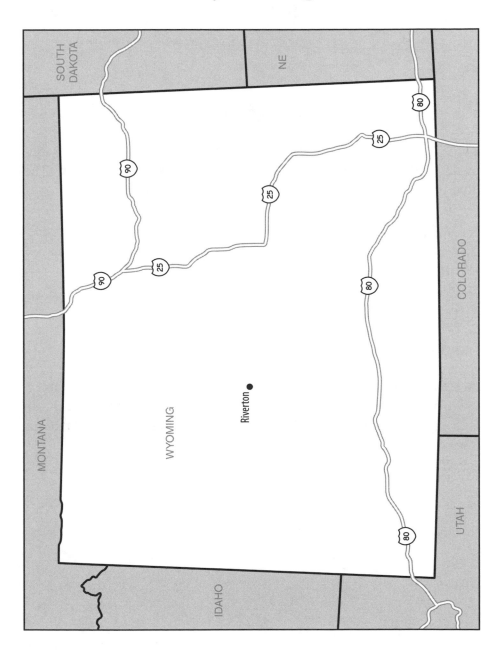

City	Casino	🚐	〰	⬭	📄
Riverton	Wind River Casino				272

WYOMING

Three Indian casinos are located in Wyoming. The largest, Wind River, owned and operated by the Northern Arapaho Tribe is listed below. The other two casinos are smaller and in more remote locations.

RIVERTON

Wind River Casino
10368 Highway 789
Riverton, Wyoming 82501
307-856-9942
www.windrivercasino.com

DESCRIPTION: The 24-hour casino features 740 slots, four gaming tables, video bingo, two restaurants and a diner. DIRECTIONS & PARKING: From I-25 exit 189, follow US-26 west for 108 miles. Parking is available for RVs.

Appendix A

Casino Comps Are For Travelers Too

What's a casino comp? "Comp" is a shortened version of "complimentary" and refers to anything the casino gives you for free in return for your playing there. There was a time when casino comps were only available to high rollers – people who spend thousands of dollars at a time. The casino would comp their hotel room, meals, even travel expenses. But nowadays casinos offer comps to virtually everyone who comes there to play.

Just about every casino has a Players Club (known by various names such as Rewards Club, Winners Circle, Total Rewards, Connection Club, Northern Rewards, Magic Money, etc), which allows patrons the opportunity to accumulate points toward comps, free meals, hotel rooms and even cash-back rewards. Players Clubs originally started as Slots Clubs and were designed to give slot machine players (low rollers) an opportunity to get comps formerly offered only to high rollers at the tables.

It doesn't cost anything to join a casino club. There are no dues, but many benefits! Players Clubs are maturing. Many casinos now also expect players at the tables to present their club card to accumulate credit toward comps. In casinos where table players are not expected to be club members, a player should always ask about being rated for comps. The casino may add table comps to slot points on the card or will simply extend comps to the player based on his or her table play. If you play both tables and slots, when you join the club, ask if your table comps and slot points will be combined.

Players Clubs have various point structures. They give gifts, cash, free meals, hotel rooms and more for accumulations of specific amounts of points. Often a Players Card can accumulate enough points in a single session to get a dollar or two or even half off a meal at the casino.

When you're playing at the casino, always make sure your card is inserted into the gaming machine before you begin. If the card reader is flashing, try re-inserting the card until the welcome message appears. Points won't accumulate unless the card is properly inserted. For table players, put your card on the table and be sure pit personnel get your information.

Why do casinos like to attach those long colorful bungee cords to their cards? Because slots players are prone to losing the card as they move around the gaming floor. The casino is hoping you'll attach the other end of that cord to yourself. But, if you lose your card while moving around the casino, take time to go back to the Club desk and get a duplicate card. Better yet, ask for two cards when you join so you'll have one at the ready should you lose the first card.

Don't think that because you are just passing through for a one or two-day visit to the casino you won't be able to accumulate enough points for comps. When going into a casino for the first time, stop at the Players Club desk and apply for a card. When you do, ask if the casino offers any incentives for new club members. Often they'll give you a free gift just for joining – things like a roll of coins to get you started on the slots, $10 of match play, restaurant meal coupons, free tee shirts, free travel bag or other logo'd items.

Casinos are continuously sponsoring special promotions that, for you, could mean a free gift, a meal coupon, free entry to a slot tournament or an entry to a drawing. Examples of some promotions include senior citizen day once or twice a week, men's and ladies night specials and special drawings. But, you won't know about these promotional comps unless you ask. Most of the time you need to be a Players Club member to participate. Some casinos extend discounts at its restaurants and gift shops for Players Club members.

Points earned on a Players Club card generally expire after one year. So if you're visiting individual casinos in different parts of the country, your card is apt to expire by the time you get around to that casino for a second visit. But this could work to your advantage; if the casino drops your name in addition to your points off their database, you can become a new member again, qualifying you for new member promotions if available.

Bottom line: familiarize yourself with club rules and take advantage of all the free "stuff" being offered by casinos.

Appendix B

How to be a Savvy Casino Discounter

Casinos are big on promotions. They are continuously offering "specials" and discounts designed to bring you into their facility and onto the gaming floor. Specific discounts are regularly offered at many of the casinos listed in this book.

Senior citizen discounts are among the most common type of discount. Most casinos cater to seniors by offering percent off food or 2-for-1 meals on "Senior Days" and some casinos even spring for free breakfast or lunch. The definition of "senior citizen" also varies – some consider 65 and older to qualify for the senior discount while other casinos define senior as 60+ 55+ or 50+. People over 50 should *always* ask about discounts.

Other frequent discounts are percent off at restaurants and gift shops for Players Club members or weekly specials at the restaurants, such as prime rib night or seafood buffets at special prices. Many casinos give Fun Books, containing valuable coupons.

Casino RV Parks will generally extend the same discounts offered at their hotel – AAA and AARP. Many also honor Good Sam and FMCA discounts and some participate in the Escapees or Passport America programs. Seasonally, casino RV Parks will run promotions such as one night free if you stay two nights or deeply discounted daily camping fees on the first two or three nights. When you make your reservation or check in, be sure to ask about current discounts. You won't know about some discounts, if you don't ask!

Two important points regarding discounts:

1) Always ask about discounts, current promotions and giveaways! We've discovered that, in many locations, if you don't request the

discount (or if you don't know about the discounts), you'll pay full price. Don't be too shy to ask about discounts!

2) Always join the Players Club when you go into a casino, even if you plan to be there only for a few hours. It doesn't cost anything to join and chances are you'll get discounts or other promotional benefits even if you don't gamble there.

Appendix C

Casinos are Hospitable to RVers

Question: What is blacktop boondocking?

Answer: Free overnight parking for self-contained RVs, typically on the paved parking area of a business establishment, with the property owner's permission.

The key phrase in this definition is *"with the property owner's permission."* Consequently whenever RVers want to stay overnight in a parking lot they must obtain permission from the property owner. RVers who often look for free overnight parking know that the places most hospitable to RVers -- those who are inclined to permit "blacktop boondocking" in their parking lots -- are casinos, 24-hour super stores and truck stops.

If you wish to secure free overnight parking, it is important to obtain authorization from management or security personnel. The casinos listed in this book are all "RV-Friendly," that is they either have an RV Park and/or they permit free overnight parking for self-contained vehicles in their lot. Blacktop boondocking at a casino is safe and secure. Casinos welcome adult campers because they know their facility is getting additional business. And the RVer gets a quiet, safe spot to rest and relax without being hassled. Since most casinos are open 24/7, security personnel are on duty all night.

But a parking lot is not a campground. When your RV is in for a free overnight stay, you are there because the property owners allow RV parking. Don't take advantage of their hospitality. During our travels we've observed blacktop boondockers who act like they own the parking lot. They put out the awning, set up table and chairs and break out the barbeque grill. Please remember, blacktop boondockers don't pay for their parking space. Therefore, the circumstances are different from a campground. When you rent a spot at a campground, you've paid for your site and you're entitled to make yourself at home – you "own" that campsite for the night. But when boondocking in a parking lot, be considerate of the property owner. Park in the area designated for RVs. If there is no specifically designated RV area, we suggest parking on the perimeter of the lot – don't take up spaces reserved for customers with cars. If there's enough space, it's OK to put out the slides, but restrict your household activity to the inside of the RV.

It is always a good idea to return the casino's hospitality by doing business with them. Treat yourself to a meal in the restaurant, buy something at the gift shop and (the obvious) participate in the gaming if you are so inclined.

We cannot emphasize enough that security personnel must be notified if you plan to stay overnight. Some will ask to see your driver's license or will ask you to complete a form showing your name, vehicle plate and drivers license number along with the date of your visit to the casino.

Even though casinos have 24-hour security, the type of security provided at a large open parking lot is not the same as at an RV park or campground. It is not wise to leave your RV unattended overnight or for any extended period. You would think this advice is just good common sense. But you'd be surprised at how many folks would leave their large expensive vehicles in a casino lot and go off to visit friends in the area for a few days. If you are foolish enough to do this, don't be surprised, when you return, to find your unattended vehicle has been towed away. Many casinos that permit overnight parking limit it to 24 hours and that's as it should be. If you are going to be in the area for more than a day or two, check into an RV Park!

Boondocking at a casino is convenient. You have the advantage of having your home with you and you can either walk or take the shuttle bus back and forth to the casino. You can play shorter more relaxing gaming sessions with breaks in between. If you are averse to crowds, you can play at odd hours and avoid peak play times. For couples, when one wants to play cards or slots and the other doesn't, there's no problem. And, of course, there's the obvious benefit – blacktop boondocking is free!

Blacktop Boondocking Etiquette

RVers should never abuse the hospitality of private businesses that allow free overnight parking. The Escapees RV Club has established eight simple rules for proper overnight parking etiquette. FMCA and other national organizations have adopted the code as a model for their members as well. Be a considerate blacktop boondocker and observe these rules:

1. Stay one night only.
2. Obtain permission from a qualified individual.
3. Obey posted regulations.
4. No awning, chairs or barbecue grills.
5. Do not use hydraulic jacks on soft surfaces (including asphalt).
6. Always leave an area cleaner than you found it.
7. Purchase gas, food or supplies as a form of thank-you when feasible.
8. Be safe. Always be aware of your surroundings, and leave if you feel unsafe.

Note: Many casinos have fee-pay RV parks or campgrounds. Some of these casinos will also allow free overnight parking in their parking lot. But others expect you to stay and pay at their RV Park and do not permit free overnight parking. If you want to dry camp in the parking lot of a casino that also has an RV Park, it's imperative to clear it with Security.

Index